THE BIRTH OF CHRIST

THE BIRTH OF CHRIST

Peter Sammons

Glory to Glory Publications

Published in Great Britain by
Glory to Glory Publications
10 Brinkman Road, Linton,
Cambridge CB1 6XF

Cover design by Roger Judd

ISBN 0-9551790-1-7

Printed and bound in Great Britain
by Bookmarque Ltd, Croydon, Surrey

Contents

PART 2 BIBLICAL ACCOUNT OF THE NATIVITY

PART 3 SOME CONTROVERSIES

To Joyce and Mark,
with sincere thanks for their love and support
during this project

FOREWORD

It is a surprising fact that, although the Western world 'celebrates' Christmas once a year, and expends literally billions of pounds, dollars and euros in the process, there are precious few books on the subject of "Christmas" itself. In spite of this, "Christmas" continues to attract interest from the media and press, especially if some aspect of "the story" can be debunked or questioned. In the UK in 2004 The Times newspaper carried a short article about the three wise men titled "*Were they wise? Or men?*"[1] Two years earlier on much the same subject, but this time a different newspaper: the London Evening Standard carried "*Three Kings ... or was it four Persian priests at the nativity?*"[2]

In the UK, over the 2004 Christmas period there were three media presentations on aspects of the 'story'. Terry Jones, a famous UK comedian, presented a radio programme aimed at rehabilitating Herod 'the Great' called "*Let's Hear it for King Herod*". BBC TV screened a documentary on the *wise men* which, allowing that it was a TV programme by a secular organisation, was remarkably "fair" but prone to drawing firm conclusions from very slim evidence. And The Economist newspaper in its final 2004 edition claimed that Emperor Augustus' census could not have happened at the time of Christ's birth – and then presented an argument for reaching this conclusion.

Whilst this short book was being prepared, in 2002 Philip Greenslade's book *The Perfect Gift*[3] was published by CWR. This is an excellent set of devotional studies of the Christmas story, and is highly recommended as such. It does not aim to evaluate the historical narrative, but rather to draw out theological lessons from it. Nearly two generations earlier Dr Leon Morris's equally recommended *The Story of the Christ Child*[4] was published, in 1960. This was also primarily a devotional study. Although both books consider certain historical evidence, neither aims to evaluate this evidence in depth.

This book, by contrast, seeks to examine various aspects of what is popularly thought of as "the Christmas story". It is hoped that readers will be blessed by God as they consider anew, or perhaps for the very first time, the amazing claims made in His Word – what we call the Holy Bible – about His Word, the Lord Jesus.

The subject is reviewed in three main sections:

1. Background
2. Biblical Account of the Nativity
3. Controversies

The biblical accounts we have of the birth of Jesus are disarmingly straightforward but found in a complex theological, historical and political setting. In spite of their simplicity, the accounts are consistent, believable and a satisfactory preamble to the life and works of Jesus, the Messiah. They are also a profound challenge in our own day, to believers and non-believers alike!

Peter Sammons

Notes
[1] *The Times*, 10 February 2004.
[2] *The Evening Standard*, 16 December 2004.
[3] Philip Greenslade, *The Perfect Gift* (CWR, 2002) ISBN 1-85345-246-7.
[4] Philip Greenslade *The Story of the Christ Child* (Marshall, Morgan and Scott, 1960).

Part One Background

1

Once, in Royal David's City

Why study the Christmas story?

On Christmas Eve each year, in Cambridge, England, the world famous King's College Chapel Choir provide a 'festival of lessons and carols' which is broadcast live by radio across the UK. The choir traditionally begins this *very* traditional service by processing into the chapel, led by a young soloist who sings unaccompanied the beautiful carol 'Once, in Royal David's City' by Cecil Alexander[1]. The words of the first verse, sung so hauntingly, are:

> Once, in royal David's city,
> Stood a lowly cattle-shed
> Where a mother laid her baby
> In a manger for his bed.
> Mary was that mother mild,
> Jesus Christ her little child.

For many people, in the English-speaking world at least, these words are familiar and often arouse warm and cosy emotions about the story of the nativity of the baby Jesus. Christmas has become, for many outside the Christian church, simply an occasion for feasting and merriment. It is fair to say that the account of the nativity of Jesus is, for some people within the church, the cause of embarrassment. True, it is a lovely story and 'wonderful for children' as it tells, in the words of another Christmas carol, how 'Love came down at Christmas, Love all lovely, Love Divine'. But it is difficult in a hard-bitten and cynical world to draw out the awesome message of Christmas and to understand the complicated history of which it is a part. So much easier to relegate Christmas to 'a time for children' —a time when the church can be uncontroversial and engage easily with the world at large; all things to all men.

Encapsulated in Cecil Alexander's carol, however, are a number of key words and phrases, each loaded with significance and which the writer wanted to impart not only to children, for whom the carol was principally written, but for adults, too:

'**Once**' – a definite event took place at a definite time in the history of the world;

'**Royal David's city**' – the event took place at a location of great importance;

'**Mary**' – for good or ill, the historical figure of Mary has had a great significance on the history of the western church;

'**Jesus**' – a name chosen by God before the child was born; a name of supreme theological significance;

'**Christ**' – the Greek title (not a proper name!) otherwise rendered as Messiah; the long promised Saviour of the Jewish people and, as the Bible makes clear, of the whole world.

It is true that many, both inside and even outside the Christian church, regret the loss of a 'meaning' of Christmas and look back, perhaps with nostalgia, to a fabled golden age of Christmas celebrations —feelings encouraged by an avalanche of Christmas greetings cards with images of fat, jolly, red-clad Santas, chirpy robins and rosy-cheeked children pulling the first presents from gorging Christmas stockings. Perhaps, all too often, it is simply a case of looking back to happier years in one's own childhood or youth when Christmas seemed so magical.

Not so romantic is the reality of Christmas for so many in the world today. In the western hemisphere the enforced jollity of the Christmas period can leave all too many feeling the bitter emptiness of loneliness. For families, brought together dutifully for a 'family celebration', Christmas can mean heightened tensions with less room for manoeuvre to escape, whilst for the poor and homeless Christmas can in reality be a crisis. No wonder that in the UK there is a charity which mobilises over the Christmas period each year to offer decent food and safe lodging for large numbers of down-and-outs, a charity called *Crisis at Christmas*. In the eastern and southern hemisphere, even in countries where Christmas is celebrated (or tolerated) the season represents no respite from grinding poverty and a very real fear of the future.

Rather than a crisis at Christmas, many yearn to discover Christ at Christmas, to experience a reality in the words of Cecil Alexander's famous carol:

> And our eyes at last shall see Him,
> Through His own redeeming love
> For that child, so dear and gentle,
> Is our Lord in heaven above;
> And He leads His children on
> To the place where He is gone.

The first Christmas was certainly a crisis for the newly married couple which travelled from Nazareth to Bethlehem. As Bishop Paul Barnett points out in his excellent book *Bethlehem to Patmos*[2] there really is nothing romantic about a pre-marital pregnancy, followed by a hastily arranged marriage and then the birth of a child near farm animals! We do capture something of that pain in the Gospel narratives, but it is seldom expressed in Christmas celebrations in church.

So, why study in detail the Christmas theme —after all, everyone knows the story, don't they? In fact, most people do not know the events *as they are recorded in the Bible*. Even many church-attending Christians are unclear about the precise details. Very little has been written, certainly in recent years, on the *biblical* account of the nativity of Jesus. The subject has been given a passing treatment in many excellent Bible study books and a number of these have been referred to and quoted in the preparation of this book. A number of written works on the life of the Lord Jesus have only a passing interest in the account of His birth. Others, sadly, have been written from a standpoint that seeks to discredit rather than evaluate the biblical narrative. Often the very people who one would expect to have an interest in defending the biblical account of the birth of Jesus have remained conspicuously silent or have simply not been granted the 'air time' that headline-grabbing biblical critics have secured. Perhaps this is because there is a certain reluctance to commit to the biblical account when so often it, along with the rest of the Bible, is denigrated. There is every temptation to keep one's head down and avoid being identified with what some see as being, in any case, a subject of only secondary importance to the Christian faith. Perhaps it is because the narrative is complex, the unknowns many and the geo-political background fiendishly difficult to summarise.

This book seeks to analyse the biblical narrative, to compare what happened with what was expected to happen by the people at the time, and to draw out the broader theological context in which the events are to be viewed. It perhaps goes without saying that this is not simply an academic exercise. The infant who was born in Bethlehem between the year 6 and 5 BC, into a poor family in a backwater of the Roman Empire, has had, beyond any reasonable contradiction, a greater influence in this world than any human before or since. His countless millions of followers, two thousand years after his birth, yield their total allegiance to Him, sometimes at the cost of their lives. The events traced out in these studies are not just history. They continue to demand a response —of belief or disbelief, of faith or of rejection. Whilst the Nativity is far from the whole story of Jesus, the account given in the Bible's Gospel narratives demonstrate a number of key truths about God:

• He cares intimately about the people of this world;

• His plan of salvation was foreshadowed by God-inspired prophets from the earliest of times;

• He identifies first and foremost with the dispossessed of this world;

• The cost of salvation was enormously high —God gave His own Son to pay the price.

The core of this book is the biblical narrative concerning the birth in Bethlehem.[3] As this narrative is split between three of the four written accounts of the life of Jesus (which are commonly called 'the Gospels'), the three separate strands have been segregated into chronological order and re-assembled into a single narrative. The author recognises that each separate narrative is integral to what each Gospel writer was reporting to his own readers, but believes that this re-packaging of the narrative does no injustice either to the narrative or to the full Gospels of which they are a part. The source and verse numbers are, in any case, all clearly stated. Only the section headings have been devised by this author, for ease of identification.

The title of Jesus principally used in these studies is *not* that most commonly found in the four Gospels, where Jesus is normally referred to simply as Jesus. William Barclay, in his important book *Jesus As They Saw Him*,[4] makes the point that, "In the Gospels [Jesus] is by far the commonest name of our Lord, for in them he is called by this simple name almost six hundred times. It is at first sight an astonishing fact that in the four Gospels the expression *Jesus Christ* occurs only four times, in Mark 1:1; Matt 1:1; John 1:17; 17:3; and the expression the *Lord Jesus* only twice, and in both cases there is doubt about it. In Luke 24:3 the reading is doubtful and Mark 16:19 is not part of the original Gospel. When the Gospel writers thought of their Lord, it was the name Jesus which came automatically to their minds and to their lips, and this is a very significant fact." It should be added that Barclay was in no way questioning the lordship of Jesus – indeed his book contains a full account of the use of the title *Lord* – he simply addressed the fact that the title is seldom used in the Gospels themselves.

In spite of this useful clarification given by William Barclay, the title used for Jesus in this series of studies is, wherever appropriate, *Lord Jesus*. This title is chosen to reflect the fact that Jesus is seen throughout the New Testament writings very much as Lord, even if the title is seldom used in the four Gospels. Sadly, the name *Jesus*, and the term *Jesus Christ*, are often misused in common parlance, sometimes even being used as swear words. We should never allow that misuse to prevent us from using His name in the proper manner, it is true to say that the phrase *Lord Jesus*, used appropriately, is a two-word theological statement of supreme importance. As the apostle Paul wrote, "No one can say 'Jesus is Lord' except by the Holy Spirit" (1 Cor 12:3).

Stages in God's plan of salvation
It is impossible to appreciate the full meaning of the birth of the Lord Jesus without recognising that His entry into the world, His subsequent life, death and resurrection from death, are part of an overall scheme devised by God to remedy humankind's state of enmity with and rebellion against God. The relationship of humans to their God is 'fallen' from the intended state of close friendship and spiritual intimacy so clearly described in the early chapters of Genesis. This condition is usually described by theologians as 'the Fall'. The Bible explains that a state of sin separates us from God and spoils our relationship with Him. Hopefully, readers will not be too disheartened to take a short excursion from our focus on the Nativity to look briefly into some weighty theology which sets the Incarnation of God (i.e. His birth into the world as a human) into a context. As this theology is an essential backdrop to the historical narrative of the Nativity, the effort will prove to be well worthwhile!

The Bible teaches that the fall of Satan, an archangel, with certain other angels, took place before the world was created. Jesus himself referred to this fall Luke 10:18, "I saw Satan fall like lightning from heaven." A fascinating glimpse of the battle in heaven that preceded Satan's expulsion is found in Revelation 12:7-12. Jesus referred to Satan's character in John 8:44, "He was a murderer from the beginning, not holding to the truth, for there is no truth in him." It seems that Satan and other rebel angels, thrown out of heaven, sought to obtain possession of the world shortly after its creation, and similar possession of mankind which had been created for special and intimate fellowship with God. In order to hurt God and to gain a measure of temporary control over His world, Satan induced mankind to rebel against God (or 'sin'), as set out in Genesis chapter 3, which led to humans becoming *spiritually fallen* beings, their previous intimate and loving relationship with God being replaced by fear and shame.

Whether Genesis chapter 3 is accepted as literal or allegorical, the essential reality portrayed in the Bible remains: humans are alienated from a God of love. Mankind's 'natural' spiritual state is dead, rather than alive. Man's innermost being (or soul) is blinded and perverted from what it was intended to be, and our physical body liable to disease and death. Most importantly, the moral disease of sin (or rebellion against God) is ever-present in the very bloodstream of the human race. So it was that humankind passed under the usurped and limited control of Satan (e.g. see Acts 26:18; Col 1:13; Heb 2:14). Certainly our broken and often disastrously flawed human relationships, whether they are between individuals, groups or nations, seem to confirm that there is something badly wrong with mankind.

Living, as we do, in an age where self-promotion and self-fulfilment are considered to represent the highest expression of human life, some readers may complain that sin – falling short of God's standards, even rebellion against God – cannot be so serious as to make a full relationship with Him impossible. Among the world's religions only Christianity teaches that sin is so serious that we cannot remedy it ourselves and need to be saved from its power and its effects. It is fair to say that most religions teach that people work and earn their way to a 'right' relationship with God by observing religious ceremonies and by doing things to appease God. This, emphatically, is not the Christian message. The Bible teaches that sin is so bad that God will not tolerate it at all. He is completely holy and completely righteous. That is how we need to be if we are to have a right relationship with Him. Since we cannot make ourselves holy and righteous, a complete and effective remedy to our condition as *spiritually fallen beings*

is necessary. Two things need to be kept in mind:
1. We are all sinful (Rom 3:23).
2. Sin is not just the awful things we easily recognise as sin (e.g. murder, robbery, violence). It is, equally, all the rebellions we have against God's right to be God in our lives. Sin, then, can be simply ignoring God.

Isn't it completely overbearing of God to be so hard on sin? To answer that question we might consider that if sin is not as serious as the Bible tells us it is, God would have found a simpler and less costly way of dealing with it than the way the Bible tells us He decided upon. This way ultimately involved the sacrifice of His Son on a cross of execution —a humiliating, disgraceful, torturous form of death, borne by the one person in history who was without sin.

In order to rescue humans from the power, grip and guilt of sin, to fully restore us to our former position which was lost in the Garden of Eden, and indeed to elevate us to a yet higher position (that of being adopted as children of God[5]), God determined on a plan of salvation. But this plan would be immensely costly because, as the apostle Paul wrote, "the wages of sin is death, but the gift of God is eternal life in Christ Jesus our Lord" (Rom 6:23). It was the Lord Jesus who was to pay the price. As the apostle Paul again wrote, "For if, when we were God's enemies, we were reconciled to him through the death of his Son, how much more, having been reconciled, shall we be saved through his life!" (Rom 5:10). The baby born in Bethlehem in 6 to 5 B.C. was born to achieve God's plan of salvation.

Did God make a mistake in allowing the fall of mankind to occur? Did He know it was going to happen and if He did, is He not at least partly responsible for the effects of sin in His world? The Bible does not give us a clear answer as to why God allowed sin to enter His world, but He certainly went to extraordinarily costly lengths to provide for all people an escape route *from* the power and consequences of sin *to* the safety of kinship with His Son. A former Principal of the Birmingham Bible Institute in the UK, H. Brash Bonsall, examined this difficult question in his excellent study book *The Person of Christ*:

"While it is plain from Scripture that God *foreknew* that the Fall of Man would occur, it must never be thought that he *foreordained* it. This would be to regard God as the author of sin, and as morally responsible for the effects of it. He *foreknew* the Fall; but He *foreordained* Redemption. The difference between the two words may be made clear by an illustration. Some years ago the Perth to London Express was travelling near the Boxmoor Tunnel at 70 m.p.h. just before the diversion from the fast to the slow line. These points should have been taken at 15 m.p.h. The train consequently left the rails and plunged over the embankment. As a result over forty people lost their lives. At the enquiry the signalman stated that he observed the train running too rapidly for safety and testified "*I saw it would happen.*" He *foreknew* there would be a train-wreck but he did not foreordain it, indeed he did all in his power to avert it. It was so with God in relation to the Fall of Man. Why He did not prevent it is a problem which the Bible does not explain. We can only take the facts as we find them and as the Bible states them to be —that is, that God's creature, Man, has fallen and that he has been redeemed. Until we have clearer light we must trust where we cannot trace".[6]

God's plan of salvation is also referred to as a plan of redemption. When the word 'redemption' or 'redeemed' is used in everyday life, it indicates that something has been bought back, or regained by payment of money or by effort. In the theological context, the word 'redeem' refers to God 'buying back' mankind, by paying the price necessitated by sin in order to return mankind to a right relationship with Himself. The Bible is certain about the fact, the process and the extent of redemption, as the following four quotations make clear:

"But now he [Christ] has appeared once for all at the end of the ages to do away with sin by the sacrifice of himself. Just as man is destined to die once, and after that to face judgement, so Christ was sacrificed once to take away the sins of many people; and he will appear a second time, not to bear sin, but to bring salvation to those who are waiting for him" (Hebrews 9:26-28).

"For he rescued us from the dominion of darkness and brought us into the kingdom of the Son he loves, in whom we have redemption, the forgiveness of sins" (Col 1:13).

"He [Jesus Christ] is the atoning sacrifice for our sins, and not only for ours but also for the sins of the whole world" (1 John 2:2).

"...... if you confess with your mouth, "Jesus is Lord" and believe in your heart that God raised him from the dead, you will be saved" (Rom 10:9).

Christ, then, swapped places with us and paid on our behalf the price of our rebellion against God. We have something to do in response —to confess that Jesus is Lord. This action has as much to do with genuine belief in Him and full acceptance of His right to be Lord of every aspct of our lives as it does with using a particular form of 'prayer of belief'. Upon our confession God then guarantees that Christ's death in our place is *the* necessary atoning sacrifice, sufficient for the needs of the whole world. The various stages in God's redemptive plan can be described as:

• Christ's Incarnation;
• Christ's redeeming death;
• Christ's Resurrection from death;
• Christ's ascension and His ministry from heaven on behalf of His people;
• Christ's future return in glory.

The latter four stages are beyond the scope of this series of studies, but need to be referred to from time to time to put the first stage into context. The Incarnation, it will be seen, was an event in history which began when a baby was born in humble circumstances in Bethlehem some two thousand years ago. The baby grew quite normally to become a man who lived in the world for a total of around thirty-three years. But what of this idea of 'Incarnation'? What exactly does it convey?

The term *Incarnation* comes from two Latin words *in*, "in" and *caro*, "flesh" and means the doctrine that at a given point in time God took upon Himself human flesh and, with it, human nature. What makes the Lord Jesus distinct from all other human beings, both before and since, is that He was without sin. He never sinned or in any way rebelled against God. He only is good enough to pay the 'wages' of sin —death. How do we know that Jesus was without sin and that therefore His death is completely adequate payment for our sins? Two answers help us here: first, there is nothing in the accounts that we have of the life of Jesus that looks remotely like rebellion against God. Everywhere the opposite is evident —that the Lord Jesus submitted Himself entirely to His Father's will. "Yet not as I will, but as you will" (Matthew 26:39) was more than simply a statement of His priorities, it was in every sense the reality at the centre of His being. Second, the Bible itself makes clear that He was without sin: "But you know that he appeared so that he might take away our sins. And in him is no sin" (1 John 3:5-6).

Who paid the price? The baby born to die

Staying with the theological aspects of Christ's Incarnation a little longer, we see that the Incarnation – God becoming flesh – is an essential factor in order for God to secure the redemption of mankind. Whilst there are many facets to this doctrine of the Incarnation, in relation to the birth of the Lord Jesus, three are particularly important:

Firstly, **Christ was born to die**. Redemption involves a substitutionary death —someone dying in the place of the guilty one. God cannot die, but Man can. Only if the Son became a man could he die. In this sense the Lord Jesus was 'born to die' as is emphasised in Hebrews 2:9, "..... we see Jesus, who was made a little lower than the angels, now crowned with glory and honour because he suffered death, so that by the grace of God he might taste death for everyone."

It should be noted that there is something in the death of the Lord Jesus which will never be experienced by His children (i.e. those adopted into His family as made clear in Hebrews 2:9-13).

When we die, even if we think or feel we are forsaken, God will be there, having promised never to leave or forsake us. But when Christ died, the Father's presence was withdrawn from the Son because He who was without sin was made sin for us (2 Cor 5:21). And this separation from God is the ultimate penalty for sin. No wonder Jesus called out from the cross, "My God, my God, why have you forsaken me?" (Matt 27:46).

Secondly, **God cannot represent man in sacrifice**, only a man can do that. The Lord Jesus became a man so that He could, on behalf of all mankind, offer His life. In Romans 5:12-21 Paul writes about the representative nature of Adam's and Christ's acts, the first in bringing sin into the world, the second in providing the gift of righteousness. "If, by the trespass of the one man [Adam] death reigned through that one man, how much more will those who receive God's abundant provision of grace and of the gift of righteousness reign in life through the one man, Jesus Christ." Because only a man could represent mankind, so it was necessary for a baby to be born into the world, who would become that representative.

Thirdly, **Christ's redemption covers all mankind** – everyone who ever lived – not just those who are saved by accepting His free gift of salvation. This means that the price is paid, but that the free gift of salvation still has to be accepted by each individual. To underline that Christ's redemption is *for all*, John the baptist said "Look, the lamb of God, who takes away the sins of the world!" (John 1:29). Reference to 'the world' in Scripture, and especially in the apostle John's writings, means the whole mass of mankind, loved by God (see John 3:16) and able to be saved, but at present under the domination of the 'prince of this world'—the devil (John 14:30). The Lord Jesus, as God's sacrificial Lamb, is, in John's words, "the atoning sacrifice for our sins, and not only for ours but also for the sins of the whole world." (1 John 2:2).

On this latter point of Christ's redemption covering all mankind, for clarity and to avoid any misunderstanding it should also be noted that this redemption is not automatic —in other words not everyone is saved. Such a belief is mistakenly taught by some both within the umbrella of the Christian church and also beyond the church. The idea is that everyone will be saved and made right with God —a superficially attractive idea, but one which is dangerous in the sense that it denies the very nature of God in that He is perfectly just, and one which runs counter to the clear teaching of the Bible on this issue. H. Brash Bonsall in *The Person of Christ* casts some light on this:

"The Bible says "Return to me; for I have redeemed thee" (Isa 44:22). One may be redeemed, but if the conditions of repentance and faith are not fulfilled, if the offer is not closed with, the redemption is without effect. Thus a cancer remedy might be discovered and offered free to all, but not all would thereby be saved. Some would never hear, some would hear and not believe, some would hear and believe but not actually take the remedy; all would die. Only those who, hearing, believed and by an *act* of faith actually took the remedy, would live. James 2:14-16 defines faith as more than an intellectual assent; it is a belief which acts.......)"[7]

The prophet Isaiah, provides a clue that it will be a person who would be needed to pay the price. And this person would go willingly to be the substitute for the sin-offering.

Sacrifice and offering you did not desire,
But a body you have prepared for me,
burnt offerings and sin offerings you did not require.
Then I said, "Here am I, I have come –
it is written about me in the scroll.
I desire to do your will, O my God;
your law is within my heart.

Isaiah 40:6-8

No longer would God be satisfied with symbolic sacrifices of animals in the temple. The days of the Jerusalem temple were numbered, in any case. In a few years it would no longer be possible for the priests to sacrifice animals on behalf of the people[8]. Now a permanent and all-sufficient sacrifice was needed, and so

God prepared a body of flesh for his Son. The sacrifice was to be made by God Himself, through the person of His Son.

The birth in Bethlehem twenty centuries ago is as relevant today as it was when those events happened. In this series of studies we look at the events themselves and at the historical and theological background in which they are set. Since for many the Bible is a little understood collection of books, we will look at how God's plan of salvation is revealed within and across these books. It is hoped that something of God's yearning love for His world, His efforts to reach His creation and to establish a right relationship with it, and of the immense cost of that redemption which began in Bethlehem, will emerge as we look deeply into the Christmas story.

This series of studies looks at the basic biblical account of the Nativity of the Lord Jesus and demonstrates that we have good grounds for believing that the accounts we have been given are complete and trustworthy. There is a real poignancy in the Christmas story. God willingly surrendered His beloved Son to be the seal of salvation, completed on the cross at Calvary —once for all. The birth in Bethlehem some two thousand years ago was the beginning of a life like no other. Perhaps this is what we need to reflect upon each Christmas time. We can take real joy and mightily celebrate the fact of the birth of the Lord Jesus! But His birth was only the beginning of the most wonderful story ever told! And the story will not be completed until Jesus returns again in glory!

We began this chapter with the opening verse of H. J. Gauntlett's famous carol *Once in Royal David's City*. Hopefully, by the end of our journey through the biblical account of Christ's birth, we will have a clearer grasp of the 'Christmas story' and where it fits in God's great plan of salvation. It is possible to intellectualise and theorise about the Christian faith, but ultimately, if it is to be accepted at all, it must be accepted with the simple faith of a child, as Jesus Himself taught (Luke 18:16-17). Perhaps, then, we will be able to make the last verse of Gauntlett's famous carol our own prayer:

Not in that poor lowly stable,
With the oxen standing by,
We shall see Him; but in heaven,
Set at God's right hand on high;
When like stars His children crowned.
All in white shall wait around.

Notes
[1] Cecil Alexander, wife of Archbishop William Alexander, Anglican Primate for Ireland, wrote the lyric in 1848 and the carol was put to music in 1849 by Henry J. Gauntlett (1805-1876)
[2] Paul Barnett, *Bethlehem to Patmos* The New Testament Story (Hodder and Stoughton, 1989), p. 28.
[3] See Chapter 5.
[4] William Barclay, *Jesus as They Saw Him* (SCM Press Ltd, 1962), p. 9.
[5] There are a number of references in the Bible to our adoption as children, e.g. see Ephesians 1:5-7 and Romans 8:15-17.
[6] H. Brash Bonsall, *The Person of Christ* (Christian Literature Crusade, 1967), p. 22.
[7] *Ibid.* p. 56.
[8] The Jerusalem temple was destroyed by the Romans in AD70 during the 'Jewish War'.

2

Salvation History

God yearns to save

No attempt is made in this book to defend the Bible as the sole revelation of God's word to humans. There are many other good books about the Bible, its history and trustworthiness. It is beyond the scope of these studies to explore such questions, though interested readers will find a wealth of helpful literature and other media on these subjects. It is therefore taken as accepted, for the purposes of this particular study of 'salvation history' that the biblical account of Christ's Nativity is accurate and reveals to us all we need to know about this momentous event. What follows below is, of necessity, a broad brush account of God's dealings with humankind as He unveiled His plan of salvation.[1]

The Bible explains that from the beginning mankind rebelled against God's right, as Creator, to be God. Whilst this rebellion was not God's plan, He definitely foresaw the effect it would have upon all humankind and determined on a plan of salvation —salvation from the grip and consequences of sin. But this would not be cheap salvation, where God winks at our wrongdoing and makes everything all right in the end. God shouldered the responsibility for Man's guilt as Jesus shouldered the cross on the road to Calvary. God progressively prepared mankind for this hugely expensive – indeed, priceless – salvation, through the two thousand years that preceded Christ. Rather than place His Son into the world straight after the Fall (described in Genesis chapter 3), God took great care to prepare humankind for this definite and final act of salvation. God prepared the human race through the calling of His chosen people, the Hebrews. To demonstrate that His priceless remedy for sin is something that could not be achieved independently by mankind, even with the knowledge of God's Law, He sent His own Son to pay the penalty for sin, *once and for all*. In the words of the apostle Paul: "....he has appeared once for all at the end of the ages to do away with sin by the sacrifice of himself. Just as man is destined to die once, and after that to face judgement, so Christ was sacrificed once to take away the sins of many people; and he will appear a second time, not to bear sin, but to bring salvation to those who are waiting for him" (Hebrews 9:26-28).

The main thrust of the Bible's message to mankind is God's immense love for His rebellious creation, who in fact deserve nothing but His judgement. Why does God love us? Because God is love (John 4:16). When the Bible says that God is love, it is saying much more than God loves, or that He is loving, or that he is lovely. It means that love is the motivation behind all that God does. Love is not just a facet of God, it is His whole nature. He is love at the core of His very being. This is not however sentimental love, a sort of amiable weakness or a good natured indulgence. If it was this sort of love it would be cheap love. Our limited understanding of God's love (and it can only be limited understanding, this side of eternity) needs to be built on God's revelation of Himself in the Scriptures, not by projecting our own ideas about love onto Him.

What does the Bible teach us about God's love? First, it is *uninfluenced*. Nothing in us can give rise to it or extinguish it. The love that we humans have for each other is influenced, or drawn out of us by something in the object of our love. God's love is not like that. His love is free, uncaused and spontaneous. In Deuteronomy 7:7-8, where God reaffirms to the Hebrews that He has chosen them to be His special people, we read, "The Lord did not set his affection on you and choose you because you were more numerous than other peoples, for you were the fewest of all peoples. But it was the because the Lord loved you .... that he brought you out with a mighty hand and redeemed you from the land of slavery...." There is no reason behind God's love for His people —He loves because He will love. This cannot be explained. Indeed to do be able to do so would require that God loves us for something outside of Himself, or something within us. No, He loves because He is love.

Second, His love is *eternal*. Being Himself eternal, and being Himself love, it follows that His love is eternal. God loved us before the earth was created, and has set His heart upon us from all eternity. This is a truth set out clearly in Ephesians 1:4-5: "For he chose us in him before the creation of the world to be holy and blameless in his sight. In love he predestined us to be adopted as his sons through Jesus Christ, in accordance with his pleasure and will...." Now this is an amazing thought for a child of God! And the only fitting response to this awesome statement is to return that love, if only we can stop ourselves exclaiming, "You surely can't mean me!"

Third, His love is *holy*. This means it is not subject to whim or sentiment, but is governed by principle. In Romans 5:21 we read, "...just as sin reigned in death, so also grace might reign through righteousness to bring eternal life through Jesus Christ our Lord." At first sight this is difficult to understand, but it means that God's love never conflicts with His holiness. On the one hand sin demonstrates its 'reign' in death —which might be described as a theological, as well as a biological, fact of life. God recognises this fact of life and has made provision for His most wonderful gift of *grace* —His free, unmerited favour and forgiveness that is bestowed upon people who truly turn to Him in faith and repentance. God's *grace* is demonstrated and proved by the opposite of death —spiritual life through the Lord Jesus. This is why God is not content for us to remain in our sinful state, He aims that we shall be holy, just as He is holy. He loves us too much to let us go on sinning. His love is holy, pure and unmixed

31

with human sentimentality. God refuses to compromise with sin —even in His own people.

Because of His uninfluenced, eternal, holy love, God yearns to save the people He has created, especially as we have been created for relationship with Him and will never find true peace until we have found that relationship. Before time began, Scripture tells us, His plan of salvation was worked out. It originated in His grace. God made a covenant of grace with Abraham, promising that through his descendants all the families of earth will be blessed. The Old Testament is to a large extent the account of God's gracious dealings with Abraham's descendants. In spite of their continual rejection of Him, God never cast them off. The historical Incarnation of the Lord Jesus was the fulfilment of His covenant (see Luke 1:68-75 in this regard).

A plan of salvation

Christ is found throughout the Old Testament. Jesus said, "The Scriptures testify about me" (John 5:39). Walking with two disciples after the resurrection, he rebuked them for their unbelief and ignorance of Scripture: "And beginning with Moses and all the prophets, he explained to them what was said in all the Scriptures concerning himself" (Luke 24:27). Later, speaking to a wider group of followers He stated, "This is what I told you while I was still with you: Everything must be fulfilled that is written about me in the law of Moses, the Prophets and the Psalms" (Luke 24:44).

Christ made it plain, therefore, that the Scriptures bore witness to Him in a general way, but also that in the Law, the Prophets and The Writings there were prophecies concerning Him *and that all these things had to be fulfilled*. The basic relationship between the Old and New Testaments, according to the Lord Jesus, was between promise in the Old and fulfilment in the New. The first words spoken by Jesus in his public ministry, recorded in Mark 1:15, were with regard to fulfilment: "The time is fulfilled, and the kingdom of God is at hand; repent and believe in the gospel." Jesus stated quite plainly to his disciples that the centuries of waiting were now over: "Blessed are your eyes because they see, and your ears because they hear. For I tell you the truth, many prophets and righteous men longed to see what you see but did not see it, and to hear what you hear but did not hear it" (Matt 13:16-17).

Christ in the Law

The 'Law' is contained in the first five books of the Bible, properly called the Pentateuch. These books contain foundation prophecies about God's salvation through Christ. So, God promised that Eve's offspring would 'crush' the serpent's head (Gen 3:15), a reference normally taken to mean Christ's victory over the devil, won on the cross at Calvary. God promised that through Abraham's descendants, all the peoples of the world will be blessed (Gen 22:18), a reference usually understood as the global spread of Christianity. Jacob, as he blessed his sons, unwittingly prophesied in Gen 49:10 that Christ would rule as King forever —this being the interpretation normally given to the sceptre not departing from Judah, but receiving the obedience of the nations.

In Deuteronomy 18:15 and 18, Moses prophesied that God would raise up a prophet like himself from the Jewish people, to whom they must listen. Moses would put his words in the mouth of this prophet, who will tell them everything that Moses commands Him. Christians see this as fulfilled literally in Luke 9:28-33. In this context, Deuteronomy 18:19 seems, then, to be a very stark warning to the Jewish nation about its rejection of the Lord Jesus.

There are also more subtle, indirect prophecies about Jesus, contained in the Law. One of the most striking is that of the Tabernacle, the place of worship which God commanded the Israelites to construct and in which would be His presence during the wanderings in the wilderness (Exodus 25 to 27). In various facets of the ancient Tabernacle, such as the altar, the laver of water, the light, the showbread, the incense and the holy of holies, Christians see a direct allusion to Jesus Christ. If an allusion could be made to only one or two such aspects of the Tabernacle as being pointers to Jesus, we might correctly be accused of wishful thinking, but the strong connection of every such aspect appears to be much more than mere coincidence.[2]

Christ in the Prophets

The books known as 'the Prophets' contain *history* (Joshua, Judges, Samuel, Kings and Chronicles, which are sometimes known as the 'former prophets') as well as *direct messages* from God to His people given at specific points in time (e.g. Ezekiel, Daniel, Amos, Jonah, etc). These latter are sometimes referred to as the 'major' and 'minor' prophets. Israel began as a theocracy ruled directly by God through Moses, then through Joshua and finally through the Judges, a number of men were chosen by God to lead Israel at different times. Israel, however, craved to be ruled by kings and, despite His warnings, continued to press this request upon God. The rule of kings, as God had warned, led to much hardship for the Hebrew nation. Through this unhappy experience, however, God was showing the Israelites the limitations of human government in order to clarify their understanding of the perfection of the future Messiah and to increase their desire for Him to be sent.

God had already made a covenant with King David, in 2 Samuel 7:8-17, to 'build him a house' and through his descendants, to 'establish his throne' forever. So the prophets began to point towards what this 'Son of David' would be. He would perfectly embody the ideals of kingship which the kings of Israel, including David, so imperfectly foreshadowed. In the Messiah's kingdom justice would replace oppression and peace would replace war. There would be no limit to the extent or duration of this future kingship, which would extend to the ends of the earth and last forever. These characteristics of the future kingdom are brought together in Isaiah's famous prophecy (Isa 9: 6,7) which Christians readily identify with Jesus:

> For to us a child is born,
> to us a son is given,
> and the government will be on his shoulders.
> And he will be called

> Wonderful Counsellor, Mighty God,
> Everlasting Father, Prince of Peace.
> Of the increase of his government and peace
> there will be no end.
> He will reign on David's throne
> and over his kingdom,
> establishing and upholding it
> with justice and righteousness
> from that time on and forever.

Whilst the prophets foretold His glory, they also foretold His suffering:

> He was pierced for our transgressions,
> he was crushed for our iniquities;
> the punishment that brought us peace was upon him,
> and by his wounds we are healed.
> We all, like sheep, have gone astray,
> each of us has turned to his own way;
> and the Lord has laid on him
> the iniquity of us all.

In this prophecy from Isaiah 53:5-6, Christians see the crucifixion of Jesus foreshadowed. Indeed Isaiah 52:13-15, followed by Isaiah 53:1-12, is the clearest prophecy of the suffering and rejection of Christ.

Christ in the Writings

The Writings (amongst which are the books that we call the Psalms and the Proverbs) point towards Jesus Christ in a number of places. Various Psalms are seen to prefigure Christ's deity, His humanity, His sufferings and His glory. The allusion in Psalm 8:6, for example, to the 'son of man' made 'a little lower than the heavenly beings', and made 'ruler over the works of your [God's] hands', is applied by the apostle Paul to Christ in his letter to the Hebrews (Heb 2:6-8). Jesus Himself quoted Psalm 22:1 from the cross as he personally experienced and fulfilled the terrible God-forsakenness of which the Psalmist wrote. In His earlier debates with the Pharisees, Jesus had quoted David's words in Psalm 110:1, "The Lord says to my Lord: Sit at my right hand until I make your enemies a footstool for your feet" as He challenged the Pharisees to explain how the Messiah could be both David's Lord and David's son (Matt 22:44; Mark 12:36; Luke 20:43).

The whole theme of wisdom in the book of Proverbs can be seen as an allusion to the coming Messiah, so that in Proverbs chapter 2 we read (verse 1), "My son, if you accept my words and store up my commands within you (verse 5) then you will understand the fear of the Lord and find the knowledge of God." Christians see this reference to God's *words* as being a reference to God's Word made flesh (John 1:1) who made His dwelling among us.

Before leaving this area of messianic prophecy, it is worth noting that Alfred Edersheim, a Jewish believer in the Lord Jesus of the late nineteenth century, and a noted biblical scholar of his time, drew up a list of 456 messianic prophecies from the Old Testament, which were supported by 558 separate quotations from rabbinic writings which confirmed them as truly messianic prophecies. And this was after deleting quite a number of prophecies which the rabbis of old considered to be messianic but which Christians reject in this class. Edersheim's book *The Life and Times of Jesus the Messiah* is still available and the full list of messianic prophecies is found in Appendix 9 to his book.[3] This is a fascinating study in its own right.

Saviour

This title of Jesus, amongst so many titles found in the pages of the New Testament, is one of the most profound. Jesus entered a world where salvation was the deepest desire in the hearts of ordinary men and women. This was a time of immense cruelty of man to man, and particularly of leaders to their people. There can seldom have been a time of such political insecurity. It was a time of tyrannical rulers who could do what they liked, and do it to anyone. The crimes of Herod "the Great" were so enormous that the slaughter of the babies in Bethlehem (in Herod's vain attempt to kill the infant Jesus) was scarcely seen as abnormal. In the Jewish historian Josephus' works, written a few years after the time of Christ, the slaughter of the little boys is not even mentioned, which some have taken to mean that it never happened, but more probably was simply an indication that this sort of behaviour towards ordinary people was not unusual.

This was an age of informers, where no one, especially in the courts of the kings and emperors, could live in security. The ancient 'gods' were on their way out. "It was not," writes William Barclay, "a case of men becoming so depraved that they abandoned their gods; it was a case of the gods becoming so depraved that they were abandoned by men."[4] The old gods were going and there was nothing to take their place except the worship of rulers, who were as depraved as their 'gods'. It was a time of superstition, when demons were seen to be everywhere waiting to injure men —indeed the number of references to Jesus casting out demons suggests this may indeed have been so. It was a time of astralism, men believing that their fate was sealed by the stars under which they were born. This in turn led to fatalism and hopelessness, a return to which we are perhaps seeing at the beginning of the third millennium. There was a consciousness of moral failure and moral helplessness —men knew they were sinners but knew no cure for sin. Small wonder, then, that they were searching for a saviour. The very title 'saviour' was prevalent at the time —any king, or even pretender to a throne, who could bring a measure of peace and security, was often called a 'saviour'.

God, in the Old Testament, is often identified as Saviour, as a short list of references will illustrate: Isa 45:15, 21; Deut 32:15; 1 Sam 10:19; Psalm 24:5; 27:9; 65:5; 79:9; 85:4-9; Micah 7:7; Hab 3:18. The Old Testament points towards a state of salvation when God will enter His Kingdom and reign. Having seen the desire for salvation in the predominantly pagan world into which Jesus was born, we see the word 'saviour' in the New Testament also applied to God:

- In Mary's song: "My spirit rejoices in God my Saviour" (Luke 1:47).
- Paul is an apostle by command of God our Saviour (1 Tim 1:1).
- God our Saviour desires all men to be saved (1 Tim 2:3).
- The living God is the Saviour of all men, especially those who believe (1 Tim 4:10).
- Paul's preaching has been entrusted to him by the command of God our Saviour (Titus 1:3).
- Everything is to be done in such a way as to adorn the teaching of God our Saviour (Titus 2:10).
- In Christ there appeared the goodness and loving kindness of God our Saviour (Titus 3:4).
- In Jude the object of praise is the only God our Saviour (see Jude 25).

Now this is an important truth to grasp: in working out God's plan of salvation, there is no tension between the stern wrath of God and the love of Jesus. It was not a case of Jesus doing something to alter the attitude of God to men, to convert the wrath of God into the love of God, or to persuade God to stay His hand, outstretched to punish. God is the Saviour God; Jesus did not live and die to change the attitude of God to men, rather he lived and died to show what that attitude is.

The Lord Jesus, also, is titled Saviour in the New Testament. The message of the angel Gabriel was that He was to be called Jesus, the Greek form of Joshua, which means 'Jehovah is salvation'. Jesus was given this name, said Gabriel, 'because He will save his people from their sins' (Matt 1:21). The Epistle to the Hebrews states plainly that Jesus, "is able to save completely those who come to God through him, because he always lives to intercede for them" (Heb 7:25). True, the title Saviour is used sparingly in the Gospels, in Matthew and Mark the title is not given; in Luke it is used only once, in the announcement of the angels to the shepherds: "Today in the town of David a Saviour has been born to you; he is Christ the Lord. This will be a sign to you: You will find a baby wrapped in cloths and lying in a manger" (Luke 2:12). In John's Gospel the title is, again, used only once. In John 4:42 the Samaritan villagers say to the woman who had spoken with Jesus, "We no longer believe just because of what you said; now we have heard for ourselves, and we know that this man really is the Saviour of the world."

Readers who are interested in a full survey of the title 'Saviour' as applied to the Lord Jesus are recommended to obtain the book *Jesus As They Saw Him* by William Barclay (and referenced in an earlier note). It looks in detail at forty-two titles applied to Jesus and how these titles would have been understood in Jesus' own day. Regarding the Lord's role as Saviour, Barclay writes: "No matter from what angle it may be approached the basic and essential idea is the idea of *rescue*, rescue from a situation in which a man is quite unable to rescue himself. It is *rescue from the past*. Through the work of Jesus Christ the penalty which man's sin deserves no longer hangs threateningly over him. The estrangement between man and God need no longer exist. The power and slavery of past sin are broken and man is no longer shackled by the chains which his own sin forged. *It is rescue for the future*. Through Jesus Christ, the living and ever-present Christ, man is no longer a slave to his own sin. He can break the habits which have been his fetters, and conquer the sins which conquered him. He is no longer frustrated and defeated; he has found the way to victorious living. He is no longer the victim of temptation; he is victorious over temptation. Salvation deals not only with a man's past; it makes him a new man and gives him a new future. It is not merely negative escape; it is positive victory. Jesus is indeed the Saviour for whom men were desperately searching, and for whom the world was waiting, and whom the world still needs."[5]

Notes
[1] Appendix 4, *Biblical Sources* and Appendix 5, *Reliability of the Biblical Sources* provide some background notes to the Bible.
[2] A full treatment of this fascinating subject is beyond the scope of

this book. Interested readers are recommended to obtain *Christ in the Tabernacle* by A. B. Simpson (Christian Publications, 1985) or a similar study.

[3] Alfred Edersheim, *The Life and Times of Jesus the Messiah* (Hendrickson Publishers, Inc., 1993).

[4] William Barclay, *Jesus As They Saw Him* (SCM Press Ltd, 1962).

[5] *Ibid.* p. 227.

3

Judaea and Galilee at the Time of the Nativity

Palestine

The modern name 'Palestine' derives from the Greek Palaestina, which comes from the Hebrew *Pleshet* ("Land of the Philistines"). Historically this was a small coastal area to the north-east of Egypt, also called Philistia. For the past 100 years the term 'Palestine' has been used by biblical historians as a sort of shorthand to describe the area covering Judaea, Samaria and Galilee. We need to be wary in using the term today, for at the beginning of the twenty-first century it has become so heavily politicised as to render its scholarly derivation almost meaningless. It is helpful to understand that the invention of the term *Syria Palaestina* by the Romans was part of a deliberate policy following the Roman-Jewish war of AD 66-70, which led to the complete defeat of Judaea, to extinguish Jewish national aspirations and to wipe the memory of Judea, Samaria and Galilee from the region. For Rome to rename the area as *Syria Palaestina* was a calculated double insult: it was designed to erase Jewish connections from the local geography in what today we might refer to as ethnic cleansing, whilst elevating the name and memory of the Israelites' ancient enemies —the Philistines. The Romans used the term Syria

Palaestina to describe the southern third of the province of Syria, including the former Judaea. The modern term 'Palestine' was not known in Jesus' day.

The scholarly name 'Palestine' was revived by the British after the First World War as an official title for the territory from the river Jordan westwards to the Mediterranean coast, lands administered at that time by Britain on behalf of the League of Nations. The area referred to as Palestine today generally extends from the Mediterranean Sea on the west to the River Jordan on the east and from the international border of Israel/Lebanon in the north to Gaza in the south. This territory was occupied in early biblical times by the kingdoms of Israel and Judah, and in the time of Christ comprised the Roman provinces of Judaea, Samaria and Galilee.

Ancient Philistia was a small but aggressive country —a loose confederation of five tiny 'city states'. Its people were Aegean – possibly Cretan – in origin and settled the maritime plain of southern Canaan during the twelfth century BC. Their territory extended from Wadi el-Arish (River of Egypt) in the south, for some seventy miles northwards to Joppa (modern Tel-Aviv) which was captured by the Philistines from the Israelites in the eleventh century BC but recaptured by King David a century later. Following the Israelite conquest of Canaan, the Philistines began a period of military and technical superiority over the Israelites, and enjoyed a near monopoly over iron making in the area. The greatest confrontations between Philistia and Israel were at the times of King Saul and King David. The Philistines failed to flourish as a people, however, and were gradually assimilated into Canaanite culture, eventually disappearing from history, leaving only the second-century Roman name "Palestine" as a monument to their presence.

The Mediterranean world at the time of Christ was controlled by Rome. Judaea, Samaria and Galilee formed a backwater, if an incessantly troublesome one, in the Roman Empire. Life in the Empire at the time of Christ was increasingly taking on the character of classical Greece. Roman civilisation was to a large extent Greek civilisation, and Greek was the 'world language' which united all the subject peoples of the east. Indeed a visitor to Palestine at the time of Christ could well have mistaken it for Greece. The 'ten cities' – in Greek, the Decapolis – of the Gospels (Matt 4:25 and Mark 5:20) took Athens as their model. They boasted temples sacred to Zeus and Artemis and each had their theatre, pillared forum, stadium, gymnasium and baths. Other Greek styled cities were Caesarea, the seat of Pontius Pilate's government, Sepphoris (a few miles north west of Nazareth) and Tiberias, which lay a few miles north east of Nazareth on the Sea of Galilee. Finally there was Caesarea Philippi, built at the base of Mount Hermon.

The many small towns and villages in Galilee and Judaea, however, completely retained their Jewish style and architecture. It was in these genuine Jewish communities that Jesus lived and worked. Nowhere do the Gospel writers refer to the Lord Jesus having lived in any of the Greek-styled cities of Palestine. Even so, Greek dress and much of the Greek way of life had penetrated even these purely Jewish communities, where the local people wore the typical tunic and cloak, shoes or sandals, often with a hat or cap for head covering. Furniture often included a bed and the Greek habit of reclining at meals was generally adopted.

Between the Old and New Testaments

Things are not, as might be expected, taken up in the New Testament where they were laid down in the Old. The period from Malachi to Matthew is one of approximately 400 years and during this time great political changes took place. At the end of the Old Testament the Persian Empire was still in power and remained so until 333 BC. Then came the Greek Empire, founded on the conquests of Alexander the Great, which dominated from 333 BC until 167 BC. After Alexander's death in 323 BC the empire was divided among four of his generals. Two of these were Ptolemy and Seleucus, each of whom founded a dynasty, the Ptolemys in Egypt and the Seleucids in Syria. They fought each other incessantly for control of 'Palestine' until 167 BC, periodically exchanging control of the area as first one side and then the other was victorious.

This period of instability was followed by another —the struggle of the Maccabees for Jewish national independence during the period 176-141 BC, which in turn was followed by the rule of a family of Jewish priest-kings, descended from the Maccabees known as the Asmonaeans (a name derived from a Hebrew word meaning 'wealthy'). The Asmonaeans remained in power for 78 years from 141 BC until 63 BC, in which year the region was conquered by the Roman general Pompey. Then began, from the point of view of the Christian Gospel narratives, a very important political development. Asmonaean rule, now under the licence of Rome, became increasingly diluted by the growing influence and power of the Herodian family, first under Antipas (see below). In 31 BC Augustus Caesar overthrew Mark Antony at the battle of Actium and the first of the Herods sought and received from the new Roman emperor, the governorship of Judaea, Samaria, Galilee, Peraea and Idumaea. The Herods, as noted above, were from the area of Idumaea, a region in the south of Judaea. According to the Jewish historian Josephus (Antiq 14.1.3.9) the Herods were not of pure Jewish descent: "It is true ......that Antipater was of the stock of the principal Jews who came out of Babylon into Judaea; but that assertion ..... was to gratify Herod, who was his son, and who by certain revolutions of fortune, came afterwards to be king of the Jews." The fact that the Herods were of Idumean stock threw a serious question into the minds of many among the Jewish populace as to the Herodians' acceptability as rulers over the Jewish nation.

The Jews of the Dispersion
During the almost continuous periods of foreign domination of 'Palestine' of the inter-testament period, the unique monotheistic Jewish religion was preserved, so faithful Jews and Christians believe, first and foremost by the power of God. The Israelites had long been a separated, *chosen* people, and vitally different from their neighbours in that they worshipped only one God.

Among the outward means by which this unique religion was preserved, one of the most important was the centralisation and focus of its worship in Jerusalem. If some of God's laws in the Old Testament appear to us to be narrow and exclusive, it must be said that it is unlikely that monotheism could have been preserved without them. In view of the religious state of the ancient world and Israel's tendency to adopt foreign 'gods' during the earlier stages of her history, strict religious isolation was necessary in order to preserve the pure worship of God from the pollution of foreign elements.

Wherever they travelled, Greeks and Romans carried their 'gods' around with them, or alternatively would adopt religions similar to their own. This was not an option for the Jews, who had one temple, in Jerusalem, and one God, the Almighty. The temple in Jerusalem was the only place that the God-appointed priesthood could offer acceptable sacrifice for the forgiveness of sins or for worship of God. On this temple focused all of Israel's sacred memories of their past and hopes for the future. The history of Israel and its future prospects were inextricably bound up with its religion. Without its religion Israel had no history, and without its history, no religion. It can be fairly said that history, religion, patriotism and hope all pointed to Jerusalem and its temple as the focus of Israel's unity.

The depressed state of the nation at the hands of various conquering enemies had not totally undermined Israel's confidence. Israel had passed through great tribulations before and had emerged triumphant from them. Even in recent history, a very great tribulation had been successfully faced, when the Syrian King Antiochus IV forbade their religion and sought to destroy their sacred books and force them into heathen worship. Worst of all, he had desecrated the temple, raising an altar there to the worship of Zeus Olympios. But God had preserved them through this, raising up Judas the Maccabee —popularly remembered as *God's hammer*,[1] who defeated the professional army of Syria with his guerrilla volunteers and then restored and purified the temple.

The Jews of Galilee, Samaria and Judaea had become, by the time of Christ's birth, a minority among the wider Jewish people. The majority of the nation comprised what was known as 'the dispersion', a term which no longer fully expressed its original meaning —the banishment by God of His people into exile as punishment for their sins. The first-century dispersion was voluntary, encouraged by economic and political considerations. But the very term 'dispersion' still expressed a measure of sorrow, of social and political isolation, felt by these dispersed Jews who continued to look towards Jerusalem as their spiritual home.

There were, in practice, two dispersions, one to the east and the other to the west. The eastern dispersion maintained close connection with 'Palestine' and in some respects was not so much a true 'dispersion', with all that the word implied, as simply a geographic separation. The western dispersion, however, began progressively to lose its close affinity with 'Palestine', as its people became more assimilated into the Greek culture in which they lived and worked. They were known as the 'dispersion of the Greeks' (see John 7:35 in this regard) or as 'Hellenists' or 'Grecians'.

The difference between the 'Hellenists' and the 'Hebrews' was far deeper than simply language. It extended to the whole direction of thought. There were intellectual influences pervading the Greek world from which it was impossible for Jews to isolate themselves. These Hellenist Jews were viewed with contempt by the Hebrew hierarchy, especially the party of the Pharisees, who openly declared the Hellenists to be far inferior to the eastern (or 'Babylonian') Jews. That such feelings, and the suspicions which they engendered, had struck deep into the popular mind is shown by the fact that, even in the apostolic church in its earliest days, disputes broke out between Hellenist Christians and Hebrew Christians arising from suspicions of unfair dealings based on factional prejudices (see Acts 6:1).

The 'Babylonian' Jews, by contrast, were viewed as more *pure* Jews. The land of Babylon and even parts of Syria were, in any case, considered by some Jews to be historically and even geographically a part of 'Palestine', as far north as Antioch. In regard to this Babylonian dispersion it should be noted that from the time of the earlier dispersion (which *was* a judgement of God - see for example 2 Chronicles 36: 11-21) perhaps only 50,000 Jews had returned whilst the wealthiest remained behind. According to Josephus, the Jewish historian, there were very large numbers, perhaps millions, of Jews in the Trans-Euphratic provinces (Antiq. 11.5.2; 15.2.2; 18.9.1 ff). To judge by the numbers of Jews killed in uprisings, for example 50,000 in Seleucia alone – according to Antiq. 18.9.9 – these figures do not seem exaggerated. Such a large and compact body naturally became a political power. Treated well under the Persian monarchy, they continued, after the fall of that empire (330 BC) to be favoured by the successors of Alexander, and were similarly favoured in the Parthian empire (beginning 63 BC) in which the Jews formed an important element in its opposition to Rome. So great was their influence that as late as 40 AD, the Roman legate avoided provoking their hostility, according to the Jewish historian and philosopher Judaeus Philo (d. AD 45-50). Even where they were numerous, however, the Jews still faced periodic and sometimes bloody persecution in these eastern lands.

The influence of the dispersion had been felt in 'Palestine' itself in other ways: even the Hebrew language, both written and spoken, had been changed by the returning Jews. Instead of the ancient characters employed, the exiles brought with them on their return the now familiar square Hebrew letters, which gradually came into general use. The language spoken by the Jews was no longer Hebrew, but Aramaean, both in Babylonia and 'Palestine'. In fact the ordinary people were quite ignorant of pure Hebrew by the time of Jesus —the older language then being the preserve of students and of the synagogue. Even there a *Methurgeman*, or interpreter, had to be used to translate into the vernacular the portions of Scripture read in the public services as well as the sermons of the rabbis. This was the origin of the so-called *Targumim*, or paraphrases of the Scripture. In the earliest times of this practice, the Methurgeman was forbidden to read his translation or write down a Targum, lest the paraphrase should be regarded as of equal authority to the original. But with the demise of pure Hebrew as a common language, their use became more and more necessary and was officially sanctioned before the end of the second century AD.

In response to these dispersions of population and the great political uncertainties of the four centuries immediately preceding Christ, the Jews placed increasing importance and emphasis on the *outward* observance and study of the letter of the Law. This is a very important point to understand, as it explains some of the opposition faced by the Lord Jesus from the religious authorities of His day. Indeed it can be argued that during this inter-testament period for many in the Jewish religious hierarchy, an unhealthy worship *of the Law* began to usurp the true worship of God, as the Hebrews slipped into religious legalism —something which the Lord Jesus strongly condemned. So it was that the *Mishnah*, or Second Law, came into being. This was originally intended to interpret and supplement the Law contained in the Scriptures. A development of the Mishnah was the *Midrash*, or investigation, a term which was applied to commentaries on the Scriptures and to preaching in general. These *Midrashim* progressively began to carry the authority of the Scripture itself and so increased the authority of the rabbis and scribes who deduced them.

We can begin to see the religious confusion of Judaism in Jesus' own day. The simplicity of God's Law was undermined by difficulties of language, by the use of interpreters to render the Scriptures into the vernacular language, the use of paraphrases of Scripture, the development of a "second Law" and to commentaries on Scripture which were treated as reverently as Scripture itself. These developments emphasised the differences between 'Palestinian' and other Jews, as well as differences between the Jewish hierarchy and the general populace. No wonder Jesus spoke of sheep without a shepherd.

The debt owed to the Babylonian Jews

As large numbers of Jews lived in the eastern lands, it was inevitable that some provision would be made for Hebrew scholarship amongst these dispersed people. Certainly all major matters concerning the Jewish faith were settled by the hierarchy in Jerusalem —ultimately by the Sanhedrin, or Council, of religious elders. It is known, for example, that the great Jewish Rabbi Hillel travelled from Babylonia to Jerusalem to advance his learning, which implies that in Babylonia there were lesser seats of learning. It is not clear how quickly the authority of these Babylonian religious schools increased and perhaps overshadowed those of Jerusalem, but it is known that this is what eventually happened.

The Jerusalem Hebrews already recognised a debt to their Babylonian brethren in the shape of Ezra, the prophet whose book forms a part of our Old Testament. He was instrumental in leading a second group of exiles from Babylonia back to Jerusalem, where he helped the people to reorganise their religious and social life in order to safeguard the spiritual heritage of Israel. Hundreds of years later, a similar debt was perceived by Jews to be owed to Hillel, the famous rabbi. And a third great rabbi, one Chija (one of the teachers of the second century AD and who is still viewed among the celebrated of rabbinical authority), was yet again instrumental in restoring Jewish learning and law at a time of crisis. "It is one of those strangely significant, almost symbolical facts of history," writes Alfred Edersheim, "that after the destruction of Jerusalem in AD 70 the spiritual supremacy of Palestine passed to Babylonia, and that rabbinical Judaism, under the stress of political adversity, voluntarily transferred itself to the seats of Israel's ancient dispersion, as if to ratify by its own act what the judgement of God had already executed."[2]

The debt owed to the Hellenists

Whilst the Hellenists were considered to be second class Jews, many Jews from the Jerusalem hierarchy would, perhaps grudgingly, have acknowledged at least one major debt owed to them. This was the translation of the Old Testament into Greek, a translation we now refer to as the Septuagint. It was impossible for the Hellenised Jewish communities to remain completely separate from their Greek surroundings and influences. Greek Jews were not a compact body, as were their eastern brethren. Rather, they were dispersed within their dispersion, living here and there as the opportunities for trade and commerce were presented. Their trades, which were the very reason for their being in 'foreign lands' were purely secular and demanded social involvement with the communities among whom they lived and worked.

When these Hellenist Jews stepped out of their own immediate family and community, they were confronted with the full force of Grecianism, which was refined and elegant. It was profound and extremely attractive. These Jews might resist, but they could not sweep Grecianism aside. The most telling strength of Grecianism was its intellectual force – its philosophy – before which these Hellenist Jews found it necessary to defend their faith in the intellectual debates in which they became embroiled. Greek philosophy penetrated everywhere. It was the very air that was breathed and the environment within which Hellenist Judaism must be preserved. Jews felt it necessary to meet argument with argument, and to do that they needed to be certain of what they believed. To be certain of what they believed they needed a translation of their Scriptures in a language they could understand.

The Septuagint translation originated in this particular need of Hellenist Jews who were ignorant of the Hebrew language. Whilst it is not clear when this great translation was begun, we do have some clear idea as to when it was finished: from the prologue to the apocryphal 'Wisdom of Jesus son of Sirach', we learn that in his days the canon of Scripture was closed and that on his arrival in Egypt, then under the rule of Euergetes, he found the so-called Septuagint translation completed. Despite there being two kings with the surname Euergetes, most scholars conclude that the one in question reigned between 247 and 221 BC. From this it follows that the canon of Scripture was at this stage fixed in 'Palestine'.

This Septuagint version, complete with its many difficulties and occasional extreme liberality in translation, became to a large extent the 'people's bible' of its time. Alfred Edersheim comments: "....we specially mark that it preserved the messianic interpretation of Genesis 49:10 and Numbers 24:7, 17, 23, bringing us evidence of what had been the generally received view two and a half centuries before the birth of Jesus. It must have been on account of the use made of the Septuagint in argument, that later voices in the Synagogue declared this version to have been as great a calamity to Israel as the making of the Golden calf...."[3]

Sects and parties at the time of Christ

In the four Gospels we read of Priests, Levites, Scribes, Pharisees, Sadducees, Herodians, Samaritans and Galileans. Most of these officials or categories appeared in the inter-testament period. Who and what were they?

The word '**priest**' occurs in the Gospels a dozen times and 'high priest' or 'chief priests' 84 times. The Jewish priesthood was ordained by God at the time of Moses, in the tribe of Levi. The function of the priests was strictly religious. After the return from captivity in Babylon, however, from the time of Ezra and Nehemiah, the civil power of the state passed into the hands of the priests, so that they were 'princes of the realm' as well as ministers of religion. The head of this order was the high priest. In the time of Christ the priests were, for the most part, persistent enemies of Jesus, being worldly in spirit and therefore quite unable genuinely to shepherd the people as their religious office required. Ultimately it was they who delivered Jesus to Pilate to be crucified.

The **Levites** were the descendants of Levi and had special religious status. They were accepted in the principal position as the 'first-born' of the Israelites, and had control of the tabernacle and its religious services —see Numbers chapter 3 for the account of their adoption by God. The priestly functions of the Levites changed over the centuries and it is today not entirely clear as to the precise relationship between the priests and the Levites, but by the time of Christ it was the Levites who performed the subordinate services associated with public worship, for example as musicians, gate keepers, guardians, temple officials, judges and craftsmen. They are only mentioned in the Gospels twice (Luke 10:32 and John 1:19).

In New Testament times the **scribes** (or "teachers of the law" in the New International Version of the Bible) were the students, interpreters and teachers of Old Testament Scriptures and accordingly were held in high esteem by the ordinary people. They were fiercely opposed to the Lord Jesus. He, in turn, denounced them for making the Word of God ineffective by their traditions (see Matt 16:21; Matt 21:15 and 23:2. See also Mark 12:28-40). The Scribes were also called lawyers (Matt 22:35; Luke 10:25; Luke 11:45-53 and Luke 14:3).

The **Pharisees** (*separated*) arose in the time of the Maccabees and were called 'separatists' in mockery by their enemies, because they 'separated' themselves from the political ambitions of the parties in their nation. They were experts in the written law and the oral law. In belief, they were conservatives, in contrast to the very liberal Sadducees. Their religious orthodoxy, however, was spiritually barren and so the Lord Jesus condemned them (e.g. Matt 12:1-2; Matt 23:1-33; Luke 6:6-7; Luke 11:37-54). It seems that in the Pharisees and Sadducees, the Israelites had two opposite and equally unacceptable extremes: legalism (the Pharisees) and license (the Sadducees). This has always been a problem, even in the Christian church. Christians see the hand of Satan in these extremes as they off-balance and distract the church from its true mission.

The name of the **Sadducees** is likely to have been derived, it is thought, from Zadok the High Priest of King Solomon's time (1 Kings 2:35). They were the aristocratic political party among the Jews, the rivals of the Pharisees. In religious belief they were the 'liberals' of their day, denying the existence of spirits, the resurrection of the dead to face judgement and the immortality of the soul. They were very much the secularists of their faith and had they been strong enough, would probably have paganised it. The Sadducees came to prominence at the time of the Maccabees and disappeared completely after the destruction of the Jewish nation in AD 70. Like the Pharisees they were condemned by Jesus (Matt 16:1-12 and Matt 22:23-33). It is ironic that, coming from two very different and often diametrically opposing viewpoints, the conservative Pharisees and the liberal Sadducees should have made common cause in opposing the man who described himself as 'the way, the truth and the life' (John 14:6) but perhaps this only reflects that their campaign of untruth came from the same root.

The **Herodians** were a political, rather than a religious party. They took their name from the family of Herod and obtained their right to rule from the Roman government. In practice they were Rome's puppet government. The Herodians were averse to any change in the political system, which favoured them so singularly, and viewed Christ as a revolutionary. They accordingly came into conflict with Jesus and were condemned by Him. (Mark 3:6; Mark 8:15 and Mark 12:13-17). Interestingly, in these passages from Mark, the Pharisees are seen allied to the Herodians against Jesus. This 'axis' might be more easy to understand, since both the Pharisees and Herodians represented 'conservatism' within Judaism, one religious and the other political.

The **Samaritans** were a mixed race living in the province of Samaria. In 722 BC the Assyrian King Sargon II took the Israelites of the northern kingdom to Assyria as captives, but left many of the poorer and weaker behind. Later, people from Cuthah, Babylon, Hamath, Sepharvaim and Ava were sent to Samaria and intermarried with the remnants of the northern kingdom, bringing with them their own idols. Esar Haddon sent to the Samaritans a priest from the tribe of Levi, who lived at Bethel, and he taught them that they should fear the Lord. The result was a sort of syncretism, where the Samaritans worshipped the Hebrew God and other gods as well. When in 535 BC the second temple was being built under Zerubbabel (Ezra 4:1-3), the Samaritans offered help, but were refused. From this time forward a bitter enmity sprang up between the Samaritans and their Hebrew neighbours, to the south and north. This enmity was still very much in evidence in the time of Christ, which gives added significance to the account of the Samaritan leper (Luke 17:16) and to the parable of the Good Samaritan (Luke 10:30-37).

The **Galileans** were an extreme party which arose in northern 'Palestine' and followed one Judas of Galilee, who began a rebellion against all foreign domination. They were insistent on their own rights and cared little for the rights of others. As political fanatics, they came into violent conflict with Pilate (Luke 13:1-3). Christ's enemies made efforts to identify Him and His disciples with this fanatical group (Matt 26:69; Mark 14:70; Luke 23:6).

It can readily be seen from this brief description of the sects and parties prominent at the time of Jesus' birth, even before considering the added complication of the conquering Romans, that 'Palestine' was a turbulent, troubled and violent region. There was certainly lawlessness in those troubled days, but more unsettling for the ordinary people of that sad and often brutal region, was that it was a time of *law with disorder*, represented most conspicuously by King Herod "the Great" himself.

The Herodians
The glorious victories of the Maccabees against the Syrian overlords culminating in 141 BC with the purification of the temple had appeared, for a moment, to be almost a return to the days of the miraculous deliverances in the Old Testament. But the moment would not last for long. The Maccabees became both high priests and kings, thus thoroughly secularising the nation state. The remainder of Maccabean rule was marked by internecine squabbling punctuated with open warfare. This period also saw the rise of the two opposing parties, the Pharisees and the Sadducees. Contention for the crown led Judas the Maccabee into an alliance with the Romans, and from that time forward there was a discernible downward spiral in the fortunes of Israel. In 63 BC, when Pompey captured Jerusalem and replaced the high priest, the last of the Maccabean rulers was effectively stripped of power and the country became a tributary of Rome, subject to the Roman governor of Syria. Shortly afterwards Gabinius, a Roman governor, divided 'Palestine' into five independent districts.

About fifty years before this, the district of Idumaea, to the south of Judaea, had been conquered by the Maccabean king John Hyrcanus I, and its inhabitants forced to adopt Judaism. After it became Judean, its administration was delegated to one Antipater, a local noble of considerable political cunning and determination. Antipater was an Edomite (an Arab from the region between the Dead Sea and the Gulf of Aqaba). A man of great wealth and influence, he increased both by marrying Kypros, the daughter of a noble from Petra, (in southwest Jordan) which was at that time the capital of the rising Nabataean kingdom. His son, Herod, although a practising Jew, was therefore of Arab origin on both sides.

Antipater successfully intervened in the unhappy civil war for the crown, which was being waged between the opposing factions of Hyrcanus II and his warlike brother, Aristobulus, finally decided in the favour of Hyrcanus II by the force of Roman arms under Pompey. King Hyrcanus II, however, was a weak character and real power was wielded by Antipater. Around 57 BC Herod, Antipater's son, met and befriended Mark Antony and became his lifelong friend. Julius Caesar also favoured the family and in 47 BC he conferred on Antipater hereditary Roman citizenship, a considerable honour. The confusing and sickening history of the Herodians is recounted by the Jewish historian Josephus. Readers who would like to follow the story in greater detail should refer either to Josephus complete works[4] or to Alfred Edersheim's full and scholarly summary in *The Life and Times of Jesus the Messiah*, referenced earlier. The following is only a brief outline.

Herod "the Great"

Herod made his political debut at the age of 25 when, in 42 BC, his father Antipater appointed him, with Mark Antony's approval, as governor of Galilee, an act which rendered Hycanus II powerless. In 40 BC the Parthians invaded Palestine, civil war broke out and Herod fled to Rome. The Roman Senate nominated him king of Judea and equipped him with an army to make good his claim. In 37 BC, at the age of 36, Herod became the unchallenged ruler of Judaea, a position he maintained for 32 years. To consolidate his new power, Herod divorced his wife, Doris, banished her and his son from court and married Mariamme, a princess of the Maccabean family. Although the marriage was primarily aimed at ending his feud with the Maccabees, Herod was, by all accounts, deeply in love with his second wife.

Herod's reign was, however, marked by a paranoid fear of rivals and his rule proved very bloody, even by the standards of the day. His wife Mariamme's uncle Antigonus (a Maccabee) had been the prime antagonist in the earlier civil war. On Herod's request he was executed by the Romans. Next to experience Herod's vengeance were the principal supporters in Jerusalem of his former rival Antigonus. Forty-five of the noblest and richest were executed. Herod then appointed an obscure Babylonian to the high priesthood, a move which aroused the active opposition of Mariamme's mother, Alexandra, who claimed the high priesthood for her son Aristobulus. Eventually Herod relented and Aristobulus, although only seventeen, was made high priest —a sad reflection of the spiritual decline in Israel. Herod had his mother in law watched from that time forward. Aristobulus, as a Maccabee and therefore still viewed favourably by many of the populace, was joyously greeted at the religious Feast of Tabernacles. Herod feared him as a rival and arranged for a bathing accident to take his life.

Alexandra denounced the murder of Aristobulus and Herod was consequently summoned to Mark Antony. Bribery of Antony and behind the scenes manoeuvring enabled Herod to weather this storm. During his absence from Jerusalem, Herod committed the government to his uncle Joseph, who was also his brother in law, having married Herod's sister, Salome. Herod's clear instruction was that, should he be found guilty by Antony, Mariamme was to be killed —she was not to be allowed to become the wife of another. Joseph told this to Mariamme, apparently to show her how much Herod loved her! But on Herod's return from Mark Antony, Salome accused her husband Joseph of impropriety with Mariamme and, when it became apparent that Joseph had told Mariamme of Herod's secret and dark instruction, Herod took this as confirmation of the charge. Joseph was executed, without even a hearing.

Serious foreign crises now supervened. During the war between the two Roman leaders Octavian and Mark Antony, the de facto heirs to Caesar's power, Herod supported his friend Antony and continued to do so despite his friend's mistress, Cleopatra, the queen of Egypt, using her influence with Antony to obtain some of Herod's best lands. After Antony's defeat at the Battle of Actium in 31 BC, Herod openly admitted to the victorious Octavian which side he had supported. Octavian, who knew Herod from his visit to Rome, believed him to be the one man likely to rule 'Palestine' in the best interests of Rome and duly confirmed him as king. He also generously restored to Herod the lands stolen by Cleopatra and in succeeding years added to them parts of the modern lands of Jordan, southern Lebanon and Syria. In order to further secure himself from possible domestic rivals, Herod had the aged deposed King Hyrcanus II executed, on the (probably) spurious grounds of intrigues with the Arabs during the earlier war.

When summoned to appear before Augustus to explain his conduct during the earlier war, Herod entrusted Mariamme to one Soemus, with the same instruction as had been given to the earlier Jospeh. Again Mariamme learned of the instruction and again Salome and others made accusations of unfaithfulness about Mariamme. Soemus was slain without a hearing and this time, Mariamme followed after a showpiece trial. Heartbroken remorse gripped Herod and brought him to the brink of suicide. Alexandria, Mariamme's mother, continued to plot the overthrow of Herod but was discovered and executed. The remnants of the Maccabean family were now few. The treacherous Salome had married another Maccabee on the death she precipitated for her first husband Joseph. She married Costobarus, the governor of Idumaea but, tiring of him, denounced him to Herod, who had Costobarus and a number of other Maccabees executed. The Maccebee family was now virtually extinct.

Herod's suspicions turned then on his own family. The king had ten wives during his eventful career, but this account focuses only on those whose offspring play a significant part in this sad history. The son of Herod's first wife, Doris, was Antipater; those of the loved Mariamme were Alexander and Aristobulus. A second Mariamme, whose father Herod had made high priest, bore a son who was named Herod (a name shared by other sons). Malthake, a Samaritan, was the mother of Archelaus and Herod Antipas. Finally Cleopatra of Jerusalem bore Philip.

The sons of the Macabbean Mariamme, as heirs presumptive, were sent to the centre of power, Rome, for their education. This was in order to pay due homage to the emperor and the political system whilst ensuring they would become known in Rome as friends of Rome. On their return to Judaea these princes were married: Alexander to the daughter of the king of Cappadicia and Arisobulus to his cousin Berenice, the daughter of Salome. Salome, for her part, continued to hate the dead Maccabean Mariamme and her offspring. The two princes, in their Maccabean pride, did not disguise their feelings towards the house of their father. At first Herod did not believe the denunciations of his sister, Salome, but eventually his own suspicions against his family took control. As a first step Antipater, the son of his first wife Doris, was recalled from exile and sent to Rome for education, a sign of disfavour to Alexander and Aristobulus. Next Herod sent the two disfavoured sons to Rome in order to place formal accusations against them before the emperor. For a while the emperor's wise counsellors were able to maintain the peace, but as time went by and further family intrigues took place in Jerusalem, Herod again laid charges against the two sons before emperor Augustus who eventually gave him full powers over them. They were duly condemned to death and, as two elderly soldiers ventured to intercede for them, some 300 supporters of a supposed plot were slaughtered whilst the two princes were strangled in prison.[5]

Antipater was now heir presumptive but, impatient for the throne, he plotted with Herod's brother, Pheroras, against his father. The wily Salome again denounced her nephew, who fled to Rome. Herod later obtained clear evidence of Antipater's failed plot and lured him back to Judaea where he was arrested. With

Augustus' permission Antipater was executed, just five days before Herod's own death. So ended a bloody and brutal reign. Small wonder that Herod feared the birth of a new king, announced by the wise men from the east. Small wonder that we read, "When Herod heard this he was disturbed, and all Jerusalem with him" (Matt 2:3). Small wonder that when Joseph was warned in a dream that Herod sought the infant Jesus, he should flee that very night. Small wonder that the slaughter of all the boys under the age of two in Bethlehem should have been ordered by Herod without a second thought. So steeped in human blood was Herod's reign that the slaughter is not even mentioned in Josephus. (Historians also believe that the highly partial Josephus, writing for a Roman audience at a difficult time for Jews, would not have mentioned the slaughter because it would have necessitated further and detailed reference to Jesus whom, of course, they had executed and whom, as a Jew, Josephus did not wish to elevate in any way).

No greater contrast could be imagined as between King Jesus, whose most magnificent act was to lay down His life for His people – sinners all – and Herod "the Great" whose most notable characteristic was his willingness to lay down the lives of others to reinforce his own wretched hold on power. Alfred Edersheim summarises Herod's reign: "We can understand the feelings of the people towards such a king. They hated the Idumaean; they detested his semi heathen reign; they abhorred his deeds of cruelty. The king had surrounded himself with foreign councillors, and was protected by foreign mercenaries from Thracia, Germany, and Gaul. (Jos Antiq. 17.8.3.) So long as he lived, no woman's honour was safe, no man's life secure. An army of all powerful spies pervaded Jerusalem —nay, the king himself would stoop to that office (Antiq 15.10.4). If pique or private enmity led to denunciation, then torture would extract any confession from the most innocent. What his relation to Judaism had been, may easily be inferred. He would be a Jew —even build the temple, advocate the cause of the Jews in other lands, and, in a certain sense, conform to the law of Judaism.... Strangest of all, he seems to have had at least the passive support of two of the greatest rabbis

—the Phillio and Sameas of Josephus (Antiq. 14.9.4; 15.1.1; 15.10.4) ...We can but conjecture, that they preferred even his rule to what had preceded; and hoped it might lead to a Roman Protectorate, which would leave Judaea practically independent, or rather under Rabbinic rule."[6]

Notes

[1] The name Maccabee may be derived from Maqqabha —a hammer

[2] Alfred Edersheim *The Life and Times of Jesus the Messiah* (Hendrickson Publishers, Inc., 1993) p. 9.

[3] *Ibid.* p. 21

[4] William Whiston *Josephus, The Complete Works* (Thomas Nelson Publishers, 1998).

[5] It is recorded in Macrobius, Saturnalia 2.4.11 that Augustus made the grim joke that it was safer to be Herod's pig than Herod's son. The king's pig was safe, on account of his studied outward observance of Judaism; his sons were not.

[6] *Op. cit.,* p. 90.

4

What Messiah did
the Jews Expect?

That first-century Jews were – and some Jews *still* are – expecting
a Messiah, is a fact of history. But what sort of Messiah did they
expect? And how did the infant born in Bethlehem who later
grew up in Nazareth differ from this expectation? Once these
pieces are slotted into the "Christmas" jigsaw, the events of the
Incarnation become much clearer as we see them in God's overall
plan of salvation. It can be stated at the outset that the basic ideas
of the rabbis concerning the Messiah were at great variance to
the reality found in the carpenter from Nazareth. This goes some
way to explain the enmity which the religious leaders of Jesus'
day displayed towards Him, but we might also observe that any
'Messiah' who did not confirm and approve the power of the
Rabbis would have been rejected by them.

John Blanchard, in his excellent short book *Why Y2K?*, subtitled "What the millennium is (really) all about", commented
on Jesus' own claim to be the Messiah. Whilst Jesus never said
"I am the Messiah", it is plain that this is what he meant his
followers – and those who opposed him – to understand. He
proved his messiahship by his deeds. The circumstances of his
birth supported, rather than detracted, from that claim and in his
dealings with the religious leaders of his day Jesus was as open
as circumstances would allow as to his true identity. In John 5:39

we read that Jesus pointed out to the Jewish religious leaders that, in spite of their "diligent" study of the Scriptures they failed to recognise that those same Scriptures "testified" about him. John Blanchard comments:

'About 2000 years before Jesus was born, God told Abraham, the founder of the Jewish nation, that through his offspring "All nations on earth will be blessed." (Gen 22:18). This means that twenty centuries before Jesus was born every other family except Abraham's was out of the running as far as producing the Messiah was concerned. Other Old Testament prophecies showed that Abraham's line of succession would run through Isaac (who was not Abraham's oldest son) Jacob (who was not Isaac's first born) and Jacob's fourth son Judah (by-passing his eleven brothers). Eleven generations later a man called Jesse was identified as being in the messianic line, and of Jesse's eight sons David was the one of whom he said that he would 'raise up ... a righteous Branch' (Jeremiah 23:5).

'In a nutshell, then, the Old Testament said that the Messiah would come from a line taken directly through Abraham, Isaac, Jacob, Jesse and David. This family tree would itself preclude most of the human race, but there were two other significant pointers. One of the messianic prophecies said that the tribe of Judah would provide Israel with all its kings *until the Messiah arrived*: "The sceptre will not depart from Judah .... until he comes to whom it belongs" (Genesis 49:10) —and Jesus was born just before Judah's government collapsed with the destruction of Jerusalem in A.D.70. The second pointer was the prophecy which told *exactly* where Jesus would be born. "But you, Bethlehem Ephrathah, though you are small among the clans of Judah, out of you will come for me one who will be the ruler over Israel." (Micah 5:2). There were two Bethlehems, one in the region of Ephrathah in Judea, and the other seventy miles to the north in Zebulon. The New Testament tells us that Jesus was born in Bethlehem in Judea, the one identified by the Old Testament prophet. (Matthew 2:1.)'[1]

Messianic prophecy

Appendix 3 to this series of studies is a simple table identifying the key events in the reports of the Nativity found in the Gospels, together with the Old Testament prophecies which point directly or indirectly toward them. The table which follows immediately below, is developed fully in W. Graham Scroggie's scholarly work *A Guide to the Gospels*,[2] but only the prophecies that concern Jesus' 'human pedigree' and birth are included here. Readers are encouraged to work through these:

	Prediction	Fulfilment
1 To be the woman's seed	Gen 3:15	Matt 1:18
2 To be born of a virgin	Isa 7:14	Matt 1:22-3
3 To be of the line of Abraham	Gen 12:3, 7	Gal 3:16
	Gen 17:7	Rom 9:5
4 To be of the Tribe of Judah	Gen 49:10	Heb 7:14
		Rev 5:6
5 To be of the House of David	2 Sam 7:12-13	Rom 1:3
	Isaiah 11:1-2	Lk 1:31-33
6 To be born at Bethlehem	Micah 5:2-3	Matt 2:6
		Luke 2:4, 15
7 To be called Immanuel	Isaiah 7:14	Matt 1:23
8 To be worshipped by Gentiles	Isaiah 60:3	Matt 2:11
9 To have a forerunner	Isaiah 40:3, 6, 9	Matt 3:1-3
	Malachi 3:1	Mark 1:2-3
10 To be incarnate by birth	Isaiah 9: 6	Luke 2:11
11 To be called out of Egypt	Hosea 11:1	Matt 2:15

There may, of course, be some debate as to whether the prophecies *were* fulfilled as identified above —indeed as to whether they were prophecies at all. It is only necessary at this point to say that these prophecies have been generally accepted through the history of the Christian church as being *messianic prophecies* and are relatively few among many that can be identified as such.

The offices of the Messiah

The word Messiah comes from the Hebrew verb *mashach* which means *to anoint*. The Messiah therefore is 'the anointed one'. In Hebrew practice anointing was associated particularly with three types of people. First and foremost, it was associated with the office of **king**. When Samuel saw the young David, the Lord said to him 'Arise and anoint him; he is the one'. So Samuel took his horn of oil and anointed David in the presence of his brothers. (1 Sam 16:12-13). Later we read of God speaking through the Psalmist, "I have found David my servant; with my sacred oil I have anointed him." (Ps 89:20). David, of course, was the greatest of the Jewish kings, but we also read of Zadok the priest and Nathan the prophet anointing Solomon (1 Kings 1:45) and Jehoiadah similarly anointing Joash (2 Kings 11:12). Secondly, anointing was associated with the office of **priest**. God's command was that the priests should be anointed and consecrated —anointing was by pouring oil over the head (Ex 29:7). Finally, anointing was associated with the **prophets** themselves; so Elijah was instructed to anoint Elisha as his successor as prophet (1 Kings 19:16) whilst Isaiah was able to claim that the Spirit of the Lord had anointed him to preach good news to the poor (Isaiah 61:1).

It is significant, therefore, that from the beginning the Messiah – the anointed one – was King, Priest and Prophet. These, of course, were three of the great offices of the Lord Jesus. He was **King** in being King of the Jews (Matt 2:2 and Matt 27:11) and by Him God's kingdom would be established, although Jesus always recognised God the Father as King ("your kingdom come" was how He taught His disciples to pray – not "my kingdom come" – Matt 6:10). He was **priest** (see Hebrews chapter 7, especially verses 23 - 5) in being of the priestly order of Melchizedek[3]. He was **prophet** to the people of His time (e.g. Luke 7:16; Luke 9:8; Mark 6:15) and also referred to himself as prophet (Luke 4:24; Matt 13:57; John 4:44). Bear in mind that the word Christ is the Greek translation of Messiah, and that from the earliest times believers linked the name Jesus with the title Christ, almost as if it were a proper name. This is the way the title is often used today, but strictly speaking we should refer to *Jesus the Christ*. The word Christ is used thirteen times in Matthew, six in Mark and twice in Luke and very often in the synoptic Gospels the word is used as a title. So, when John the Baptist began his ministry, people wondered whether he was *the Christ* (Luke 3:15). At Caesarea Philippi Peter first referred to Jesus as *the Christ* (Matt 16:16; Mark 8:29). Jesus Himself did not deny the title (Luke 22:67). To give Jesus the title Christ is the same as calling Him Messiah.

There is no doubt that the New Testament presents Jesus as Messiah. This was the basis of the teaching of the apostle Paul, particularly when he preached to Jews. After his Damascus road experience of conversion, Paul amazed the Jews who knew him as a zealous anti-Christian, by proving in their synagogues that Jesus was the Christ (Acts 9:22). His message in Thessalonica was that, "This Jesus I am proclaiming to you is the Christ" (Acts 17:3). Again, in Corinth, "Paul devoted himself exclusively to preaching, testifying to the Jews that Jesus was the Christ" (Acts 18:3). Not only Paul, but Apollos in Ephesus, "vigorously refuted the Jews in public debate, proving from the Scriptures that Jesus was the Christ" (Acts 18:28). So there is clear and unmistakable evidence that the early preaching of the Christian church presented Jesus as the Messiah.

The Jews expected the Messiah to be intrinsically a part of Israel: the Messiah was thought of as the seed of Abraham, as the 'son' in a unique sense, as well as the 'son of David'. They saw the whole of the Old Testament as a picture in which the figure of the Messiah was clearly discernible. There was a belief, referred to in detail by Alfred Edersheim, that all the miracles and deliverances of Israel's past would be re-enacted, only in a much wider manner, in the days of the Messiah. Israel's whole history was seen as symbolising its future and in this past/future perspective, says Edersheim, we should understand two sayings of the Talmud: "All the prophets prophesied only of the days of the Messiah (Sanh 99a), and, "The world was created only for the Messiah' (Sanh 98b)[4].

The Messiah as the Son of David

The belief in the coming Messiah was closely associated with the covenant relationship of Israel to God, who had chosen Israel to be His special people. Sovereignly, God had entered into the unique relationship with Israel in which He took them to be His unique people and He in turn would be in a unique way, their God. The Jewish people pledged themselves to keep and obey God's laws (Exodus 24:1-8) and believed, both in their religious convictions and in their popular sentiment, that one day the nation would enter into the visible state of honour, glory and supremacy which they believed to be their right. The Messiah would be the agent of God who would bring about this destiny.

The messianic dream was at first very simple: it was a dream of peace and prosperity to be accomplished under a king of David's line. Sometimes the vision centred not so much around an individual king, but a dynasty of kings of the Davidic line. Later the ideal assumed rather more superhuman proportions, but the idea of the Messiah as a son of David was never totally lost. In 2 Samuel we read how King David decided to build a temple to the Lord, but that Nathan the prophet told him that this honour was reserved for his son Solomon. Nathan also spoke God's great promise to David: "Your house and your kingdom shall endure forever before me, your throne shall be established forever" (2 Sam 7:16). Succeeding prophets repeated the promise, interpreting the messianic vision in its light. This was to be a dream that never died:

A shoot will come up from the stump of Jesse; from his roots a Branch will bear fruit ..... In that day the root of Jesse will stand as a banner for the peoples; the nations will rally to him, and his place of rest will be glorious.

Isaiah 11:1, 10

"The days are coming" declares the Lord, "when I will raise up to David a righteous branch, a King who will reign wisely and do what is just and right in the Land. In his days Judah will be saved and Israel will live in safety. This is the name by which he will be called: The Lord Our Righteousness.

Jeremiah 23:5f

They will serve the Lord their God and David their king, whom I will raise up for them.

Jeremiah 30:9

In those days and at that time I will make a righteous Branch sprout from David's line; he will do what is just and right in the land.

Jeremiah 33:15

For this is what the Lord says: 'David will never fail to have a man sit on the throne of the house of Israel, nor will the priests, who are Levites, ever fail to have a man stand before me continually to offer burnt offerings, to burn grain offerings, and to present sacrifices.

Jeremiah 33:17

I will make the descendants of David my servant and the Levites who minister before me as countless as the stars of the sky and as measureless as the sand on the seashore.

Jeremiah 33:22

I will place over them one shepherd, my servant David, and he will tend them; he will tend them and be their shepherd.

Ezekiel 34:23

Afterwards the Israelites will return and seek the Lord their God and David their king. They will come trembling to the Lord and to his blessings in the last days.

Hosea 3:5

In that day I will restore David's fallen tent. I will repair its broken places, restore its ruins, and build it as it used to be.

Amos 9:11

On that day the Lord will shield those who live in Jerusalem, so that the feeblest among them will be like David, and the house of David will be like God, like the Angel of the Lord going before them.

Zechariah 12:8

Once and for all, I have sworn by my holiness – and I will not lie to David – that his line will continue for ever and his throne endure before me like the sun; it will be established forever like the moon, the faithful witness in the sky.

Psalm 89:35-37

What are we to make of the mysterious prophecy concerning a *shoot* emerging from the stump of Jesse? And what of the *righteous branch*? What do these prophecies in particular signify? The branch became another name for the Messiah. This was because in spite of God's clear promise to David that his throne would last forever, it appeared from the time of King Nebuchadnezzar who had destroyed Judah, as though the royal throne had been chopped down like a tree —sawn right down to the roots and destroyed. For six hundred years from the time of Jeconiah (also rendered Jehoiachin) no descendant of David had held the throne. As we have already seen, King Herod who tried to kill the infant Jesus in Bethlehem, was not a true Jew, but a second-generation Edomite —to all intents and purposes, a foreign king.

Mary's line of descent from David was unbroken (see chapter 11), however Jesus would not have been born in Bethlehem had Joseph's descent not also been from David. So, from the apparently dead stump of David's fallen family tree, a shoot would suddenly emerge. Prophecies concerning the branch spanned 300 years. First Isaiah foretold some 760 years BC, at a time when David's descendants still ruled, that David's tree would become a stump remaining where it was felled, but the stump would remain as a holy seed. (Isaiah 6:13). This was elaborated further in Isaiah 11 verses 1 and 10. A shoot would emerge which would bear fruit and be a banner to the peoples (not 'people' —a sign that the new king's dominion would extend beyond Israel). The theme continues in Isaiah 53, perhaps the most messianic of all the messianic prophecies, speaking as it does of the atoning death of the Lord Jesus. In verse 2 we read, "He grew up before him like a tender shoot, and like a root out of dry ground."

A hundred and fifty years later, the prophet Jeremiah was also inspired to speak of the Branch. At this time the royal tree had been destroyed by Babylon. But Jeremiah was given the words we read above, about a "righteous branch" emerging. Perhaps a hundred years after this, the prophet Zechariah was given a similar picture. "Listen," he wrote, "O high priest Joshua and your associates seated before you, who are symbolic of things to come: I am going to bring my servant, the Branch". The theme of the Branch is explored thoroughly by Dr E K Victor Pearce in his book *Prophecy*. Having pointed out that Zechariah speaks of the Branch removing the guilt of the world in a single day (Zech 3:9), he writes: "Mary's line crossed with Joseph's at Zerubbabel's name ... and, as Mary's cousin was a priest, it meant that Jesus would be both priest and king. As priest, his atoning sacrifice would remove Earth's guilt in a single Good Friday. No wonder that, in Chapter 4, there were to be joyful shouts of 'Grace, grace, unto the stone which had become the head of the corner' and Zerubbabel would be the Davidic ancestor 'not by might, nor by power, but by my Spirit says the Lord.'"[5]

Could there be a clearer picture of the infant born into a poor family in an obscure backwater of the ancient world's mightiest empire, yet who would rule not by might, nor power, but by God's spirit? A picture of one born not by the agency of a human father, but by the agency of God's spirit.

The Messiah as nationalist leader

The image of the Messiah in the collective mind of the Jewish nation, was one of Israel's exultation through its Messiah, rather than salvation for the world. The rabbinic ideal was not of 'a light to the Gentiles' (Isaiah 42:6; Isaiah 49:6). Accordingly, there was a fundamental antagonism between the rabbis and Christ, quite irrespective of the manner in which Jesus carried out His work. The purely nationalistic elements, which formed the greater part of the rabbinic expectation of the future Messiah, never entered Jesus' teaching about the kingdom of God. Jesus so fundamentally separated Himself from the ideas of messiahship prevalent during His day, that it is of no surprise that he was not widely recognised as the Messiah. Furthermore, it is important to note that the doctrine of original sin, and the sinfulness of the whole human nature, were not held by the ancient rabbis. So, whilst they recognised the effects of sin, and of sin in Adam, the rabbis saw no need for a Redeemer who, as the second Adam, would restore what Adam had lost. These doctrines are fully developed and made explicit only in the New Testament, although Christians would argue that they can be fully deduced from the Old Testament as well.

What was the Jewish expectation of the nature, person and qualifications of the Messiah? Two inferences can be made from rabbinic writings and from Old Testament prophecies viewed as messianic. First, the idea of a divine personality, and of the union of two natures in the Messiah, was alien to the rabbis —and even, at first, to Jesus' own disciples. Second, Jewish orthodoxy viewed the Messiah as far above any human being, any prophet or even any angel. The boundary line between the Messiah and God was, in the rabbis' estimation, very narrow, so that when the reality of the Messiah Jesus finally burst upon the minds of the disciples, they had no difficulty in worshipping Jesus as Son of God. These two inferences accorded with ancient Jewish teaching. Beginning with the Septuagint rendering of Genesis 49:10 and Numbers 24:7, 17, we gather that the kingdom of the Messiah was higher than any earthly kingdom, and destined to rule all earthly kingdoms. The rendering of Ps 72:5, Ps 100:3, and especially Isaiah 9, goes much further, however. They teach the existence of the Messiah before his entry onto the world stage —before the moon (Ps 72), before the morning star (Ps 110), and eternal (Ps 72).

And what of the other rabbinic writings that held such sway in Jesus' time? What clues did they give about the Messiah? There are a number of these and they are dealt in some detail by Alfred Edersheim in *The Life and Times of Jesus the Messiah* (see for example Book 2, Chapter 5), and also in William Barclay's *Jesus As They Saw Him.*[6] The treatment below is necessarily brief:

The third book of the **Sibylline Oracles** which, with a few exceptions, date from over 150 years BC, presents a picture of messianic times. Here, the Messiah is the King sent from heaven who would "judge every man in blood and splendour of fire" (Sybill Or. 3.285, 286).

This is repeated in a reference to "the King whom God will send from the sun" (Sybill Or. 3. 652). The writings go on to present an eternal superhuman kingdom (Sybill Or. 652-807). Such a kingdom, it might be added, would have a superhuman King. In the so-called **Book of Enoch** which most historians believe to be dated in its oldest parts (chapters 1-36 and 72-105) from 150 to 130 BC, there are messianic references to 'the Woman's son' (Enoch 62.5) and 'the Son of Man' (e.g. Enoch 48.2; 62.7; 69.29) amongst other obscure titles.

Still more explicit is a collection of eighteen psalms, dating from the century before Christ, which are now known as the **Psalms of Solomon**. These are quoted quite extensively in Barclay's *Jesus As They Saw Him* (see pp 98-100), from which the following very limited extracts are taken:

> Behold, O Lord, and raise up unto them their king,
> the son of David
> At the time in which thou seest, O God,
> that he may reign over Israel thy servant.
> And gird him with strength that he may
> shatter unrighteous rulers,
> And that he may purge Jerusalem
> from nations that trample her down to destruction.
> Wisely, righteously, he shall thrust out sinners

from the inheritance.
He shall destroy the pride of the sinner as a potter's vessel.
With a rod of iron he shall break in pieces their substance,
He shall destroy the godless nations with the word of his
mouth;
At his rebuke nations shall flee before him......

And he shall gather together a holy people,
whom he shall lead in righteousness,
And he shall judge the tribes of the people that have been
sanctified by the Lord his God......
For he shall know them, that they are all sons of their God.

This, then, was the Davidic Messiah that was expected by most
Jews at the time of Christ. He would be the picture of a nationalistic
king. Gentiles have no part in His future kingdom. The Lord Jesus,
this humble carpenter from Nazareth, this Prince of Peace of Isaiah
9:6, and the God of peace celebrated in the New Testament, was
very far from the rabbinic expectation. To those Jews who still
await the Messiah, the essentially nationalistic king who will
exalt Israel is still very much in contemplation. How different is
this expectation from those beautiful words from Isaiah chapter 9
which point to a holy and peaceful kingdom where righteousness
and justice flourish:

For unto us a child is born,
to us a son is given,
and the government will be on his shoulders.
And he will be called
Wonderful counsellor, Mighty God,
Everlasting Father,
Prince of Peace.
Of the increase of his government and peace
there will be no end.
He will reign on David's throne
and over his kingdom,

> establishing and upholding it
> with justice and righteousness
> from that time on and for ever.

Isaiah 9:6-7

Finally, what of the birth of this superhuman king Messiah? Alfred Edersheim takes up the story: "It is not without hesitation, that we make reference to Jewish allusions to the miraculous birth of the Saviour. Yet there are two expressions which convey the idea if not of superhuman origin, yet of some great mystery attaching to his birth. The first occurs in connection with the birth of Seth. 'Rabbi Tanchuma said, in the name of Rabbi Samuel: Eve had respect [had regard, looked forward] to that Seed which is to come from another place. And who is this? This is Messiah the King' (Ber. R. 23, ed. Warsh. p. 45b). The second appears in the narrative of the crime of Lot's daughters (Gen 19:32): 'Is it not written, "that we may preserve a son from our father"' but "seed from our father". This is that seed which is coming from another place. And who is this? This is the King Messiah.' (BerR. 51 ed. Warsh p 95a). I am, of course, aware that certain Rabbinists explain the expression "seed from another place" as referring to the descent of the Messiah from Ruth - a non-Israelite. But if this explanation could be offered in reference to the daughters of Lot, it is difficult to see its meaning in reference to Eve and the birth of Seth".[7]

All this may be difficult to follow without a thorough grounding in Jewish messianic prophecy and rabbinic writings, but it should by now be abundantly clear that the Messiah expected at the time of Jesus (and indeed later) was a superhuman king who would lead Israel to new heights of domination among the nations of the world and who would, in all probability, throw off the yoke of Rome. It was precisely this vision of the Messiah that the Lord Jesus rejected and which led him into conflict with the Jewish religious authorities, whose power base they felt to be threatened by this prophet from Nazareth.

Notes

[1] John Blanchard *Why Y2K?* (Evangelical Press, 1999), p. 48.

[2] W. Graham Scroggie DD *A Guide to the Gospels* (Pickering & Inglis Ltd, 1948), p. 482.

[3] Melchizedek —a mysterious biblical personality whose name means "king of righteousness". The historical record about this priest king is contained in Genesis 14:18-20; Psalm 110:4 and Hebrews 5:10, 6:20 and 7:1-17. A good Bible Encyclopaedia will provide useful background about Melchizedek's place in messianic prophecy.

[4] *Op. cit.* p. 115.

[5] Dr E. K. Victor Pearce *Prophecy*, Vol. 3 in the Evidence for Truth series (Eagle, 1998), p. 63.

[6] William Barclay *Jesus As They Saw Him* (SCM Press Ltd, 1962).

[7] *Op. cit.* p. 125.

5

The Biblical Account
of the Nativity

We have, up to this point, attempted to 'set the scene' by assembling in 'jigsaw' fashion a composite picture made up of biblical, theological and historical data which, taken together, comprise the stage upon which the Lord Jesus would accomplish His earthly ministry. It is hoped that we have indeed assembled a broad 'picture' in which the Nativity, which we are about to review, is a key focal point: but a focal point cannot be fully appreciated outside the context of the broader picture. Liken it if you will, to a Christmas card depicting the nativity scene: if the picture was of nothing but a baby lying on a bed of straw, we would recognise little from the image. But put the baby on its bed of straw, in an animal feeding trough, and place this in a cattle stall, with the figures of a concerned man and woman looking on, perhaps with a number of rough dressed shepherds in attendance, and a complete scene, indeed a message, is recognised. God prepared mankind for the entry of His Son into the world through the events described in the Old Testament. By the time of Jesus, the desire for a Messiah was palpable amongst the Jewish nation, and perhaps amongst other peoples as well. Yet it seems that most were looking in the wrong place, as did the 'Wise Men' from the East, shortly after Jesus was born.

There were two ways in which this series of studies might have reviewed the biblical account of the Incarnation. We might have taken the various events in sequence and then analysed them, looking at the history, the context and the interpretation of the events themselves. Such an analysis may have value, but would be unduly long and disjointed. The alternative, and the method actually chosen, is to look at the historical and theological setting in which the events occurred, only then reviewing the accounts of Christ's birth contained in the Gospels. This is what we set out to do in this study. It will be followed by studies of the key characters and events reported in the biblical narrative, together with some of the controversies that have attended the traditional understanding of the Nativity.

We obtain our understanding of the events from the witnesses John, Matthew and Luke. Their accounts are written from different perspectives although for the same basic reason— that their readers will put their faith in the Lord Jesus by *believing* in Him. It is only by reading all three accounts that we achieve the full biblical account of Christ's Nativity. In this chapter, the writer has taken each Gospel account, segregated the various events contained in them and reassembled them into a single narrative, believed to be in the correct chronological sequence, as follows:

A. John 1:1-5   The Word

B. Matt 1:1-17   The Genealogy (cp. Luke 3:23-38)

C. Luke 1:5-25   John the Baptist's birth announced

D. Luke 1:26-56 Annunciation of birth of Jesus Christ, Mary, Elizabeth, Mary's song

E. Luke 1:57-66 The birth of John the Baptist

F. Luke 1:67-80 Zechariah's prophecy about John the Baptist (cp. John 1:6-9)

G. Matt 1:18-25 Joseph's dream and decision

H. Luke 2:1-20 The birth of Jesus Christ; the visit of the shepherds

I. Luke 2:21-38 The baby Jesus presented at the temple in Jerusalem

J. Matt 2:1-12   The visit of the Wise Men (Magi)

K. Matt 2:13-18 The flight into Egypt and the slaughter of the innocents
L. John 1:10-14 To all who received Him....

This sequence commences in pre-history (A) and concludes in the theological statement (L) that to all who receive Jesus, to those who believe in His name, He gives the right to become children of God. Only one of the two genealogies is included, partly because no purpose would be served in including what is basically repetitive information, partly because they start from opposite points (Luke working from Jesus backwards and Matthew working from Abraham forwards); partly because Luke includes his genealogy well into his account of the life of Jesus whereas Matthew includes his as an integral part of the account of Jesus' birth and partly because they do not match —a matter we will investigate in Chapter 11. Apart from the genealogy included in Luke, all the relevant narrative is included.

A word of explanation is necessary about the position of (G), Joseph's dream and decision. We presume that when Mary returned from visiting her cousin Elizabeth she was between one and three months into her pregnancy, leaving Elizabeth's house about the time that Elizabeth gave birth to John. Travelling back to Nazareth we again presume that Mary quickly told Joseph of her condition. It is quite possible that (F) and (G) happened at the same time or that their order should be reversed. For this study, however, it is felt that the details of John's birth should be kept together, then moving to Joseph's side of the narrative which in turn leads naturally to the birth of the Lord Jesus.

The text is taken, with permission, from the New International Version of the Bible. The bold headings are devised for the purposes of these studies, as are the comments on the probable timing. The verse numbers are, of course, those from each Gospel as appropriate. Readers may, therefore, notice some slight variation in style between the three Gospel witnesses, but apart from this the various strands of the overall account mesh with each other quite satisfactorily. Note that the period covered by the "Christmas" account may be as long as two years, judging from the fact that the visit of the wise men was to a house (Matt 2:11) not a stable and that Herod, in his attempt to exterminate Jesus, gave orders for all infant boys up to the age of two years should be slaughtered (Matt 2:16). All this indicates that Mary and Joseph settled, temporarily, in Bethlehem after the birth. This writer's investigation calculates the story from September/October of 7 BC to late 5 BC.

BIBLICAL ACCOUNT OF THE BIRTH OF JESUS

A. John 1:1-5 The Word
Time: pre-history
1 In the beginning was the Word, and the Word was God. 2 He was with God in the beginning.
3 Through him all things were made; without him nothing was made that has been made. 4 In him was life, and that life was the light of men. 5 The light shines in the darkness, but the darkness has not understood it.

B. Matt 1:1-17 The genealogy (cp. Luke 3:23-38)
Time: most of the Old Testament historical period
1 A record of the genealogy of Jesus Christ the son of David, the son of Abraham:
2 Abraham was the father of Isaac, Isaac the father of Jacob, Jacob the father of Judah and his brothers, 3 Judah the father of Perez and Zerah, whose mother was Tamar,
Perez the father of Hezron, Hezron the father of Ram, 4 Ram the father of Amminadab, Amminadab the father of Nashon, Nashon the father of Salmon, 5 Salmon the father of Boaz, whose mother was Rahab, Boaz was the father of Obed, whose mother was Ruth, Obed the father of Jesse, 6 and Jesse the father of King David.
David was the father of Solomon, whose mother had been Uriah's wife, 7 Solomon the father of Rehoboam, Rehoboam the father of Abijah, Abijah the father of Asa, 8 Asa the father of Jehoshaphat, Jehoshaphat the father of Jehoram, Jehoram the father of Uzziah,

9 Uzziah the father of Jotham, Jotham the father of Ahaz, Ahaz the father of Hezekiah, 10 Hezekiah the father of Manasseh, Manasseh the father of Amon, Amon the father of Josiah, 11 and Josiah the father of Jeconiah and his brothers at the time of the exile to Babylon.

12 After the exile in Babylon: Jeconiah was the father of Shealtiel, Shealtiel the father of Zerubbabel, 13 Zerubbabel the father of Abiud, Abiud the father of Eliakim, Eliakim the father of Azor, 14 Azor the father of Zadok, Zadok the father of Akim, Akim the father of Eliud,

15 Eliud the father of Eleazar, Eleazar the father of Mattan, Mattan the father of Jacob, 16 and Jacob the father of Joseph, the husband of Mary, of whom was born Jesus, who is called Christ.

17 Thus there were fourteen generations in all from Abraham to David, fourteen from David to the exile in Babylon, and fourteen from the exile to the Christ.

C. Luke 1:5-25 John the Baptist's birth announced
Time: Fifteen months prior to Jesus' birth?
September of 7 BC?

5 In the time of Herod King of Judea there was a priest named Zechariah, who belonged to the priestly division of Abijah; his wife Elizabeth was also a descendent of Aaron. 6 Both of them were upright in the sight of God, observing all the Lord's commandments and regulations blamelessly. 7 But they had no children, because Elizabeth was barren; and they were both well on in years.

8 Once when Zechariah's division was on duty and he was serving as priest before God, 9 he was chosen by lot, according to the custom of the priesthood, to go into the temple of the Lord and burn incense. 10 And when the time for the burning of the incense came, all the assembled worshippers were praying outside.

11 Then an angel of the Lord appeared to him, standing at the right side of the altar of incense. 12 When Zechariah saw him, he was startled and was gripped with fear. 13 But the angel said to him: "Do not be afraid, Zechariah; your prayer has been heard.

Your wife Elizabeth will bear you a son, and you are to give him the name John. 14 He will be a joy and a delight to you, and many will rejoice because of his birth, 15 for he will be great in the sight of the Lord. He will never take wine or other fermented drink, and he will be filled with the Holy Spirit even from birth. 16 Many of the people of Israel will he bring back to the Lord their God. 17 And he will go on before the Lord, in the spirit and power of Elijah, to turn the hearts of the fathers to their children and the disobedient to the wisdom of the righteous - to make ready a people prepared for the Lord."

18 Zechariah asked the angel, "How can I be sure of this? I am an old man and my wife is well on in years."

19 The angel answered, "I am Gabriel. I stand in the presence of God, and I have been sent to speak to you and to tell you this good news. 20 And now you will be silent and not able to speak until the day this happens, because you did not believe my words, which will come true at their proper time."

21 Meanwhile, the people were waiting for Zechariah and wondering why he stayed so long in the temple. 22 When he came out, he could not speak to them. They realised he had seen a vision in the temple, for he kept making signs to them but remained unable to speak.

23 When his time of service was completed, he returned home. 24 After this his wife Elizabeth became pregnant and for five months remained in seclusion. 25 "The Lord has done this for me," she said. "In these days he has shown his favour and taken away my disgrace among the people."

D. Luke 1:26-56 Annunciation of birth of Jesus Christ; Mary and Elizabeth; Mary's song
Time: March 6 BC?

26 In the sixth month, God sent the angel Gabriel to Nazareth, a town in Galilee, 27 to a virgin pledged to be married to a man named Joseph, a descendent of David. The virgin's name was Mary. 28 The angel went to her and said, "Greetings, you who are highly favoured! The Lord is with you."

29 Mary was greatly troubled at his words and wondered what kind of greeting this might be. 30 But the angel said to her, "Do not be afraid, Mary, you have found favour with God. 31 You will be with child and give birth to a son, and you are to give him the name Jesus. 32 He will be great and will be called the son of the Most High. The Lord will give him the throne of his father David, 33 and he will reign over the house of Jacob for ever; his kingdom will never end."

34 "How will this be," Mary asked the angel, "since I am a virgin?"

35 The angel answered, "The Holy Spirit will come upon you, and the power of the Most High will overshadow you. So the holy one will be called the son of God. 36 Even Elizabeth your relative is going to have a child in her old age, and she who was said to be barren is in her sixth month. 37 For nothing is impossible with God."

38 "I am the Lord's servant," Mary answered. "May it be to me as you have said." Then the angel left her.

39 At that time Mary got ready and hurried to a town in the hill country of Judea, 40 where she entered Zechariah's home and greeted Elizabeth. 41 When Elizabeth heard Mary's greeting, the baby leaped in her womb and Elizabeth was filled with the Holy Spirit. 42 In a loud voice she exclaimed: "Blessed are you among women, and blessed is the child you will bear! 43 But why am I so favoured, that the mother of my Lord should come to me? 44 As soon as the sound of your greeting reached my ears, the baby in my womb leaped for joy. 45 Blessed is she who has believed that what the Lord has said to her will be accomplished!"

46 And Mary said:

"My soul glorifies the Lord 47 and my spirit rejoices in God my Saviour, 48 for he has been mindful of the humble state of his servant. From now on all generations will call me blessed, 49 for the Mighty One has done great things for me - holy is his name. 50 His mercy extends to those who fear him, from generation to generation. 51 He has performed mighty deeds with his arm; he has scattered those who are proud in their inmost thoughts. 52

He has brought down rulers from their thrones but has lifted up the humble. 53 He has filled the hungry with good things but has sent the rich away empty. 54 He has helped his servant Israel, remembering to be merciful 55 to Abraham and his descendants forever, even as he said to our fathers."

56 Mary stayed with Elizabeth for about three months and then returned home.

E. Luke 1:57-66 The birth of John the Baptist
Time: June 6BC?

57 When it was time for Elizabeth to have her baby, she gave birth to a son. 58 Her neighbours and relatives heard that the Lord had shown her great mercy and they shared her joy. 59 On the eighth day they came to circumcise the child, and they were going to name him after his father Zechariah, 60 but his mother spoke up and said, "No! He is to be called John."

61 They said to her, "There is no one among your relatives who has that name." 62 Then they made signs to his father, to find out what he would like to name the child. 63 He asked for a writing tablet, and to everyone's astonishment he wrote, "His name is John." 64 Immediately his mouth was opened and his tongue was loosed, and he began to speak, praising God. 65 The neighbours were all filled with awe, and throughout the hill country of Judea people were talking about all these things. 66 Everyone who heard this wondered about it, asking, "What then is this child going to be?" For the Lord's hand was with him.

F. Luke 1:67-80 Zechariah's prophecy about John the Baptist
(cp. John 1:6-9)
Time: June 6BC?

67 His father Zechariah was filled with the Holy Spirit and prophesied:

68 "Praise be to the Lord, the God of Israel, because he has come and has redeemed his people. 69 He has raised up a horn of salvation for us in the house of his servant David 70 (as he said through his holy prophets of long ago), 71 salvation from our

enemies and from the hand of all who hate us - 72 to show mercy to our fathers and to remember his holy covenant, 73 the oath he swore to our father Abraham: 74 to rescue us from the hand or our enemies, and to enable us to serve him without fear 75 in holiness and righteousness before him all our days.

76 And you, my child, will be called a prophet of the Most High; for you will go on before the Lord to prepare the way for him, 77 to give his people the knowledge of salvation through the forgiveness of their sins, 78 because of the tender mercy of God, by which the rising sun will come to us from heaven 79 to shine on those living in darkness and in the shadow of death, to guide our feet into the path of peace."

80 And the child grew and became strong in spirit; and he lived in the desert until he appeared publicly to Israel.

G. Matt 1:18-25 Joseph's dream and decision
Time: June/July 6BC?

18 This is how the birth of Jesus Christ came about: His mother Mary was pledged to be married to Joseph, but before they came together, she was found to be with child through the Holy Spirit. 19 Because Joseph her husband was a righteous man and did not want to expose her to public disgrace, he had in mind to divorce her quietly. 20 But after he had considered this, an angel of the Lord appeared to him in a dream and said, "Joseph son of David, do not be afraid to take Mary home as your wife, because what is conceived in her is from the holy Spirit. 21 She will give birth to a son, and you are to give him the name Jesus, because he will save his people from their sins."

22 All this took place to fulfil what the Lord had said through the prophet: 23 "The virgin will be with child and will give birth to a son, and they will call him Immanuel - which means "God with us."

24 When Joseph woke up, he did what the angel of the Lord had commanded him and took Mary home as his wife. 25 But he had no union with her until she gave birth to a son. And he gave him the name Jesus.

H. Luke 2:1-20 The birth of Jesus Christ; the visit of the shepherds
Time: late December of 6BC?

1 In those days Caesar Augustus issued a decree that a census should be taken of the entire Roman world. (2 This was the first census that took place while Quirinius was governor of Syria.) 3 And everyone went to his own town to register.

4 So Joseph also went up from the town of Nazareth in Galilee to Judea, to Bethlehem the town of David, because he belonged to the house and line of David. 5 He went there to register with Mary, who was pledged to be married to him and was expecting a child. 6 While they were there, the time came for the baby to be born, 7 and she gave birth to her firstborn, a son. She wrapped him in cloths and placed him in a manger, because there was no room for them in the inn.

8 And there were shepherds living out in the fields near by, keeping watch over their flocks at night. 9 An angel of the Lord appeared to them, and the glory of the Lord shone around them, and they were terrified. 10 But the angel said to them, "Do not be afraid. I bring you good news of great joy that will be for all the people. 11 Today in the town of David a Saviour has been born to you; he is Christ the Lord. 12 This will be a sign to you: You will find a baby wrapped in cloths and lying in a manager." 13 Suddenly a great company of the heavenly host appeared with the angel, praising God and saying,

14 "Glory to God in the highest, and on earth peace to men on whom his favour rests."

15 When the angels had left them and gone into heaven, the shepherds said to one another, "Let's go to Bethlehem and see this thing that has happened, which the Lord has told us about." 16 So they hurried off and found Mary and Joseph, and the baby, who was lying in the manger. 17 When they had seen him, they spread the word concerning what had been told them about this child, 18 and all who heard it were amazed at what the shepherds said to them. 19 But Mary treasured up all these things and pondered them in her heart. 20 The shepherds

returned, glorifying God for all the things they had heard and seen, which were just as they had been told.

I. Luke 2:21-38 The baby Jesus presented at the temple in Jerusalem
Time: early January of 5BC?

21 On the eighth day, when it was time to circumcise him, he was named Jesus, the name the angel had given him before he had been conceived. 22 When the time for the purification according to the law of Moses had been completed, Joseph and Mary took him to Jerusalem to present him to the Lord 23 (as it is written in the Law of the Lord, "Every firstborn male is to be consecrated to the Lord") 24 and to offer a sacrifice in keeping with what was said in the Law of the Lord: "a pair of doves or two young pigeons".

25 Now there was a man living in Jerusalem called Simeon, who was righteous and devout. He was waiting for the consolation of Israel, and the Holy Spirit was upon him. 26 It had been revealed to him by the Holy Spirit that he would not die before he had seen the Lord's Christ. 27 Moved by the Spirit, he went into the temple courts. When the parents brought in the child Jesus to do for him what the custom of the law required, 28 Simeon took him in his arms and praised God saying:

29 "Sovereign Lord, as you have promised, you now dismiss your servant in peace. 30 For my eyes have seen your salvation, 31 which you have prepared in the sight of all people, 32 a light for revelation to the Gentiles and for Glory to your people Israel."

33 The child's father and mother marvelled at what was said about him. 34 Then Simeon blessed them and said to Mary, his mother: "This child is destined to cause the falling and the rising of many in Israel, and will be a sign that will be spoken against, 35 so that the thoughts of many hearts will be revealed. And a sword will pierce your own soul too."

36 There was also a prophetess, Anna, the daughter of Phanuel, of the tribe of Asher. She was very old; she had lived with her husband seven years after her marriage, 37 and then was a widow until she was eighty four. She never left the temple but worshipped night

and day, fasting and praying. 38 Coming up to them at that very moment, she gave thanks to God and spoke about the child to all who were looking forward to the redemption of Jerusalem.

Editor's Note: *Apparently the Holy family returned briefly to Nazareth (Luke 2:39) —possibly with the intention of winding-up their affairs there prior to a permanent move to Bethlehem. Such a journey would probably have been undertaken slowly, after which they returned to Bethlehem and lived in a house (Matt 2:11).*

J. Matt 2:1-12 The visit of the Wise Men (Magi)
Time: mid to late 5BC?

1 After Jesus was born in Bethlehem in Judea, during the time of King Herod, Magi from the east came to Jerusalem 2 and asked, "Where is the one who has been born king of the Jews? We saw his star in the east and have come to worship him."

3 When King Herod heard this he was disturbed, and all Jerusalem with him. 4 When he had called together all the people's chief priests and teachers of the law, he asked them where the Christ was to be born. 5 "In Bethlehem in Judea," they replied, "for this is what the prophet has written:

6 " 'But you, Bethlehem, in the land of Judah, are by no means least among the rulers of Judah; for out of you will come a ruler who will be the shepherd of my people Israel' "

7 Then Herod called the Magi secretly and found out from them the exact time the star had appeared. 8 He sent them to Bethlehem and said "Go and make a careful search for the child. As soon as you find him, report to me, so that I too may go and worship him."

9 After they had heard the king, they went on their way, and the star they had seen in the east went ahead of them until it stopped over the place where the child was. 10 When they saw the star they were overjoyed. 11 On coming to the house, they saw the child with his mother Mary, and they bowed down and worshipped him. Then they opened their treasures and presented him with gifts of gold and of incense and of myrrh. 12 And having been warned in a dream not to go back to Herod, they returned to their country by another route.

K. Matt 2:13-18 The flight into Egypt and the slaughter of the innocents
Time: late 5BC?

13 When they had gone, an angel of the Lord appeared to Joseph in a dream. "Get up," he said, "take the child and his mother and escape to Egypt. Stay there until I tell you, for Herod is going to search for the child to kill him."

14 So he got up, took the child and his mother during the night and left for Egypt, 15 where he stayed until the death of Herod. And so was fulfilled what was said through the prophet: "Out of Egypt I have called my son."

16 When Herod realised that he had been outwitted by the Magi, he was furious, and he gave orders to kill all the boys in Bethlehem and its vicinity who were two years old and under, in accordance with the time he had learned from the Magi. 17 Then what was said through the prophet Jeremiah was fulfilled:

18 "A voice is heard in Ramah, weeping and great mourning, Rachel weeping for her children and refusing to be comforted, because they are no more."

L. John 1:10-14 To all who received Him
Time: Now!

10 He was in the world and though the world was made through him, the world did not recognise him. 11 He came to that which was his own, but his own did not receive him. 12 Yet to all who received him, to those who believed in his name, he gave the right to become children of God - 13 children born not of natural descent, nor of human decision or a husband's will, but born of God. 14 The word became flesh and made his dwelling among us. We have seen his glory, the glory of the One and Only, who came from the Father, full of grace and truth.

6

Jesus

Whilst 'Jesus' was the name given by God to the infant born in Bethlehem, in the opening verses of the John's Gospel we read of a special and puzzling title: "In the beginning was *the Word*, and the Word was God. He was with God in the beginning. Through him all things were made; without him nothing was made that has been made. In him was life, and that life was the light of men. The light shines in the darkness, but the darkness has not understood it." Why was John inspired to title Jesus, first, as the Word?

A number of answers have been advanced offering at least a partial explanation. First, we consider how the people of Jesus' own day would have understood by the title, before looking at how it has been viewed in later times. The earliest Christian preaching was by Jews to Jews who would readily have understood the concept of the Messiah. As the gospel spread it was necessary to address a wider world, not steeped in Old Testament teaching. After Judaea and Galilee (and, to a lesser extent, Samaria) it was the Greek/Roman world that was the first to encounter Christianity. It became necessary to find ways to communicate the lordship of Jesus to the Greek mindset. John found this in the powerful concept of *the Logos* —the Word.

As a Jew, John would have approached the concept of the Word firstly in a Jewish way. A word was not seen as being simply a sound in the air, it was an effective power, almost a unit of energy. Words did not only *say* things, words *did* things. In the creation, every act in the creation process commenced: "And God said ...." A Jew would have understood John's description of Jesus as *the Word* to be the very motive and creative power of God. The prophet Jeremiah said that the Lord's word was like fire, like a hammer that breaks a rock in pieces (Jer 23:29). God's word, we read in Isaiah, "...will not return to me [God] empty handed but will accomplish what I desire and achieve the purpose for which I sent it" (Isaiah 55:11).

In Jewish thought, also, the concept of wisdom was held in high esteem; see for example, Proverbs 8. Wisdom was the companion of God before the World began, and His helper in creation (Prov 8:22-30). Wisdom was seen to exist almost as a person at God's side. The Greek word Logos conveys more than just the idea of a word. It can also be translated 'mind' or 'reason', again suggesting something of the intimacy of the Word with God. These two meanings need to be kept in mind, because the English word 'Word' in this context is quite inadequate to convey the full force of what John saying. The idea of the Logos had come powerfully into Greek consciousness via the Greek philosopher Heraclitus who lived five centuries before Christ. He taught that, although the universe was in a constant state of flux, it was still a dependable universe and the 'law' in operation was the Logos —the mind, the reason, on which the whole order of the universe depends. This concept was further developed among the Greek philosophers in the centuries that followed.

The most sophisticated Greek view of the Logos was developed by Philo, an Alexandrian Jew (a Hellenist) born in 20 BC. In this man Greek and Jewish thought mingled. He was a prolific writer and in his books (according to William Barclay) the word Logos appears some 1,200 times. "To him Logos is the image of God and in a unique sense the bridge between God and man. The Logos is God's instrument of creation, God's mind stamped on the universe, the tiller by which God steers the world, the bond which holds the world together, the High Priest through whom

God communicates with men."[1] The Word, then, is a means of communication. People communicate primarily through words. In Jesus God spoke to men in a way that He had never done before, and has never done so since. In Jesus everything that God said to mankind became incarnate in a person. The word is a means of revelation. A word expresses a thought and Jesus is the perfect expression of the mind of God.

Such was the Jewish and Greek appreciation of the concept of *the Logos*, the Word of God. In modern times, church leaders have stressed the love of God —and rightly so. God is the great Lover. Because He is love, he is always seeking ways of communicating that love to his creatures. The Old Testament shows how God communicated with His people by delivering them from their enemies, by establishing the temple ritual and the priesthood and through special messengers —the prophets. Jesus, however, is much greater than any Old Testament prophet. He not only brought God's words to His people, He *was* that Word. The apostle John continued his theme on the Word: "The Word became flesh and made his dwelling among us. We have seen his glory, the glory of the One and Only, who came from the Father, full of grace and truth" (John 1:14). In human relationships, a word may be heeded or spurned. The modern church emphasises that this is also true of God's Word. Because God has spoken to us through His Son, there is a heavy responsibility upon us to respond to that Word. As the writer to the Hebrews said: "In the past God spoke to our forefathers through the prophets at many times and in various ways, but in these last days he has spoken to us by his Son, whom he appointed heir of all things, and through whom he made the universe. The Son is the radiance of God's glory and the exact representation of His being, sustaining all things by his powerful word" (Heb 1:1-3).

The power in a Name
Names can be powerful and meaningful in their own right, even causing strong emotions, as any parent who has had the difficult task of choosing a name can recognise! Many people in history

have been given popular titles inspired by their achievements or their notoriety, titles that have become instantly recognisable as a 'celebration' of the person and what they did. So we have all heard of Alexander *the Great*, of William *the Conqueror*, of *Bloody Mary*, and of John *the Baptist*. Slightly less well known may be the English King Ethelred *the Unready*. From biblical times we have already met Judas Maccabeus —*God's Hammer*, a popular title given because of his stunning victories over the Persians. One of Jesus' own disciples is principally remembered not for what he did but for the simple fact that he was an adherent of a political movement: Simon *the Zealot*.

The Lord Jesus was given many titles which can be seen as both affirmations of what He was and confessions of faith in Him. W. Graham Scroggie lists in his *Guide To The Gospels* fifty-two such titles given to Jesus,[2] but it is the simple name 'Jesus' by which the Lord is most often referred to in the Gospels —almost six hundred times, in fact. The name Jesus emphasises the real humanity of the Lord. Whilst to us it has become a sacred name, and we would consider it irreverent to give the name to any child today (though in some Latin societies this is not an uncommon practice), in New Testament times Jesus was one of the most common names for a boy. 'Jesus' is the Greek form by which the Old Testament name Joshua (e.g. as in the Book of Joshua) is translated. Whilst a common name when Jesus was born, by the second century AD it was rapidly dying out. Among Jews it had become a hated name whilst among Christians it was too sacred for common use.

Ordinary though the name Jesus was, it was nevertheless a significant one. In the ancient world names were seen as being very meaningful, often describing something about the person to whom it was given. The name Jesus was given to our Lord by the direct instruction of God (Matt 1:21), and indeed this name might have been thought somewhat irregular by people at the time because it was customary to name eldest sons after their fathers. We would note, in this regard, that Jesus had no biological father, so in His name may be found some clue as to His heavenly Father.

The Jewish rabbis had a saying: "Six persons received their names before they were born, namely, Isaac, our great lawgiver Moses, Solomon, Josiah, Ishmael and the Messiah." Jewish belief was that God would directly command what the name of the Messiah must be.

In both Hebrew and Greek the name Jesus has a special meaning, being in a sense, a one word summary of the work that the Lord was sent to do. In Hebrew the name Joshua means, variously, 'Jehovah is my help', or, 'Jehovah is rescue', or, 'the help of Jehovah'. In Matt 1:21 we read, "...you are to give him the name Jesus, because he will save his people from their sins." The very name Jesus, therefore, marks Him out as Saviour. "He is God's divinely appointed and divinely sent Rescuer," writes William Barclay, "whose function it is to deliver men from their sins. He came to rescue men from the estrangement and the alienation from God which is the consequence of their past sins, and for the future to liberate them from the bondage to sin, from the moral frustration and the continuous and inevitable defeat which are the result of sin. He came to bring friendship for fear, and victory for defeat."[3]

To the Greek mind a connection was made between the name Jesus and the verb *iasthai*, which means *to heal*. The connection between the two words is only in the sound, but the Greeks made much of the idea of Jesus as the healer of the bodies and souls of men. Jesus was the only one who could bring health to the body in its physical pain and renewal of the soul polluted by the spiritual disease of sin. It was no accident, therefore, that Jesus was given His name, for it summarises the things He came to do and which *only* He could do. He came to be the divine rescuer of men from the consequences and the grip of sin.

Jesus, Man and God

The traditional Christian view is that the baby born in Bethlehem is both God and Man, an astounding thought and a stumbling block for many, notably the Jehovah's Witnesses in the Western world and Moslems in the east. How did this doctrine develop?

Is it biblical? What did Jesus Himself have to say? We will try to answer these questions as we evaluate whether anyone other than God, Himself, could ultimately pay the debt owed for rebellion (sin) against Himself.

The first point to make is that Jesus was a real, complete and ordinary human being. He was born like us and developed through childhood to adulthood in a completely normal way. In the Bible we read that he ate, drank, slept, sweated, became tired, felt pain and emotion. Ultimately He died. He was also tempted to sin as we are, even in a quite unprecedented way by the devil himself (Luke 4:1-13), although Jesus did not surrender to the temptation and so we can say with certainty that He was without sin. Just as He taught His disciples to pray, so Jesus Himself needed to pray, to remain in close intimacy with His heavenly Father. He acknowledged He could do nothing without His Father's power and taught only what His Father had shown Him (John 8:28). In spite of all Jesus' undoubted supernatural power, He was fully dependent on His heavenly Father, so He stated plainly that He did not know the time when He would return —this was known only by His Father (Mark 13:32).

So why do Christians equate God with Jesus? The foundations of the belief are in the Bible itself —indeed it should be said that the doctrine is based on viewing the Bible as an organic whole; the doctrine is alluded to, albeit indirectly, throughout the unveiling of salvation history. It should be added, straight away, that Christians do not claim to have a perfect understanding of this Incarnation - of God becoming flesh. We can, however, say that the evidence is overwhelming as this following short study will illustrate:

* What can we say of God? He is...

One and only	Isaiah 44:6 (and Gal 3:15-20)
Unchangeable	James 1:17
Invisible	Col 1:15
Infinite	1 Kings 8:27
Holy	1 Peter 1:15-16
Spirit	John 4:24

* His unity
Deuteronomy 6:4
Gal 3:20 (see also verse 16)
1 Tim 2:5
James 2:19

* Father, Son and Holy Spirit
Matt 28:19 (name, not names!)
2 Cor 13:14
Heb 1:8
1 Peter 1:2

* "I AM"
Exodus 3:13-15 —God reveals His name to Moses

* Jesus uses the phrase 'I am' to describe His attributes
John 8:58 —before Abraham was born, I AM!
John 6:48 —the bread of life
John 10:7 —the gate
John 10:11 —the good shepherd
John 10:36 —God's son
John 11:25 —the resurrection and the life
John 14:10 —in the Father and the Father is in me (see also John 10:30)
John 15:1 —the true vine

It is plain that Jesus was claiming the divine co-existence of God the Father and Himself, the Son. So it was that the people in His own home town rose up against Him (Luke 4:29) when He compared Himself to Elijah. "My Father is always at work to this very day, and I, too, am working," said Jesus in John 5:17. The Gospel writer continues: "For this reason the Jews tried to kill him; not only was he breaking the Sabbath, but he was even calling God his own Father, making himself equal with God" (John 5:18). It is true that nowhere did Jesus ever say unambiguously 'I am God', but He nevertheless made some explicit statements leading to this conclusion. Thus "I and the Father are one" (John 10:30) is the most obvious, but is reinforced by, for example, "All that belongs to the Father is mine" (John 16:15), and, "All authority in heaven and on earth has been given to me" (Matt 28:18). So, whilst we read in Acts 10:36 that Jesus is Lord of all, elsewhere we read that, "the Lord your God is God in heaven above and on the earth below" (Joshua 2:11), and similarly in Genesis 28:13 we read of God introducing Himself to Jacob as, "I am the Lord, the God of your father Abraham and the God of Isaac."

Since the earliest days of the church, Christian belief has been that the man Jesus is also God. Not a man with god-like qualities, nor God *appearing* in human guise, but God the eternal Logos who "became flesh" (John 1:14). Four great ecumenical Councils of the fourth and fifth centuries AD wrestled with the mysteries of the godhead, and each clarified an important aspect of it. The Council of Nicea (AD 325) affirmed that Jesus is truly God, and the Council of Constantinople (AD 381) confirmed that He is truly man. The Council of Ephesus (AD 431) clarified that, although God and Man, He is one Person. Finally the Council of Chalcedon (AD 451) confirmed that, although one person, Jesus is both God and man perfectly. These beliefs have been reaffirmed both by Roman Catholics and the Reformers down through the centuries.

Critics of the doctrine of the Trinity often ask how God can be in two places at once. We might as well ask how God can create a universe, or how he can raise from the dead someone who has been crucified. The very question, perhaps, tries to lock the infinite God into a one-dimensional Being, easily comprehended by the finite minds of simple men. It has been rightly observed, *we can call Jesus God, but we cannot call God Jesus*. God continued to control the universe in His omniscience, omnipotence and omnipresence when the man Jesus was on this earth. However, in the man Jesus we meet absolutely and completely God in His personal relationship with men. We see perfectly, in Jesus, God, in His attitude to, and in His relationship with, men. Although this mystery is in the fullest sense incomprehensible to humans, this is God as He has revealed Himself: as three distinct persons

—one in three and three in one.

Notes

[1] William Barclay *Jesus As They Saw Him* (SCM Press Ltd, 1962), p. 426.

[2] W. Graham Scroggie DD *A Guide To The Gospels* (Pickering & Inglis Ltd, 1948), p. 519.

[3] *Op. cit. Jesus As They Saw Him* p. 12.

7

Mary and Joseph

The two people most directly involved in the account of the Lord Jesus' birth are, of course, Mary and Joseph. The Gospels begin their report with the viewpoint of Mary, to whom the announcement, or annunciation, of Jesus' impending birth is first given. It is only later that Joseph is made a part of the drama and this is (presumably within a few days) *after* he has been told that Mary is pregnant. We will follow the reports in the biblical order therefore, beginning with Mary and later looking at Joseph's role in the events.

Mary
Any study of Mary may fall on or between a number of possible errors and needs to be undertaken diligently and reverently, bearing in mind the subject matter. The two most extreme errors are, first, those of disbelievers in the virgin conception who either wittingly seek to slur or unwittingly acquiesce in the slurring of Mary's reputation, and second, those who elevate the virgin mother to a position not entertained anywhere in Scripture. This latter error is sometimes referred to as Mariolatry —the worship of Mary. It is not intended to look in any detail at Mariolatry as it is beyond the scope of this book. Instead we seek to allow the Scriptures themselves to place the correct parameters on Mary's position

within the Christian faith. It *is* necessary, however, to look in detail at the former error as this is the proposition most frequently advanced by critics of the biblical account of the Nativity.

Why should the virgin conception have proved so controversial through the ages? Is it not slightly absurd, for example, for people who claim to believe in a supernatural, creative God, also to believe that somehow, the management of a birth without the agency of a human father is beyond Him? The reason for controversy is simply that both sides of the debate recognise the doctrine to be vitally important. In spite of this, some who are (or claim to be) adherents of the Christian faith, maintain that the doctrine is unimportant and that one can deny the virgin conception and still be a mainstream Christian. They say that the virgin conception is only referred to in two New Testament scriptures (Matt 1:18 and Luke 1:34-5) and once in the Old Testament (Isaiah 7:14), and so what the Bible deals with so scantily cannot be of great importance.

Most Christians would argue in reply that the doctrine of the virgin conception is indeed of fundamental importance, because only in this way can we begin to understand how God, the second person of the Trinity, could become a man and take human nature into *eternal union* with His divine nature. If the 'virgin birth' is false we have less ground on which to base the other essential truth of Christ, that of His sinlessness. And of course the legitimacy of His birth also comes into question. It would seem bizarre, to say the least, that a holy God should look down over His creation with all the options no doubt at His disposal for creating new life and decide upon an illegitimate birth to be the method to bring His holy and sinless Son into the world!

The two passages in the New Testament in which the fact of the virgin conception are clearly reported are of considerable importance:

This is how the birth of Jesus Christ came about: His mother Mary was pledged to be married to Joseph, but before they came together, she was found to be with child through the Holy Spirit.

Matt 1:18

" How will this be," Mary asked the angel, "since I am a virgin?" The angel answered, "The Holy Spirit will come upon you, and the power of the Most High will overshadow you. So the holy one will be called the son of God. Even Elizabeth your relative is going to have a child in her old age, and she who was said to be barren is in her sixth month. For nothing is impossible with God."

Luke 1:34-35

The correct placing of these verses in the original texts has never been seriously doubted; practically every ancient manuscript includes them, except a mutilated copy of a manuscript of the Ebionites (a Jewish/Christian sect that denied Christ's deity and which deleted many other things that alluded to His deity), and one Syriac reading of Matt 1:18 which is certainly wrong, but which critics sometimes claim may have predated other manuscripts. This says that Joseph begat Jesus —but then goes on to narrate the virgin birth, something the critics are less willing to own up to!

The second passage was written by Luke, who was a physician and therefore an educated man, who had accompanied the apostle Paul on his missionary journeys. These journeys encompassed many of the locations where the Gospel events took place. Whilst Paul was in prison in Caesarea, undergoing protracted investigations by the Roman procurators Felix and Festus (see Acts 24 and 25) Luke may well have had time to travel within Judaea and Galilee to interview surviving witnesses.[1] These witnesses may have included Mary herself. (Allowing that Mary was no more than eighteen years in 6 to 5 BC when Jesus was probably born, and knowing as we do that Luke accompanied Paul on his second missionary journey, AD 49-52, then Mary would have been in her late sixties at the time that Luke had an opportunity to meet her. Obviously this is supposition, but without doubt there would have been plenty of eye-witnesses still alive at the time.) Is it in any way credible that the apostle Paul, of whom Luke was a close companion over many years (see Col 4:14; 2 Tim 4:11; Philemon

24) was unaware of the virgin conception? Yet nowhere in his writings does Paul seek to deny it. If anything, he confirms it as he writes to the Galatians (Gal 4:4), "...when the time had fully come, God sent His son, born of a woman, born under law...." It is difficult to see why Paul would otherwise have made this statement, unless it was to affirm that the Lord's conception was undertaken in a supernatural manner.

Detractors argue that the Greek word *parthenos* translated 'virgin' actually means 'young girl'. This is disingenuous. Both the word and the context make it blindingly obvious that in Luke 1:34 Mary was referring to the fact that she had had no physical relationship with a man. Furthermore, the word *parthenos* always and unequivocally means virgin. It is interesting, in this regard, that the Hebrew word translated virgin in the messianic prophecy of Isaiah 7:14 is *almah*. The word *almah* usually, though not invariably, signifies a virgin. It was translated in the Greek Septuagint by the uncompromising word *parthenos*, which has only one meaning. The Septuagint was the Hellenist Jews' standard translation of the Hebrew Scriptures into Greek until the first century AD.[2] As Christians used the word *parthenos* to defend the virgin conception of the Lord Jesus, and made the Septuagint generally the Christian Bible, and as the Hebrew text was in any case undergoing revision in the first century, the first century Jews ceased to use the Septuagint and prepared a succession of revised Greek translations, in which *almah* was translated not by *parthenos* but by *neanis* —a young woman. A clear indication that the Jews were responding to the Christians' testimony about the Lord's miraculous conception —by altering their own Scriptures.

As we will, at a later stage, look in greater detail at the controversy surrounding the virgin conception, we will leave the subject here with the thought that Christians, at least, need to be clear where they stand on this issue and why. It really is not adequate to say, 'on balance I believe in the virgin conception', as some do, as though it is somehow difficult to believe in this aspect of the Incarnation, in the light of some perceived weight of contrary evidence, but on a balance of probabilities the story is given a reluctant vote of 'likely to be true, all things taken in the round'! Thinking logically through the statement 'on balance I believe' it quickly becomes apparent that for any person making such a statement *belief* is the one thing most assuredly absent —only a vague acquiescence to the likelihood that the biblical account is true.

Returning to Mary, it is noted that her humanness was no different from that of any other human person. She was, however, someone who rejoiced in God her Saviour (Luke 1:47) and was chosen by God to bear Jesus because she was 'highly favoured' (Luke 1:28), which implies that in some way the quality of her life and character was such that God found in her a *very* suitable person in the outworking of His great plan of salvation. Biblically, we can go no further than this. "She was a sinner as truly as any other woman," says H. Brash Bonsall, "and saved by grace through faith in the atoning work of the Son, like others. She was a Jewess of the lineage of David through his son, Nathan, and was chosen to be the privileged instrument whereby the second person of the Godhead should lay hold of humanity and permanently unite human nature with his own divine nature. Mary's blood, but not Joseph's, flowed in His veins. The lineaments of Mary's face would doubtless show in His own. Our Saviour was a Jew." [3]

The announcement of the birth of Jesus, when the angel Gabriel came and spoke to Mary, can only have taken a few minutes. The Bible does not tell us where the appearance of the angel took place. It would have been somewhere private —probably in her own home. First, the angel tells Mary not to be afraid! No doubt any human person upon meeting such a spiritual creature would feel fear and apprehension. To allay those fears, Gabriel immediately tells her that she has found favour with God; in other words, the angel has not appeared as a portent of doom. Without further introduction or explanation, Gabriel goes on to tell Mary that she "will be" with child (note she is not already with child) and will give birth to a son, who is to be named Jesus. There is no pause here for a reply. Mary needs more information before she can make an appropriate response. Gabriel gives it: "He will be great and will be called the Son of the Most High. The Lord will give him the throne of his father David, and he will reign over the house of Jacob forever; his kingdom will never end."

Mary now has the essential information. To our modern minds, we might have liked some additional details, some additional assurance, some promise relating to our own personal interests! But not Mary. She has listened to the message and, in a limited way, understands what she is being told. To have told her any more would surely have been too much for her to bear. Jesus Himself would later teach His disciples, "do not worry about tomorrow, for tomorrow will worry about itself. Each day has enough trouble of its own." It is only appropriate that the same lesson should have been applied to Mary. The reference to 'his father David' seems not to have caused any surprise or difficulty to Mary. She obviously would have been aware of her own lineage and the fact that there is no question by Mary of the Davidic aspect of the angel's announcement supports the view that Jesus' Davidic descent is provided by both his mother's and Joseph's side of the family (see later, the debate about the genealogies).

Mary's immediate response to the angel Gabriel's announcement is highly practical: 'How will this be, since I am a virgin?' She does not complain or argue, or even display fear; she simply questions the practicality of what has been announced. Gabriel then provides more information. The third person of the Trinity, the Holy Spirit, will come upon Mary and undertake the necessary extra-physical action that will translate her in her present state of virginity to the state of being a virgin 'with child'. It is again beyond the scope of this study to look in detail at the person and the work of the Holy Spirit. Suffice to say that, in much the same way as He 'comes upon' all believers to a greater or lesser extent at the point of 're-birth' (see John 3:16), so in the same way the Holy Spirit 'came upon' Mary and worked the miracle that we call the virgin conception. Having told Mary that the Holy Spirit will come upon her, Gabriel adds that, 'the power of the Most High will overshadow' her. So it may be seen that, in a way we need not fully understand, the virgin conception was brought about by two of the three persons of the Trinity, so as to enable the physical birth into the world of Jesus.

Gabriel goes on to provide a little more information, although it has not been requested. The holy one (Jesus) will be called the Son of God. Also Mary's childless cousin Elizabeth, though elderly in terms of child bearing, is in her sixth month of pregnancy, "...For nothing is impossible with God." The fact that Gabriel mentions Elizabeth's miraculous, though physically normal, pregnancy in this way suggests that Mary may not have known about it, or that if she did, it is now being revealed to her as a miracle brought about by God. Although we cannot be sure whether Mary knew about Elizabeth's condition or not, the text tells us that she "straightway" went to be with Elizabeth, to support her at a time when they shared so much in common. She stayed with Elizabeth for three months, presumably until John was born (Luke 1:56), at which point we may assume that Mary was herself pregnant, though not in a physically obvious way.

Mary's response to Gabriel's announcement has been admired by Christians for twenty centuries. "I am the Lord's servant. May it be to me as you have said." There is in those words a humility and courage that needs to be learned and followed by all Christians. God always works for us and (if we let Him) with us. "We know that in all things God works for the good of those who love him, who have been called according to his purpose" (Rom 8:28). We are not told that in all things we will have an easy ride, or that all circumstances will be pleasant or conducive to our 'walk' with the Lord. Mary surely understood this. She did not fight against what God had chosen her for. She did not say "I'd rather you chose someone else" in the way that Moses did when he was chosen for his great mission (Exodus 4:13). Her acquiescence was not feeble or resigned. It was, rather, humble but with a strength of purpose and a simplicity rarely matched. Humility is, of course, a characteristic not much favoured by our world! But a right reckoning of our position before God – which is really what humility is – is highly favoured by God. With such people He is able to accomplish mighty acts.

God was gentle in this process. He did not cause the miracle of conception to occur without informing Mary, as presumably He might have chosen to do. He was gentle with Mary as He is gentle with all his children —not pushing us further or faster than we can manage. He revealed to Mary only such knowledge as she could cope with. Mary's humility in not asking for more information is, it needs to be repeated, one that Christians should take to heart. Not that God would have us to be dull witted or disinterested participants in His purposes, but that sometimes it has to be sufficient for us to know only partly what God's purposes are and to trust Him for the rest. As the apostle Paul wrote, "Now we see but a poor reflection as in a mirror; then we shall see face to face. Now I know in part; then I shall know fully" (1 Cor 13:12). So for us, some things will only be fully understood as and when God eventually allows us to look back over our lives from His perspective.

We may presume that Mary could have rejected God's plan for her, as individual Christians sometimes reject God's plan for their lives. But Mary was chosen because she was highly favoured and she was so favoured, we assume, because God knew she would not reject His purposes for her. John Stott in his book *The Authentic Jesus* points out that it was a great privilege for Mary to be chosen to give birth to the 'Son of the Most High God', in the words of the Good News version of the Bible. But it was also an awesome and costly responsibility, involving a readiness to become pregnant before she was married, so exposing herself to the shame and suffering of being thought an immoral woman. As Stott comments with his characteristic clinical accuracy, the humility and courage of Mary in accepting God's plan for her stand in stark contrast to the attitudes of church-based critics who deny the biblical account.[4]

Being specially chosen by God, and with His Holy Spirit very much at work in her life, we should not be surprised at Mary's magnificent 'song' of praise (Luke 1:46-55) which reveals many deep spiritual truths. Mary's response to the announcement of her pregnancy is to rejoice in God and glorify Him. She recognises that she is immensely blessed and correctly predicts that all generations will see her as such. God, she acknowledges, is merciful to those who have a godly fear of Him, a fear (it might be added) that comes from a close relationship with Him, which is not the same as the God-aversion which often characterises those who rebel against Him. The proud, in stark contrast with Mary herself, will ultimately face the defeat of all that they have put their pride in, something which Mary calls being 'scattered'. In God's economy, it is the humble who are lifted high, contrasted sharply with mighty rulers who are brought down from their high places. It is the 'hungry' (the spiritually hungry) who are fed with good things, whilst the 'rich' (those who in their pride believe that they have all the answers and can look down on others) who will be sent away, empty. These are spiritual truths that are as relevant today as the day that Mary first 'sang' them.

Comparing Mary with Zechariah

The annunciation to Mary is the second that Gabriel has made concerning an impending birth. We follow the events in Luke chapter 1:

In the time of Herod King of Judea there was a priest named Zechariah, who belonged to the priestly division of Abijah; his wife Elizabeth was also a descendent of Aaron. Both of them were upright in the sight of God, observing all the Lord's commandments and regulations blamelessly. But they had no children, because Elizabeth was barren; and they were both well on in years.

Once when Zechariah's division was on duty and he was serving as priest before God, he was chosen by lot, according to the custom of the priesthood, to go into the temple of the Lord and burn incense. And when the time for the burning of the incense came, all the assembled worshippers were praying outside.

Then an angel of the Lord appeared to him, standing at the right side of the altar of incense. When Zechariah saw him, he was startled and gripped with fear. But the angel said to him: "Do not be afraid, Zechariah; your prayer has been heard. Your wife Elizabeth will bear you a son, and you are to give him the name John. He will be a joy and a delight to you, and many will rejoice because of his birth, for he will be great in the sight of the Lord. He will never take wine or other fermented drink, and he will be filled with the Holy Spirit even from birth. Many of the people of Israel will he bring back to the Lord their God. And he will go on before the Lord, in the spirit and power of Elijah, to turn the hearts of the fathers to their children and the disobedient to the wisdom of the righteous – to make ready a people prepared for the Lord."

Zechariah asked the angel, "How can I be sure of this? I am an old man and my wife is well on in years." The angel answered, "I am Gabriel. I stand in the presence of God, and I have been sent to speak to you and to tell you this good news. And now you will be silent and not able to speak until the day this happens, because you did not believe my words, which will come true at their proper time."

Luke 1:5-20

In the appearance of the angel to Zechariah, one promise among the prophecies given by the angel seems to have taken root in the elderly priest's mind —that of a son. The doubt which Zechariah expressed was almost subconscious: "How can I be sure of this? I am an old man and my wife is well on in years." It is this demand for a sign that most distinguishes Zechariah from Mary. Jesus himself condemned the demand for 'signs' (Matt 12:38-39; John 4:48) so God's displeasure at those who demand such signs should not surprise us. The tongue that failed to praise God but instead asked for a sign, got one! It was struck dumb!

We cannot help but compare Mary's simple belief and acceptance with Zechariah's unbelief. To our modern minds, the 'punishment' of Zechariah for his unbelief may seem harsh. At one level, it could be said that all he had done was to seek a little more information about this momentous event. There must, however, have been something in Zechariah's unbelief which was dishonouring to God. It might also be said that God, in His wisdom, sealed Zechariah's lips in such a way that he was unable to attract attention to the impending birth of his own son, John, nor to the vastly more important birth of Mary's son. Such news as Zechariah might have published abroad, had he been able to speak, would almost certainly have reached the ears of the religious authorities and probably the ears of King Herod, too. We know what Herod's likely reaction would have been. Had Zechariah not been 'shut up' for the period of his wife's pregnancy, the boy's subsequent life would have been impossible, even had he escaped Herod's interest. As it was, Zechariah was unable to speak during the period from the announcement until the eighth day after John's birth —probably the full nine months of a normal pregnancy. He must have done a great deal of thinking and praying during this time. His period of silence was a necessary one of personal preparation, giving him time to think through the implications of what Gabriel had announced to him. How wonderful it was that when Zechariah's tongue was finally loosed, it was immediately turned to the praise of God! (Luke 1:64).

It is deeply symbolic that the Gospel account in Luke should begin in the temple, indeed in the inner sanctuary of the temple – in the Holy Place – wherein was located the golden altar of incense. This was close to the heavy curtain (or veil) that separated the outer chamber from the Holy of Holies. It was to this altar of incense that Zechariah would have taken the incense, already lit with burning coals. It was in this place that the angel Gabriel appeared to Zechariah to announce that his son would prepare the way for the Lord. The symbolism is found in the fact that it was in order to open up a permanent way to the Holy of Holies (in other words, to God Himself) that Jesus came, confirmed by the tearing of the veil from top to bottom as Jesus died on the cross (Matthew 27:51). No more would there be any need for priests to officiate as intermediaries between man and God. In Jesus' own words, His task had been finished (John 19:30; see also Heb 10:11-22) and in His death was created the new priesthood —that of all believers (1 Peter 2:9; Rev 1:6; Rev 5:10).[5]

Mary's period of pregnancy

Following the glorious announcement by the angel Gabriel of the impending birth of the Redeemer-King to Mary, we have seen that the only additional information she requested was to ask *how* she could be connected with it. The words she spoke were not words of doubt, or a demand for a sign, but only of willing self-surrender. The angel pointed her to the fulfilment of Israel's glorious hope, that of the Messiah, a hope that would have been as ever-present in the mind of a faithful Israelite as is today's similar hope among Christians of the Lord's second coming in glory and triumph. The hope of the Saviour was not strange to Mary —the only strange thing to this humble young woman was that *she* could have a part in His advent. Although Mary had not asked for a sign, she was never the less graciously given one —that of her own cousin Elizabeth.

The first thought and as far as we know, the first action, of Mary after the angel Gabriel had left her was to travel from Galilee to the hill country of Judea to be with her cousin Elizabeth. This would not have been a journey undertaken lightly. We do not know what domestic arrangements Mary had to put in place in order to undertake it, but it marked the beginning of a period in her life involving travel and uncertainty. Truly, for Mary life would never be the same again. To be with Elizabeth was vitally important to this young woman. It would enable her to open her heart to someone who would readily understand what she was going through and who might in a very real way be able to minister to Mary, while she in turn helped Elizabeth in her period of pregnancy.

It can have been no ordinary welcome that awaited Mary in Elizabeth's house. We may presume that, although unable to speak, Zechariah had been able to impart to Elizabeth a little of the momentous announcement concerning their son, and this in turn would have suggested the near advent of the Messiah. Luke sketches in the detail for us: "At that time Mary got ready and hurried to a town in the hill country of Judea, where she entered Zechariah's home and greeted Elizabeth. When Elizabeth heard

Mary's greeting, the baby leaped in her womb and Elizabeth was filled with the Holy Spirit. In a loud voice she exclaimed: "Blessed are you among women, and blessed is the child you will bear! But why am I so favoured, that the mother of my Lord should come to me? As soon as the sound of your greeting reached my ears, the baby in my womb leaped for joy. Blessed is she who has believed that what the Lord has said to her will be accomplished!" (Luke 1:39-45). So these two Spirit-filled women were a comfort to each other.

We know nothing of Mary's pregnancy except that it must have been normal in all respects apart from the conception. The first three months of the period were spent, as we know, with Elizabeth. It is not clear from the text whether Mary stayed until John's birth or left shortly before. "Mary stayed with Elizabeth for about three months and then returned home" is the simple detail supplied by Luke. Now, having returned home, Mary needed urgently to share her secret with her betrothed, Joseph.

Joseph

It is likely that Joseph and his intended, Mary, were closely related. Certainly both were of the lineage of David (see Chapter 11 on the genealogies). Mary could also claim kinship with the priesthood, being a 'blood relative' of Elizabeth who, as we know, was the wife of Zechariah, a priest. This suggests that Mary's family shortly before had held higher rank than that which the humble maiden now enjoyed, because custom was that the priesthood only married into such families. At the time of their betrothal, Joseph and Mary were extremely poor, as appears from the facts firstly that Joseph was a carpenter, a humble trade, and secondly that after Jesus was born, the offering made by the grateful parents in the temple was the lowest that the religious law allowed: a pair of doves or two young pigeons. A wealthier family, by contrast, would have offered a lamb (Lev12:7-8).

First century Jewish culture recognised two methods of betrothal: firstly in the presence of witnesses, either by the solemn word of mouth or by some prescribed formality, with the added pledge of a sum of money (however small) or some gift of money's worth; or secondly by writing (the so-called *Shitre Erusin*[6]); either way, the ceremony concluding with a prayer of blessing over a cup of wine tasted in turn by each of the betrothed. From that point the couple were betrothed 'man and wife', their relationship as sacred as if they were already married. Any breach of betrothal was considered as adultery. Betrothal could not be broken except by regular divorce. In spite of the betrothal and the fact that it might be many months before the actual marriage, the betrothed would not come together as man and wife. It was in this extremely solemn and serious way that Mary and Joseph were bound together.

It is the account of the Nativity given in Matthew's Gospel which provides Joseph's side of the story, and is written from his perspective. We take up the thread in chapter 1 verse 18, after Matthew's explanation of the genealogy of the Lord Jesus:

"This is how the birth of Jesus Christ came about: His mother Mary was pledged to be married to Joseph, but before they came together, she was found to be with child through the Holy Spirit. Because Joseph her husband was a righteous man and did not want to expose her to public disgrace, he had in mind to divorce her quietly. But after he had considered this, an angel of the Lord appeared to him in a dream and said, "Joseph son of David, do not be afraid to take Mary home as your wife, because what is conceived in her is from the holy Spirit. She will give birth to a son, and you are to give him the name Jesus, because he will save his people from their sins."

All this took place to fulfil what the Lord had said through the prophet: "The virgin will be with child and will give birth to a son, and they will call him Immanuel – which means "God with us."

When Joseph woke up, he did what the angel of the Lord had commanded him and took Mary home as his wife. But he had no union with her until she gave birth to a son. And he gave him the name Jesus."

To the great and good man Joseph we owe a great deal. He displayed calm, courage, faith, obedience and honour which were evidently his essential characteristics. We do not know in what manner or with what words Mary shared her divine secret with her betrothed. It would be gratuitous prying for us to share this detail and would not in any way advance our understanding of the Lord Jesus if we did. The Bible treats the whole subject, as we would expect, with great delicacy. We are shown first that Joseph, having received the news and being a righteous man, wanted to do what he considered to be the best thing for himself and his betrothed, to divorce her quietly. Joseph could legally divorce his betrothed either publicly or privately, whether from change of feeling, or because he had found just cause for the action. Less honourable men might have wanted to take revenge by publicly disgracing their betrothed, but this was not the decision that came to Joseph. His private divorce would have left it open to doubt as to the grounds on which he had chosen to do so.

We might surmise that Joseph, as Mary, was selected by God to fulfil the legal role of father to the divine child, because he also was highly favoured. There was, no doubt, some combination of characteristics in the man Joseph which attracted God's attention to him as being suitable to fulfil a supremely difficult role. We might go further and suggest that God nurtured and encouraged Joseph as he developed to manhood to prepare him for the great task that God had set before him.

However conscious Mary was of the circumstance that had led to her condition, it must have been painful for her to have shared the news with Joseph. However deep his love for and trust in the woman he had chosen to be his wife, only a direct communication from God could dispel the doubts in his mind. It was that which he now received. The fact that the announcement came to him in a dream would more readily have disposed him to accept it as being from God. In popular Jewish custom a good dream was one of three things considered to be marks of God's favour ('A good king, a fruitful year, and a good dream'). In the dream, 'an angel of the Lord' appeared and delivered the message: "Joseph son of

David, do not be afraid to take Mary home as your wife, because what is conceived in her is from the holy Spirit. She will give birth to a son, and you are to give him the name Jesus, because he will save his people from their sins."

In these fifty one words, the angel gave Joseph sufficient information on which to take Mary as his wife. Being addressed as 'son of David' would have grabbed his attention —it was an unusual salutation! The reference to his betrothed immediately brought the message 'home' and no doubt matched the matter that was most singularly on his mind. The naming of the unborn Messiah, as we have already seen, agreed with popular notions (the idea being that God would name six people from before their birth: Isaac, Ishmael, Moses, Solomon, Josiah and the Messiah) and the symbolism of such a name was rooted in Jewish belief. The name itself, *Jeshua* (Jesus) was explained as meaning that He would save His people from their sins —one commonly understood office of the expected Messiah. No doubt Joseph understood this as referring to the people of Israel. His mind now set at rest on the issue of Mary's faithfulness, Joseph could no longer hesitate. His duty towards the virgin mother and the unborn child demanded an immediate marriage which would afford not only physical, but also moral protection for both. So we read in Matthew 1:24-5, "When Joseph woke up, he did what the angel of the Lord had commanded him and took Mary home as his wife. But he had no union with her until she gave birth to a son. And he gave him the name Jesus."

Joseph made three distinct contributions to the history of the Incarnation. Firstly, **he protected the good name of Mary and of the Lord Jesus**, who was commonly accepted as the natural son of Joseph and Mary (e.g. Matt 13:55; Luke 2:48; John 1:45). Secondly, he **provided materially for the infant Jesus and his mother** through his trade a carpenter (Matt 13:55), a trade which the Lord Himself adopted until He began His public ministry. In Mark 6:3 Jesus is called 'the carpenter' —and some have inferred from this fact that by this time Joseph had died. And thirdly, **Joseph transmits to Christ his 'crown rights'** as

Joseph represented in himself the regal-legal line. Being a direct descendant of David through Solomon he possessed the crown rights. "But for the misfortune of his race," writes H. Brash Bonsall "he would have been known not as the carpenter of Nazareth but as King Joseph I and, by Jewish law, he could pass on these rights to his foster son, Jesus the Christ."[7] Alfred Edersheim makes a similar point as he refers to the prophecy in Isaiah 7:15: "Never had the house of David sunk morally lower than when, in the words of Ahaz, it seemed to renounce the very foundation of its claim to continuance; never had the fortunes of the house of David fallen lower, than when a Herod sat on its throne, and its lineal representative was a humble village carpenter...."[8] What a contrast then, between the noble Joseph who should have held the throne of Israel, and the corrupt and ignoble Herod who actually sat on it!

The Lord Jesus and His parents as a family

We have considered some of the personal virtues in Mary and Joseph that help us to understand God's pre-selection of them through a long historic process which predated both of them and stemmed from their ancestor King David. That Mary was a good woman and Joseph a good man, there can be no doubt on the basis of biblical evidence.

The biblical records about the practical aspects of the Incarnation, especially the Nativity which brought it about, are strictly limited. We are given only the barest essentials to enable us to identify the Lord Jesus as God's promised Saviour. We perceive the reality of his birth which leaves us no doubt that, although His conception was unique, in every other way He was a normal human being and lived a normal human life. He fully identifies with those He had come to save and, in theological terms, perfectly and completely stands in the place of those who repent and believe, to face the holy wrath of God. (e.g. Rom 3:25; Rom 5:10-11; 2 Cor 5:21; 1 Peter 1:18-19; 1 John 4:10). The biblical account of the Nativity does not give us any additional information which could serve to distract attention from the holiness and uniqueness of the Lord Jesus. To do so would be to run the very real risk of our admiration of these parents, chosen by God, becoming an unhealthy or even dangerous veneration of them. Such veneration is to be given only to the Lord Jesus, who is 'the First and the Last' (Rev 1:17) and to whom all authority in heaven and on earth has been given (Matt 28:18).

What limited additional information we are given about the parents of the Lord Jesus shows us their humanity and fallibility, counterweights, perhaps, to their obvious virtues of humility and courage. So, despite the fact that both Mary and Joseph had had direct personal revelations from God via angelic messengers about the nature of their eldest son and the ministry He would undertake, despite also the visit of the shepherds, and their testimony – which Mary pondered in her heart (Luke 2:19); despite the amazing exclamations of Simeon and Anna in the temple; despite the visit of the *Magi* ('wise men') and the amazing and deeply symbolic gifts they presented; and despite the clear evidence of God's hand being upon them and preserving them against the threat of Herod and delivering them to the safety of temporary residence in Egypt – in spite of all these evidences – still they misunderstood their eldest son.

So it was that, twelve years later, when Jesus was taken to Jerusalem to celebrate the feast of Passover (presumably with His siblings, although they are not mentioned) and Jesus stayed behind after His parents had set out for the return journey to Nazareth, when they eventually located Him in the temple, they gently rebuked him, pointing out to Him that they had been searching anxiously for Him (Luke 2:41-52). Jesus responded with the simple question "Didn't you know I had to be in my Father's house?" Luke points out (verse 50), "...they did not understand what he was saying to them." and repeats once more that, "Mary treasured all these things in her heart." Similarly, after Jesus has begun His ministry, we read in Matthew 12:46-49 that Jesus' mother and brothers came to speak with Him. The context suggests (though this is only supposition) that they were a family delegation and had come to question Jesus, or even to persuade Him to return

116

with them. This was at a time of growing controversy and we cannot know what pressure His mother and brothers were under, as an indirect form of attack against Him. Jesus, without rushing to meet this family delegation, uses it as an opportunity to teach a spiritual truth— that His mother and brothers are those who do the will of His Father in heaven.

We also have a hint, but only a hint, that in some way Jesus was gently displeased by His mother bringing to Him, at a wedding feast in Cana, the problem that the host had run out of wine. Presumably such a domestic crisis would have been embarrassing, even shameful to the hosts, but not something, one would imagine, that demanded the intervention of God's Son. So Jesus says to His mother, "Dear woman, why do you have to involve me? My time has not yet come" (John 2: 4). But out of Mary's perhaps mistaken motive – we do not know that Mary expected Jesus to perform a miracle – comes Jesus' first miracle, a miracle that, although *prima facie* trivial in nature, nevertheless carried a deeper spiritual significance: the master of the banquet is unaware that he has delineated this deeper spiritual significance as he exclaims "Every one brings the choice wine first and then the cheaper wine after the guests have had too much to drink; but you have saved the best till now!" The best that was saved until last was God's own Son, who had been preceded by so many prophets, each of whom had, in their way, pointed towards Him.

Mary and Joseph, then, shared the characteristic of all those who came into contact with Jesus, be they friends, family or disciples: they misunderstood Him. We cannot blame them for this. Had they fully understood their eldest son, fully understood His Divinity and His mission, then they would have found it impossible to be truly His parents. As a consequence of this He would have been unable to have led a normal human life (normal, it might be added, except that He never rebelled against His heavenly Father and therefore never sinned). Had Jesus been understood for who He was, then He could not in any meaningful sense have been subject to His parents —such knowledge would then have broken the bond of true humanity which the Lord Jesus shares with us. We could not then have become His brethren and a very basic part of His mission could not then have been fulfilled— to be our kinsman-redeemer. We can apply this thought more generally: had Jesus' Divinity not been kept a mystery whilst He was on earth, then the thought of His Divinity would have proved so engrossing to the people of His time, that His humanity, with all its lessons, could not have shone through. We would never have been able to see Jesus *the man*, and one crucial part of our salvation would have become wholly impossible.

Only one more thought needs to be added to complete our review of the Lord Jesus and His parents as a family unit. Some have held that the virgin Mary remained perpetually as a virgin. This is not supportable by the canon of Scripture. First, within the account of the Nativity itself, we read in Matthew 1:25 that Joseph had no union with Mary *until* she gave birth to a son. This clearly implies that their marriage became in every way normal after the Lord Jesus' birth. Second, there are a number of references to Jesus' siblings, which we have already seen. They are Matt 12:46-49; Matt 13:55-56 and Luke 8:19-21. James and Jude, cited as two of Jesus' brothers, are thought by many scholars to be the authors of the epistles of those names. The reference to 'all his sisters' in Matt 13:55 implies that there were at least three of these.[9] We are left, then, with the clear message that the Lord Jesus' family was a normal human family, and in this very normality we find our identity with Christ as a human who lived in every way as we do, with the singular exception that He never sinned. And this is the great guarantee of our salvation —for only He could pay the debt to God caused by our sins.

Notes

[1] "I myself have carefully investigated everything from the beginning" (Luke 1:3).

[2] For more detailed information, see Appendix 4, *Biblical Sources*.

[3] H. Brash Bonsall *The Person of Christ,* Volume 1: The Doctrine (CLC, 1967), p. 36.

[4] John Stott *The Authentic Jesus* (Marshall Morgan and Scott, 1985), p. 65.

[5] At this point we need to look at some weighty theology: After the fall of mankind God provided a way of salvation and forgiveness whereby each individual sinner could find atonement for his sin *in anticipation of the cross*. We find instances of Abel, Noah, Abraham and others approaching God by way of sacrifice. Truly repenting and believing, and because of the shed blood of the innocent animal which had been sacrificed, the individual found forgiveness and peace with God. It appears similarly, that heads of families could sacrifice for their households and that patriarchs could sacrifice on behalf of their people. *All this was in anticipation of the cross* —but the essential requirement of the individual remained unchanged, i.e. faith in God and belief in the blood. The end of the era of animal sacrifice coincided with the sacrifice of Jesus Christ on the cross. This is God's final and complete way of salvation for man, opening the new and living way to God. The veil in the Holy of Holies was torn from top to bottom and once again, as at the very beginning of time (before sin spoiled man's relationship with God) every human has direct access to God. And so becomes possible the priesthood of all believers who offer spiritual sacrifices to God, e.g. of their personal consecration, of souls won for Christ and of praise and thanksgiving. There is no longer any requirement for priests, who are redundant.

[6] See Alfred Edersheim *The Life and Times of Jesus the Messiah* p. 105.

[7] *Op. cit. The Person of Christ Volume 1: The Doctrine,* p. 44.

[8] *Op.cit. The Life and Times of Jesus the Messiah*, p. 110.

[9] Others have held, in support of the idea of a perpetual virginity, that Jesus' brothers and sisters were Joseph's offspring by a former marriage, the former wife presumably having died. This strikes one as an inventive method of getting around the 'problem' of Jesus' siblings, but virtually impossible. Why should God have chosen a widower? Would there not have been a surprising age difference between Joseph and Mary had he already sired a large

family? Why do we not read of some or all of these siblings being present at the Nativity of the Lord Jesus? Such inventions appear more as a prop to the error of Mariolatry, referred to earlier, than a serious contribution to understanding Jesus' family.

8

Bethlehem, Tax Census and Birth

Bethlehem

In those days Caesar Augustus issued a decree that a census should
be taken of the entire Roman world. (This was the first census that
took place while Quirinius was governor of Syria.) And everyone
went to his own town to register.

So Joseph also went up from the town of Nazareth in Galilee
to Judea, to Bethlehem the town of David, because he belonged
to the house and line of David. He went there to register with
Mary, who was pledged to be married to him and was expecting
a child. While they were there, the time came for the baby to be
born, and she gave birth to her firstborn, a son.

Luke 2:1-6

Matthew 2:1 and Luke 2:4-7 state that the Lord Jesus was born
in Bethlehem. The town of Bethlehem lies on a ridge about 2,500
feet high some six miles south and slightly west of Jerusalem in
the Judean hills. In Old Testament history Bethlehem was the
home of David, son of Jesse, (1 Samuel 16:1) and was therefore
the 'town of David' (1 Sam 20:6 and Luke 2:4 —in older English
translations of the Bible sometimes rendered 'city of David').
King David however, decided to make his capital at Jerusalem and

121

Bethlehem remained a 'town' as it is called in John 7:42. Older translations, such as the Revised Standard Version, render this, perhaps more correctly in view of its small size in Herod's day, as 'village'. The prophet Micah thought of Bethlehem as of great potential importance when he wrote of it as being the home of the future messianic ruler (Micah 5:2) and this is certainly how the town was viewed in Herod's day (Matt 2:4-5).

The name Bethlehem is rendered in Arabic, *Bayt Lahm* ("House of Meat") and in Hebrew *Bet Lehem* ("House of Bread") The town is certainly an ancient settlement being (possibly) mentioned in the Amarna Letters —14th century B.C. diplomatic documents found at Tell el-Amarna, Egypt. The Hebrew meaning of *Bet Lehem* ("House of Bread") is doubly significant when we consider Christ's controversial assertion that He is *the Bread of Life*. The account of Jesus using this title is found in John 6:25-59. "But here is the bread that comes down from heaven," said Jesus (verse 50), "which a man may eat and not die. I am the living bread that came down from heaven." This was extremely controversial at the time, but provides a much deeper significance to the ancient Hebrew name of David's town.

Bethlehem is first mentioned in the Bible in relation to Rachel, who died on the wayside near there (Gen 35:19), and is the setting for most of the Book of Ruth, one of David's ancestors. It was in Bethlehem that David was anointed as king of Israel (1 Sam 16) by the prophet Samuel. The town was fortified by Rehoboam, David's grandson and the first king of Judah after the division of the state between Israel and Judah (2 Chronicles 11). Following the return of Jewish exiles to Judah after their Babylonian Captivity (516 BC and after), the town was progressively repopulated by the Hebrews. Much later, a Roman garrison was stationed in Bethlehem during the second Jewish revolt led by Bar Kokhba (AD 135).

The site of the Nativity of Jesus was identified by Justin Martyr, a second century Christian apologist, as a manger in a cave close to the village. The cave, which is today under the nave of the Church of the Nativity in the heart of Bethlehem, has been venerated by

Christians ever since. It is frankly impossible to state whether or not this was the precise site of Jesus' birth. Christians should always be wary of the danger of venerating things or places, rather than the One who provided them. It might be added that it is a fact (and believing Christians would add, a wise and godly fact) that no details or artefacts of Jesus or any of His disciples have survived. This may well be God's protection against the possibility of superstition taking hold among His people. The only fully dependable records we have, Christians believe, are those of the Bible itself.

Not only Old Testament prediction via the words of Micah, but also rabbinic teaching, pointed directly to Bethlehem as the birthplace of the Messiah. Micah 5:2 was universally understood at the time of Jesus' birth as identifying Bethlehem as the birthplace of the Messiah. Besides this, the practice of using *Targumim* to translate and interpret Scripture from Hebrew to other languages pointed in the same direction. Thus the *Targum Jonathan*, mentioned in Alfred Edersheim stated this to be the case.[1] Similarly, the *Talmud* (scholarly interpretations of the *Mishna* — the codification of Jewish Law) contained references to the belief, such as one citing an imaginary conversation between an Arab and a Jew, where Bethlehem is named as the Messiah's birthplace. (Mentioned in Edersheim again —see reference below)

Whilst the birth in Bethlehem is affirmed by Matthew and Luke, neither Mark or John mention the fact. There is, however, in John's Gospel an oblique reference to the Bethlehem birth, in the context of a contemporary debate about the Lord Jesus among his fellow countrymen. So in John 7:40-43 we read: "On hearing his words, some of the people said 'Surely this man is the Prophet?' Others said 'He is the Christ'. Still others asked, 'How can the Christ come from Galilee? Does not the Scripture say that the Christ will come from David's family and from Bethlehem, the town where David lived?' Thus the people were divided because of Jesus." We see in these verses the fact that John also understood The Lord's birth to have taken place in Bethlehem —otherwise he would presumably have commented upon it.

Nothing less likely than the circumstances of the Gospel accounts of the birth in Bethlehem would have suggested itself to Jewish minds: a boy born of a visitor from Nazareth, not a native of Bethlehem, to participate in a counting of the people, or census, carried out at the instruction of a heathen emperor, and executed by one so universally hated as Herod, the emperor's puppet king. These facts would have been totally repugnant to all Jewish expectations.[2] Had the Gospel writers wanted to create a legend around Jesus' birth, in order to persuade Jews of the messiahship of Jesus, they would surely have chosen a more likely and more conducive scenario! If the account of the circumstances which brought Mary and Joseph to Bethlehem had no basis in fact, but was simply a plot to locate the birth of a Nazarene in the royal town of David, then it must be pronounced a most clumsily devised plot. There is nothing to account for the origin of such a 'legend', either in parallel events in the past, or from contemporary expectations. So why, apart from their belief in its truthfulness, should the Gospel writers have connected the birth of the Lord Jesus with what was most repugnant to Israel?

The tax census
The census is by no means a modern invention. Practised in ancient times, it was used then, as today, for two extremely reasonable purposes. It provided the relevant information firstly for drafting men for military service and secondly for tax. In subject countries it was the second of these that most concerned Rome. Without exacting tribute from its foreign possessions, Rome could not with its own resources have sustained its magnificent and extravagant style.

There has been some debate in recent years as to the reliability of Luke's report of the Tax Census called by the Emperor Augustus. Some arguments have been scholarly, but others decidedly not! The problem revolves around the fact that P. Sulpicius Quirinius (sometimes written as Cyrenius), who undertook the census on behalf of the emperor, is known to have carried out such a census in AD 6, when he became governor of Syria. At this time

Judaea was absorbed into the Syriac territory as part of Quirinius' responsibility to 'wind-up' the estate of Herod's son Archelaus who had by this time been banished to Vienna by the Emperor as a result of various misdemeanours. Jesus was born, as best can be reckoned, in 6-5 BC. Luke 2:2 says, "this was the first census that took place while Quirinius was governor of Syria." But he did not become governor of Syria until ten years later. Did Luke make a mistake? Worse, did he make the story up?

If Luke had been in the business of making up stories, he would not have done so about such an event. He would surely have selected some other, less controversial but more nebulous reason to prise Mary and Joseph out of Nazareth and locate them in Bethlehem. After all, Luke knew full well about the census in AD 6 —he referred to it in Acts 5:37! So, we appear to have a major dating problem, indeed Paul Barnett suggests that it is probably the major historical problem in the New Testament.[3] Let us be precise, then, about the nature of this problem. Luke refers to Mary's conception of Jesus as being "in the time of Herod, King of Judea" (Luke 1:5 and 36) and to Jesus' birth as occurring "while Quirinius was governor of Syria" (Luke 2:2). A ten year gap separates the two events from our present understanding of history.

Some scholars believe that Luke made a glaring error, yet this would be most remarkable for an educated man who wrote both his Gospel account and the book of Acts some years after the event and was certainly aware of the latter census under Quirinius. It also does not fit neatly with the idea of a witness who himself "carefully investigated everything from the beginning" (Luke 1:3). A number of points therefore need to be made:

1. The problem is confined, as Paul Barnett points out, to one very short sentence of eight Greek words. While the most likely translation is, "This was the first census that took place when Quirinius was governor of Syria," it is possible that the correct rendering should be: "This was the first census that took place *before* Quirinius was governor of Syria." In other words, it is telling us that the census that took place before that of the well known

census in AD 6, so that the two are not confused. This is certainly a possibility: while the translation may have become corrupted, it might well have been an objective of Luke to emphasise that the census was *not* the famous Quirinius/Syriac one, so his readers were quite clear that Jesus was born in the time of Herod.

2. It is possible that such a census coincided with the oath of loyalty that all the people made to Herod and Augustus in 7 BC. (See point 5 below.) If so, this would virtually coincide with Jesus' presumed date of birth and with the triple conjunction of Jupiter and Saturn which occurred that year and which may have been the 'star' followed by the wise men from the east.

3. The supposed error should be compared with the precision with which Luke writes in the very next chapter (Luke 3:1-2), "In the fifteenth year of the reign of Tiberius Caesar – when Pontius Pilate was governor of Judea, Herod tetrarch of Galilee, his brother Philip tetrarch of Iturea and Traconitis, and Lysanius tetrarch of Abilene – during the high priesthood of Annas and Caiaphas...." This accurate information proves that Luke was well aware of the complex division of the former Herod's kingdom, including the part of it then under direct Roman rule.

4. At the time of the famous Quirinius census, in AD 6, the census applied only to the people of Judea, not Galilee, where Mary and Joseph were. So it is highly unlikely that the betrothed couple would have responded to a census covering Judea only. It is far more likely that the census was an earlier one covering Judea *and* Galilee, both then under the control of Herod 'the Great'.

5. Whilst Herod 'the Great' had been Rome's useful puppet king during most of his reign and had paid considerable honours to his Roman overlords (naming buildings after Augustus, naming his Jerusalem palace 'Caesarium' and so on), and most crucially kept the peace within his borders, towards the end of his reign Herod did incur the Emperor Augustus' deep displeasure. And this would have been about the time that the Lord Jesus was born.

The cause of Augustus' displeasure was Herod's invasion of the neighbouring kingdom of the Nabataeans. Herod made two attempts to placate and curry favour with Augustus, both of which backfired badly: first in 7 BC he issued an order that all people in his kingdom should take an oath of loyalty to himself and to Augustus. Six thousand Pharisees refused to comply for religious reasons and faced severe punishment, but Herod relented under domestic pressure. The aged Herod, losing his grip mentally as well as physically, now ordered that a giant golden eagle, symbol of Rome, should be affixed on the great gate of the Jerusalem temple. Angered by Herod's blatant disregard for Jewish religious laws against idolatry, two leading rabbis incited their followers to remove the offending symbol. For their pains Herod had them burned alive. Now desperate to please Rome, upon Emperor Augustus' issuance of a decree concerning an empire-wide census, could it be that Herod over-enthusiastically carried out the decree, insisting not only on registration, but on registration in 'ancestral homes'? This would have been a more 'Jewish' way of performing the necessary census and perhaps made it appear less Roman to a predictably hostile Jewish audience.

Whilst one, or a combination, of these possible answers to the problem may fully resolve it, there appears to be a much simpler solution. This is suggested in Werner Keller's influential and popular book *The Bible As History.* [4] Keller explains that Cyrenius the Governor was actually the senator P. Sulpicius Quirinius, who is known to historians from other Roman documents. The Emperor Augustus certainly rated highly the outstanding abilities of Quirinius both as an administrator and as a soldier. He was born in modest circumstances in the Alban hills near Tusculum, a place that was reckoned to be among the favourite resorts of wealthy Roman families. In AD 6 Quirinius was sent as legate to Syria. Coponius was sent with him from Rome to an appointment as the first procurator of Judea.

Between AD 6 and 7, Quirinius and Coponius carried out an administrative census for the Romans, but this certainly cannot be the one referred to by Luke, as by this time Jesus would have been over ten years old. According to Luke's narrative the census ordered by Caesar Augustus took place in the year Christ was born. For a long time, says Werner Keller, it seemed as if Luke had made a serious mistake in his research. It was only when a fragment of a Roman inscription was discovered at Antioch that a surprising fact emerged: that P. Sulpicius Quirinius had been the Emperor's legate in Syria on an earlier occasion —in the days of Saturninus the pro-consul. At that time Quirinius' assignment had been solely a military one. He had led a campaign against the Homonadenses, a tribe in the Taurus mountains of Asia Minor. Quirinius set up his seat of government as well as his headquarters in Syria between 10 and 7 BC. This would explain why Luke emphasised that, "this was the first census while Quirinius was governor of Syria" —he wanted to make sure his readers understood he was talking about events in 6 BC, *not* AD 6. For the Judean and Galilean elements of the earlier census, Herod would have acted as Quirinius' agent.

So much for the scholarly objections to the account of the census. Readers who have access to the internet may have visited sites which purport to debate the accuracy of the Bible. These sites approach the subject from an atheist point of view and their scholarship is often questionable. One such website visited by the author made two objections to "the story". The first was that there "was no universal census at the time of Jesus birth" and then goes on to cite the 'problem' that we have just considered, i.e. Quirinius carried out his famous census in AD 6.[5]

The second 'problem' was that 'chaos would have resulted'! The argument is put forward: "Caesar, according to Luke, decided that everyone would have to return to the town from which they descended. Who could imagine the efficient Romans requiring millions in the empire to journey hundreds of miles to villages of millennium-old ancestors merely to give in a tax form!" This objection is rather quaint, the idea that the Romans, who thought little of nailing thousands upon thousands of vanquished foes to a forest of execution crosses should baulk at the idea of mounting a census, however inconvenient to their subject peoples! As we have seen however, it appears that Herod may well have interpreted the Emperor's call for a census in his own way. The Romans would have been unlikely to have objected to this, providing the resulting tax revenues were in due course collected and paid to Rome.

The census and Joseph and Mary

So Joseph also went up from the town of Nazareth in Galilee to Judea, to Bethlehem the town of David, because he belonged to the house and line of David. He went there to register with Mary, who was pledged to be married to him and was expecting a child.

Luke 2:4-5

We can now follow the course of the Gospel narrative. In consequence of the decree of Caesar Augustus, Herod directed a general registration in the Jewish, rather than the Roman manner. In most practical points the two would be similar: country people being required to register in 'their own city' —meaning the town to which the village or hamlet where they were born was attached for administrative reasons. We might think of this in modern terms as the 'catchment area' of the major town. Certainly most people would not be required to travel far, as most people were born, lived and died in the same place. Indeed it is possible there may have been local dispensations for certain categories of subjects to enable them to register elsewhere. But this does not seem to have been the case with Joseph.

According to the Jewish mode of registration, their people were enrolled according to *tribes*, *families* or clans and the *house* of their fathers. As the ten tribes of Israel had not returned to Judaea and Galilee *as tribes*, but rather as individuals and mixed-tribe groups, this could only be undertaken in a very limited way, although it would be simple enough for people to be registered in their 'own city' where the *house* and *lineage* of each person was recorded. In the case of Joseph and Mary, whose lineage from King David was known, it was most important that the unborn infant should be born in David's city, and no doubt Mary and Joseph realised this in some limited way —the angel had, after all, told them that their son would inherit "the throne of his father David" (Luke 1:32). Furthermore, it was important that the birth should be recorded there. We might readily recognise, for all too obvious reasons, that Mary and Joseph were probably glad to leave Nazareth and if possible seek a new home in Bethlehem. In these circumstances Mary, now the 'wife' of Joseph, though in fact continuing the correct relationship of betrothal, would certainly accompany her husband to Bethlehem, even though the law did not require her presence.

The impression is certainly formed that the couple intended to stay in Bethlehem; the fact that Herod ordered the destruction of boys up to two years of age, and the reference to the wise men coming to worship the infant in a *house* (Matt 2: 11) both suggest that the couple stayed on in Bethlehem after the birth. And the fact that it took a warning in a dream to persuade Joseph to quit Bethlehem also lends weight to the idea that Mary and Joseph had intended to settle permanently.

No room at the inn – the birth of the Lord Jesus

The journey from Nazareth in Galilee to Bethlehem in Judaea would have been something a little in excess of ninety miles, including likely detours. The way would have been long and tiring, whatever route was taken from Nazareth. In all probability the route chosen would have been that most often followed by Jews, out of their strong desire to avoid the hated Samaria, along the eastern banks of the Jordan and by the fords of Jericho. Travel down the Jordan valley would have taken them past the Gentile city of Scythopolis, through the bleak Judaean desert, on through the oasis city Jericho, and then by a slow ascent of some 4,000 ft through the ravines up to Jerusalem. This route would have taken at least six days to travel, but Mary's condition would certainly have necessitated a slower pace.

Although passing through one of the warmest regions of 'Palestine', the likely time of year (winter, as we shall see later) must have increased the difficulties of the journey. It must have been with a sense of great relief that the couple reached the rich fields that surrounded the ancient 'House of Bread' and, passing through the valley leading into the town, no doubt recalled some of the former glories associated with the names of Ruth and Boaz, of Jesse and of David himself.

There was a distinct contrast, however, between that glorious past and the circumstances of the present for, as the travellers reached the heights of Bethlehem, the most prominent object in view was the great castle to the south-east of the town which Herod 'the Great' had built, and immodestly named after himself, as Herodium. Whilst Mary and Joseph could not yet realise the danger to which the king would shortly put them and their unborn son, they would probably have been aware of the fearsome reputation of the castle and the king whose name it bore. Herodium was a fortress palace, which became the final resting place of the bloody king, who would soon be buried there. In all, along the borders of his kingdom and for internal control, Herod possessed no fewer than eleven fortresses, of which Herodium near Bethlehem and Herodium in Jordan were his own constructions. The remainder had been built by Maccabean and Hasmonean leaders and later re-fortified and improved by Herod.

Josephus says that Herodium near Bethlehem was built on an artificial hill (which remains to this day) and was lavishly decorated by Herod. The site was chosen because it was where, in 40 BC, Herod fought and won an important battle against the Hasmoneans and their Parthian supporters (*War* 1:13:8:265). Of the castle-palace itself, Josephus tells us: "He bestowed much curious art upon it with great ambition, and built round towers all about the top of it, and filled up the remaining space with the most costly palaces round about, insomuch that not only the sight of the inner apartments was splendid, but great wealth was laid out on the outward walls, and partitions and roofs also. Besides this, he brought a mighty quantity of water from a great distance, and at vast charges, and raised an ascent to it of two hundred steps of the whitest marble...." (*War* 1:21:10:419-420.)[6] It was no doubt from this self-congratulatory fortress that Herod's soldiers issued forth to carry out his order to slaughter the infant boys in Bethlehem and surrounding parts.

The first necessity for Joseph and Mary on reaching Bethlehem was to find shelter and rest. The little town was crowded with those who had travelled from outlying districts to register their names. Had the visitors from Galilee known anyone in the town personally, they would have found their house fully occupied. Even the inn[7] was filled, and the only available space was the place where cattle were normally stabled. It should be noted at this point that Luke's account does not state categorically that the place of Jesus' birth was a stable. It is only conjecture, though entirely reasonable and likely to be true, that the place was a stable. Mary placed the new born baby in a manger *because there was no room for them in the inn.* It is possible that a manger was taken from a stable and used in some other place, but the three references to the manger (Luke 2:7, Luke 2:12 and Luke 2:16) clearly imply there was something unusual and very humble about the circumstances of the Lord's birth.

"Bearing in mind the simple habits in the east," writes Alfred Edersheim, reflecting on the use of a stable, "this scarcely implies what it would in the west; and perhaps the seclusion and privacy from the noisy, chattering crowd, which thronged the khan, would be all the more welcome."[8] We cannot help, however, being amazed that the King of Glory, the Creator of the world and the author of moral perfection should have chosen to allow His Son to be born in such circumstances. Plainly in this circumstance there is in evidence a real-life parable being acted out. The King of Glory had become the Servant-King, identifying first and foremost with the poor of this world, and with the social outcasts. Not for Him all those things that the world holds so dear: wealth, comfort and position. For the Saviour, only a borrowed stable. Far from men's deference, all that the Lord received was mankind's meanest left-overs.

The point is fairly made that the Greek word rendered "inn" in most Bible translations (Luke 2:7 —there was no room for them at *the inn*) should perhaps more correctly be rendered "lodging house". Very similar Greek words are used in Luke 9:12 and Luke 19:7, where the context is about finding lodgings. The New Testament Greek word used by Luke for what we might call a 'commercial inn' is quite different (as used in Luke 10:34). The idea often advanced today is that Joseph would have sought to stay with relatives in Bethlehem and that the domestic housing arrangements for most poor folk in biblical times involved humans living and sleeping on a raised platform, whilst animals occupied a lower "ground floor" space. So humans and animals lived in very close proximity, as animals would be brought into the 'house' at night, for protection from predators and the elements. The argument is heard that, because Bethlehem was overcrowded, and the upper space was filled to capacity, Mary and Joseph were forced to sleep (and Mary to give birth) in the lower space, amongst the animals. The theory may be correct but there are some possible flaws, as we now consider.

Firstly, Joseph may indeed *not* have sought relatives in Bethlehem. He came from Nazareth, so any relatives may have been quite distant. Although the rules of hospitality would probably have demanded that even distant relatives should provide lodging, Joseph may not have sought them out. He left Nazareth with Mary for good reasons, we have already conjectured —to leave behind any tittle-tattle about the timing of the child's birth. Lodging with even distant relatives would surely soon have reignited unwelcome explanations. Modern Jehovah's Witnesses, who deny Christ's deity and have made it an article of faith not to celebrate or acknowledge Christmas in any form, question many elements of our 'traditional' understanding of the Nativity. They say that the placing of a child in a manger signifies only that the device also made an excellent crib, even when placed in a house —or on the ground floor of a built dwelling. However Luke's triple reference to the use of a manger (Luke 2:7, 12 and 16) may be to emphasise the unusual nature of this aspect of the Lord's birth. Whilst we cannot be totally sure of this aspect of the account, it seems equally likely that indeed the traditional view is correct. Mary and Joseph arrive in a strange town, overcrowded on account of the tax census, and fail to find proper lodging. Instead an outhouse of some sort is offered to them and they accept, with no other option.

Others who doubt the idea that a borrowed stable could be the location of the Lord's birth have suggested that a wise and honourable man like Joseph would never have allowed his wife to bear a child in such a place. But this view simply ignores the exigency of the situation —*there was no room at the inn*. These same critics argue that we must stretch our imagination a long way to believe that there was not one innkeeper in the whole of Bethlehem who could offer reasonable accommodation to the weary travellers —and that it is inconceivable that Almighty God would allow His Son to be born in a borrowed stable. They perhaps forget that his body was to be laid in a borrowed grave (Matt 27:60; John 19:41). No, the Gospel writers leave us in little doubt that the circumstances of the Lord's birth were in every way testing and humbling.

Although in our modern view, it may seem important to possess details of the event of the Lord Jesus' birth – after all, the most important birth in history – the Gospels provide none. All we are given by Luke is: "While they were there, the time came for the baby to be born, and she gave birth to her firstborn, a son. She wrapped him in cloths and placed him in a manger, for there was no room for them in the inn" (Luke 2: 6-7).

The Gospels were never intended to provide a biography, nor even the material for one. They were provided so that, in the words of John, "you may believe that Jesus is the Christ, the Son of God, and that by believing you may have life in his name" (John 20:31). Commenting on this lack of detail, Edersheim writes:

"It is better that it should be so. As to all that passed in the seclusion of that 'stable' – the circumstances of the 'Nativity', even its exact time after the arrival of Mary (brief as it must have been) – the Gospel narrative is silent. This only is told, that then and there the Virgin-Mother 'brought forth her firstborn Son, and wrapped him in swaddling clothes, and laid him in a manger." Beyond this announcement of the bare fact, Holy Scripture, with indescribable appropriateness and delicacy, draws a veil over that most sacred mystery. Two impressions only are left on the mind: that of utmost earthly humility, in the surrounding circumstances; and that of inward fitness, in the contrast suggested by them. Instinctively, reverently, we feel it is well it should have been so. It best befits the birth of the Christ —if He be what the New Testament declared Him."[9]

But the humble circumstances provide strong indirect evidence of the truthfulness of the account we have in the Bible. If it was the outcome of Jewish imagination, then where is the basis for it in terms of contemporary expectation? Would Jewish legend have portrayed the Messiah as being born in a stable, to which lowly circumstance His mother had been reduced on account of a tax census by a foreign power? All contemporary Jewish thought would have run contrary to this! Opponents of the authenticity of the Gospel accounts of the Lord's birth are bound to face and answer this. It might be added, no myth would ever have been given with such scantiness of detail —the essential features of legend and of tradition are that they always seek to portray their heroes with glory, and to provide detail in their accounts that emphasise this heroic portrayal. In both these respects, a sharper contrast with the Gospel narratives could hardly be imagined.

The visit of the shepherds

And there were shepherds living out in the fields near by, keeping watch over their flocks at night. An angel of the Lord appeared to them, and the glory of the Lord shone around them, and they were terrified. But the angel said to them, "Do not be afraid. I bring you good news of great joy that will be for all the people. Today in the town of David a Saviour has been born to you; he is Christ the Lord. This will be a sign to you: You will find a baby wrapped in cloths and lying in a manger." Suddenly a great company of the heavenly host appeared with the angel, praising God and saying, "Glory to God in the highest, and on earth peace to men on whom his favour rests."

When the angels had left them and gone into heaven, the shepherds said to one another, "Let's go to Bethlehem and see this thing that has happened, which the Lord has told us about." So they hurried off and found Mary and Joseph, and the baby, who was lying in the manger. When they had seen him, they spread the word concerning what had been told them about this child, and all who heard it were amazed at what the shepherds said to them. But Mary treasured up all these things and pondered them in her heart. The shepherds returned, glorifying God for all the things they had heard and seen, which were just as they had been told.

Luke 2:8-20

We can perhaps imagine the traditional scene in our mind's eye —so often have we seen it depicted in Christmas cards and children's books: a clear mid-winter sky, stars glistening brilliantly in the clear, cold night air. This was before the days of atmospheric and 'light pollution'! Even today the 'firmament' in the southern hemisphere glows with an intensity that many of us who live in northern climes do not fully appreciate. Perhaps huddled around a small fire, trying vainly to keep the night chill at bay, sit a handful of shepherds. Silhouetted faintly behind them we can see the shapes of a large flock of sheep scattered across the hillside. A shepherd's crook or two may lean against a small boulder. Suddenly a brilliant light bursts upon the scene, illuminating the startled faces of the shepherds —and, in the words of the famous carol, "the angel of the Lord came down and glory shone around."

Jewish tradition regarding the birth of the Messiah is also illuminating. It was a settled conviction that the Messiah was to be born in Bethlehem, as we have already seen. So too was the belief that the Messiah was to be revealed from *Migdal Eder* - 'the tower of the flock' according to the Targum Pseudo-Jon on Genesis 35:21. (This concerns the death of Rachel at Bethlehem Ephrathah —after the death and burial of his wife, Jacob pitched his tent at Migdal Eder, near Bethlehem). This *Migdal Eder* was *not* the watchtower for the ordinary flocks of sheep which pastured on the barren hills beyond Bethlehem, but lay close to the town, on the road from Jerusalem.

Jack Finegan refers to third-century writings of husband and wife pilgrims Eusochium and Paula (circa 386 AD) and their first visit to Bethlehem. Paula travelled from the traditional cave of the

Nativity in Bethlehem "a short distance down the hill to the tower of Eder, that is 'of the flock', near which Jacob fed his flocks, and where the shepherds keeping watch by night were privileged to hear the words 'Glory to God in the highest and on earth peace, goodwill towards men.' Hebrew Migdal Eder means "tower of the flock" (as the same words are translated in Micah 4:8) and in Genesis 35:21 Jacob is said to have journeyed on from Rachel's tomb "and pitched his tent beyond the tower of Eder". Hence, says Jack Finegan, "it was evidently supposed that the place where Jacob pastured his flocks was the same as that where the later shepherds heard the angel's message."[10]

Here we return to the helpful work of Alfred Edersheim: he points out that a passage in the Mishnah (Shek 7:4) leads to the conclusion that the flocks which pastured at Migdal Eder were destined for temple sacrifices. The Mishnah, says Edersheim, "expressly forbids the keeping of flocks throughout the land of Israel except in the wilderness —and the only flocks otherwise kept, would be those for the temple-services........ accordingly, the shepherds who watched over them, were not ordinary shepherds. The latter were under the ban of Rabbinism, on account of their necessary isolation from religious ordinances and their manner of life, which rendered strict legal observance unlikely, if not absolutely impossible. The same Mishnic passage also leads us to infer that these flocks lay out *all the year round*, since they are spoken of as in the fields thirty days before passover – that is, in the month of February, when in Palestine the average rainfall is nearly greatest. Thus, Jewish tradition in some dim manner apprehended the first revelation of the Messiah from that *Migdal Eder*, where shepherds watched the temple-flocks all the year round."[11]

This is a wonderful testimony to the fore-planning of God. Jesus was foreshadowed as the Lamb of God from the earliest of times. So the lamb is seen as being an acceptable sacrifice throughout the Old Testament (e.g. Gen 22:7; Ex 12:3; Lev 3:7; Isaiah 1:11). Although Jewish teaching saw a connection of the Messiah to Migdal Eder, in the sense that the Messiah would first be revealed from there, it is plain that Jewish teaching in no way fully understood the Messiah as being the Lamb of God, a truth only fully revealed in the death and resurrection of Jesus. When John the Baptiser pointed out Jesus to his followers, he said, "Look, the Lamb of God, who takes away the sin of the world!" (John 1:29, 36). We are not, wrote Peter, ransomed with perishable things like silver or gold, but with "the precious blood of Christ, a lamb without blemish or defect" (1 Peter 1:18-19). When Philip met the Ethiopian official in Acts chapter 8, he found him reading the passage from Isaiah 53:7, "... he was led like a lamb to the slaughter, and as a sheep before a shearer is silent, so he did not open his mouth." Beginning from here and in these terms Philip explained to the Ethiopian the gospel of Christ.

The lamb, of course, has always been a symbol of innocence, meekness, lowliness and gentleness. It is also a symbol of dependence. God is the Shepherd of men (Ps 23:1) and we are the sheep of his pasture (Ps 100:3). No one is more dependent than the lamb is upon the shepherd. The lamb is a symbol of trust and dependence, expressing the trust and dependence of Jesus on God His Father. Among Jews the lamb was singularly *the* animal of sacrifice. So we read in Genesis 22:7 the question of Isaac to his father Abraham: "where is the lamb for the burnt offering?" and Abraham's answer: "God himself will provide the lamb." In this, Christians see Abraham's unwitting prophecy of the Messiah —after he had sacrificed the lamb miraculously provided by God, Abraham called the place "The Lord Will Provide" (Gen 22:14). Some two thousand years later the Lord again provided a Lamb without blemish for slaughter —this time on the cross at Calvary.

It is of the deepest significance, therefore, that the angels should have announced the birth of the Messiah first to shepherds whose role in life was to care for the temple's sacrificial lambs. "Do not be afraid. I bring you good news of great joy that will be for all the people. Today in the town of David a Saviour has been born to you; he is Christ the Lord. This will be a sign to you: You will find a baby wrapped in cloths and lying in a manger." It was the Saviour who had been born for all the people. The shepherds' awe, surprise and fear would quickly have given way to excitement as they heard from the angel that what they were witnessing was not judgement upon them, but news of great joy. They reacted straightaway: "Let's go to Bethlehem and see this thing that has happened, which the Lord has told us about." Finding the family in a small village like Bethlehem would have presented little difficulty. Even by the primitive conditions of the time, Jesus' birth (probably) in a stable was unusual and therefore remarkable, and no doubt news about it would have spread quickly among the village people.

"So they hurried off and found Mary and Joseph, and the baby, who was lying in the manger. When they had seen him, they spread the word concerning what had been told them about this child, and all who heard it were amazed at what the shepherds said to them." As temple-shepherds, no doubt one of the places to which they carried this amazing news was the temple itself. Whilst the chief priests may have heard the news, and probably scoffed at it (who, after all, would expect such an announcement to be made to lowly, unwashed men of the field?) others would have heard and believed. In this way, we may speculate, Simeon and Anna's minds and hearts were prepared to meet the baby who would be brought to the temple just eight days later.

Circumcision and naming in the temple

On the eighth day, when it was time to circumcise him, he was named Jesus, the name the angel had given him before he had been conceived. When the time for the purification according to the law of Moses had been completed, Joseph and Mary took him to Jerusalem to present him to the Lord (as it is written in the Law of the Lord, "Every firstborn male is to be consecrated to the Lord") and to offer a sacrifice in keeping with what was said in the Law of the Lord: "a pair of doves or two young pigeons".

Luke 2:21-24

After their exhausting journey from Nazareth to Bethlehem, followed by the immediate birth of the Lord Jesus and the visit just hours later of the shepherds with their amazing account of the message from the angel, Mary and Joseph must have wondered what might happen next. As a faithful Jewish couple, anxious to fulfil all the requirements of the Law, it was to the temple in Jerusalem that Mary and Joseph next travelled, now with the new born infant. There were two reasons for this: first to dedicate and name the infant, and second to present Mary for the rite of purification.

The first of these was the circumcision, representing the voluntary and willing subjection to the conditions of the Law, but also an acceptance of the privileges of the covenant between God and His chosen people. Just as, some thirty years later, Jesus would present Himself to John the Baptiser to go through the symbolic rite of baptism (Matt 3:13-15), so now His parents brought Him to the temple for the symbolic rite of circumcision as required by the Law (Gen 17:9-14). The ceremony took place, in the usual way, on the eighth day when the child was given the name Jesus (*Jeshua* in Hebrew).

The firstborn son of every household was, according to the Law (Numbers 18:16), to be "redeemed" of the priest for the price of five shekels of silver 'according to the Sanctuary shekel'. To this simple scriptural Law, rabbinic tradition had added many needless and even repulsive details. For example, the earliest period of presentation was thirty-one days after birth, to make the legal month quite complete. The child must be the first born of his mother, neither father or mother must be of Levitic descent and the child must be free of all bodily defects which would have disqualified him from the priesthood. It was greatly dreaded that a child should die before his "redemption". If, however, his father died before the child's redemption, then the child was to redeem himself when of age. The redemption could be made by any priest and attendance at the temple was not a prerequisite.

The requirements for the purification of the mother after childbirth are set out in Leviticus 12. This requires the mother to wait thirty-three days before making the necessary offering to the priest. Rabbinic tradition had increased this to forty-one days after the birth of a son, and eighty-one days after the birth of a daughter so as to make sure the biblical requirements were quite complete! In fact there was no connection between the time of the circumcision of the child and the purification of the mother. In special circumstances the circumcision might be delayed for days —in the case of sickness for example, when the ceremony would wait until recovery. Equally, the purification of the mother might take place at any later time. Typically, it might be delayed until attendance at one of the great religious feasts in Jerusalem brought the mother to that city.

So it was that a mother could in some circumstances offer several sacrifices of purification at the same time. Further, the woman was not required to be personally present. Her offering could be presented by a member of the laity who daily partook in the religious ceremonies on behalf of the districts from which they came. However, mothers who were within easy travelling distance of Jerusalem, and especially the more zealous among them, would attend the temple in person. In such cases, when possible, the redemption of the firstborn and the purification of the mother would be combined. And this was, according to Luke, the case with Mary and her son. So, the holy family travelled from Bethlehem to the temple for this solemn and serious rite. The baby Jesus would have been presented to the priest, with two short prayers of blessing: one for the law of redemption and one for the gift of a firstborn son. After this the redemption money would be paid.

The rite of purification, as already noted, could be carried out without the presence in person of the mother. It consisted of a sin-offering for the Levitical 'defilement' symbolically attaching to the beginning of life, and a burnt offering which marked the restoration of communion with God. The sin offering consisted in all cases simply of the sacrifice of a turtle dove or a young pigeon. For the burnt offering, wealthier people would bring a lamb for sacrifice, but poorer people could instead bring a turtle dove or a young pigeon. The temple price for the meat and drink offerings was set once a month and special officials assisted the intending offerors. Quaint as it may sound to modern readers, those poor women who bought the turtle dove or young pigeon as an offering would need to deal with the 'superintendent of turtle-doves and pigeons'. Located in the *Court of the Women* were thirteen trumpet-shaped chests for money contributions of various types. Into the third of these the mother would drop the price of her sacrifice. An offeror of the poor's offering, such as Mary, would not need to deal directly with any sacrificing priest —instead the poor's trumpet chest would be opened at a certain time of the day and half the contents applied to burnt-offerings and the other half to sin-offerings. And so sacrifices were provided for a corresponding number of those who were to be purified, without either shaming the poor, needlessly disclosing the nature of the impurity or causing unnecessary logistical difficulties to the temple authorities.

The contrasts in the account of the Lord Jesus' Nativity are striking: together with every humiliation suffered by the infant and His family, there were wonderful affirmations from heaven of His priceless worth. So, although He was born of the poor and humble maiden from Nazareth, yet His birth was announced by an angel. Although He was laid to sleep in a cattle feeding trough, yet a shining host from heaven heralded His entry into the world. Although He was not recognised for whom He was by most, yet He was accorded His royal office in the worship of the wise men. Although a despot sought His life, yet His parents were Divinely warned of the danger and brought Him to a place of safety. And now, when the poor mother of Jesus could only bring the 'poor's offering' yet there would be another affirmation of His greatness from two people, an elderly man and an elderly woman, in each of whom burned the true spirit of the Old Testament.

"Now there was a man living in Jerusalem called Simeon, who was righteous and devout. He was waiting for the consolation of Israel, and the Holy Spirit was upon him. It had been revealed to him by the Holy Spirit that he would not die before he had seen the Lord's Christ. Moved by the Spirit, he went into the temple courts. When the parents brought in the child Jesus to do for him what the custom of the law required, Simeon took him in his arms and praised God saying:

'Sovereign Lord, as you have promised, you now dismiss your servant in peace. For my eyes have seen your salvation, which you have prepared in the sight of all people, a light for revelation to the Gentiles and for Glory to your people Israel.'

The child's father and mother marvelled at what was said about him. Then Simeon blessed them and said to Mary, his mother: 'This child is destined to cause the falling and the rising of many in Israel, and will be a sign that will be spoken against, so that the thoughts of many hearts will be revealed. And a sword will pierce your own soul too.'

There was also a prophetess, Anna, the daughter of Phanuel, of the tribe of Asher. She was very old; she had lived with her husband seven years after her marriage, and then was a widow until she was eighty four. She never left the temple but worshipped night and day, fasting and praying. Coming up to them at that very moment, she gave thanks to God and spoke about the child to all who were looking forward to the redemption of Jerusalem."

Luke 2:25-38

As they entered the temple courts, Joseph and Mary were met by a man whose venerable figure must have been well known at the temple to worshippers and temple officials. The aged Simeon combined three characteristics of true Old Testament piety, in distinct contrast to the Pharisees who so boastfully claimed that piety as their own. Firstly he was deeply concerned about *justice*, waiting as he was for the consolation of Israel. Secondly he had a genuine *fear of God*, being righteous and devout, in stark contrast to the Pharisees who heaped burden upon spiritual burden onto the ordinary folk of their day. Thirdly, Simeon had a genuine *longing expectancy* of the near fulfilment of God's great promises to his fellow Israelites. Coming 'in the Spirit' into the temple, Simeon took the infant in his arms and burst into rapt thanksgiving. God had fulfilled His word —Simeon would not see death until he had seen the Christ. Now this elderly and most loyal servant could be 'dismissed in peace'; he had witnessed the salvation so long awaited. He had seen the glorious light that would illuminate the heathen world as well as the land of Israel. Everything breathed by Simeon was a rich fragrance of all that was best in the Old Testament.

His unexpected appearance, and even more unexpected words no doubt reinforced the sense of awe in Mary and Joseph. Whatever unspoken questions may still have lingered in their minds, the aged Simeon began to supply the answer. It was as if the whole history of the Christ upon the earth was flashing before Simeon's mind's eye. Jesus was to be a stumbling block to many, a sign which would be spoken against, and the sword of deep personal sorrow that would pierce His mother's own heart.

Simeon's was not the only amazing prophetic utterance that day. A sad mystery surrounds Anna, who approached the group just as Simeon finished his prophecy. She was elderly —some eighty-four years of age. The early pain in the loss of her husband had been followed by many years of mourning, fasting and prayer, never leaving the temple. Alfred Edersheim comments that Anna was: "one of those in whose home the tribal genealogy had been preserved. We infer from this, and from the fact that it was that of a tribe which had *not* returned to Palestine, that hers was a family of some distinction. Curiously enough, the tribe of Asher alone is celebrated in tradition for the beauty of its women, and their fitness to be wedded to High-priest or King."[12]

Deepest in Anna's soul was a yearning for *the* promised 'redemption', and now that redemption had arrived in the flesh. In contrast to Simeon's rejoicing in the 'salvation' of Israel, Anna gave thanks for Israel's 'redemption'. The mother who was shortly to pay the redemption money for her firstborn son was told by Anna that Jesus was Himself the redemption for which Jerusalem had so long waited. We can still, even at the distance of two millennia, feel with Anna the desperate need of redemption for her unhappy people: the hopeless state of Anna's own tribe, never to return from exile, the desperate political state of Israel, riven for generations by internecine warfare and now under the iron rule of a psychopathic despot, the submission of Israel to an all-powerful and all-pervasive heathen foreign emperor, and the unhappy moral, social and religious condition of her own Jerusalem. All these sad factors kindled in Anna and Simeon, and all like-minded servants of Israel's Holy God, a great longing for the promised time of 'redemption'.

Notes

[1] *Op. cit. The Life and Times of Jesus the Messiah* p. 143.

[2] As evidence of the feelings of Jews towards a tax census, see *Josephus* Antiq. 18.1.1, although note this was a *later* tax census.

[3] Paul Barnett *Bethlehem to Patmos* (Hodder and Stoughton,1989), p. 26.

[4] Werner Keller *The Bible As History* (Hodder and Stoughton, 1956), p. 327.

[5] I have referred to this census as 'famous' because it is well documented in Josephus' *Antiquities* 17.13.5 and 18.1.1.

[6] William Whiston, A.M. *Josephus, The Complete Works* (Thomas Nelson Publishers, 1998).

[7] There has been some question as to whether the 'inn' is as we understand the term. The view has been expressed that it would be a guest-chamber attached to a house, but most scholars hold that the word translated 'inn' is, as we understand it, a place where travellers stay, in exchange for payment.

[8] *Op. cit. The Life and Times of Jesus the Messiah*, p. 130.

[9] *Ibid.*, pp. 130-131.

[10] Jack Finegan *The Archaeology of the New Testament* Revised Edition (Princeton University Press, 1992), p. 40.

[11] *Op. cit.* pp. 131f.

[12] *Ibid.* p. 140.

9

Wise Men and Flight to Egypt

The prologue to Luke's Gospel draws to a close with the Presentation of the baby Jesus in the Jerusalem temple and acknowledgement of His status made by devout ordinary people, rather than the religious leaders. Luke recommences his account of the Lord Jesus' life and work some twelve years later when He returned to the Jerusalem temple with His family to celebrate the feast of Passover. The writer Luke, however, leaves us with one small puzzle: in 2:39 he tells us that after the Presentation, the Holy Family returned to Galilee to their own home town, where Jesus grew in wisdom and grace.

The 'Christmas' narrative continues in Matthew, however, in the account of the visit of the wise men from the East, which took place *in Bethlehem at least six months later*, as we shall see. Who then is right, Luke or Matthew? In practice there is no real conflict here. Luke in his account jumps twelve years and quite correctly states that Jesus' home town was during most of that time Nazareth. Matthew lingers with the Nativity and infancy of the Lord Jesus, however, and covers the short exile to Egypt and final return to Nazareth.

We may infer the likely movements of the Holy Family in this way: Mary and Joseph, having initially left Nazareth in order to register in Bethlehem, travelled the ninety odd miles to Bethlehem where Jesus was born. For reasons we do not know, the couple decided to settle in Bethlehem —certainly it would remove them from the narrow-minded gossip of Nazareth, and surely Bethlehem as 'David's City' would have seemed the 'right' place to bring up their new son. They had, no doubt, certain domestic matters to wind-up: some living quarters to dispose of, and Joseph's carpentry tools would probably need to be sold or moved from Nazareth to Bethlehem so he could resume his trade. So, following the Presentation of Jesus in the temple, the couple returned briefly to Nazareth but shortly afterwards travelled back to Bethlehem with the intention of settling permanently there. It is to the Gospel of Matthew that we turn for the final details of the infancy of the Lord Jesus:

The visit of the wise men

After Jesus was born in Bethlehem in Judaea, during the time of King Herod, Magi from the east came to Jerusalem and asked, "Where is the one who has been born king of the Jews? We saw his star in the east and have come to worship him."

When King Herod heard this he was disturbed, and all Jerusalem with him. When he had called together all the people's chief priests and teachers of the law, he asked them where the Christ was to be born. "In Bethlehem in Judaea," they replied, "for this is what the prophet has written: 'But you, Bethlehem, in the land of Judah, are by no means least among the rulers of Judah; for out of you will come a ruler who will be the shepherd of my people Israel.' "

Then Herod called the Magi secretly and found out from them the exact time the star had appeared. He sent them to Bethlehem and said "Go and make a careful search for the child. As soon as you find him, report to me, so that I too may go and worship him."

After they had heard the king, they went on their way, and the star they had seen in the east went ahead of them until it stopped over the place where the child was. When they saw the star they were overjoyed. On coming to the house, they saw the child with his mother Mary, and they bowed down and worshipped him. Then they opened their treasures and presented him with gifts of gold and of incense and of myrrh. And having been warned in a dream not to go back to Herod, they returned to their country by another route.

Matt 2:1-12

Magi, as the *New International Version* of the Bible correctly names the 'wise men' (rendered incorrectly but very poetically as 'kings' in the famous and lovely carol by the American John Henry Hopkins, 'We Three Kings of Orient Are'[1]) is the term used in the Septuagint, and also by Philo, Josephus and other ancient writers.[2] It describes both magicians practised in ancient 'magical arts' as well as Eastern (especially Chaldean) priest-sages who appear to have held deep philosophical knowledge, not untinged with superstition, based on their exhaustive researches and study of ancient learning. It was these latter priest-sages, rather than magicians, to which Matthew refers in his Gospel. The number of Magi is not stated, but it is a widespread assumption that there were three, on account of the number of gifts given. Their number, however, is of no consequence.

This 'priestly' caste of the Medes and Persians in New Testament times were dispersed over various parts of the East. Magi are thought to have emerged in what we now think of as Arabia. Certainly there was trade and political interaction between Judaea/Galilee and 'Arabia' generally. Indeed, from about 120 BC to the sixth century of our own era, the kings of the area now occupied by Yemen professed the Jewish faith.[3] The presence in those same Eastern lands of large numbers of Jews of the *diaspora* would have enabled the Magi to obtain first-hand information about the great hope of a Messiah which the Hebrews held so dear. It is likely that they were familiar with the much-studied prophecy of Numbers 24:17 which promised that "a star will come out of Jacob; a sceptre will rise out of Israel." Paul Barnett, in his excellent book *Bethlehem to Patmos*, notes that the Septuagint, the Greek translation of the Hebrew Old Testament, had rendered Numbers 24:17 as, "a star shall come forth out of Jacob, a man shall arise out of Israel" and that this prophecy was so widely known, that it is also found in the writings of the Roman historian Tacitus (Macrobius, Saturnalia, 2:4:11).[4]

Some time after the Presentation of the infant Jesus in the temple and after the Holy Family returned from Nazareth to Bethlehem, there arrived in Jerusalem Magi with a strange message. They had witnessed the rising of a star which they regarded as announcing the birth of the Jewish Messiah-King and accordingly had travelled to Jerusalem to pay homage to him. They arrived in the Jewish capital not, we may assume, because they expected to find him there but because they thought that in Jerusalem they would receive information about where he might be found. They addressed themselves first to the head of the nation, King Herod.

Herod 'the Great', we have already noted, was fast losing his mental and physical grip in the twilight of his life. Whilst he had been an excellent client-king of the Romans, rivalling Emperor Augustus in the lavishness and extent of his building programmes and, as Josephus the Jewish historian notes, "was on more friendly terms with Greeks than with Jews" (Antiq. 19:7:3:329), he had upset his own people with the heavy burden of tax that funded his opulent lifestyle and building projects. There were good reasons, perhaps, for members of his family to plot his succession. He had had, after all, ten wives and nineteen children, but none could feel safe while he lived. An increasingly relevant factor at the close of Herod's life was the numerous illnesses that dogged him. In Josephus we read of the period shortly before his death: "Herod's distemper became more and more severe to him, and this because these his disorders fell on him in his old age, and when he was in a melancholy condition; for he was already almost seventy years of age, and had been brought low by the calamities that happened to him about his children, whereby he had no pleasure in life, even when he was in health; the grief that Antipater was still alive aggravated his disease, whom he resolved to put to death now, not at random, but as soon as he should be well again" (*War* 33:1.647). The incident with the golden eagle and the consequent bloody confrontation with the Jewish religious authorities occurred at this time.

Josephus continues 'After this, the distmeper seized his whole body, and greatly disordered all its parts with various symptoms; for there was a gentle fever upon him, and an intolerable itching all over the surface of his body, and continual pains in his colon, and dropsical tumours about his feet and an inflammation of the abdomen – and a putrefaction of his privy member, that produced worms. Besides this he had difficulty of breathing upon him and could not breath but when he sat upright, and had convulsion of all his members; insomuch that the diviners said those diseases were a punishment upon him for what he had done to his Rabbis' (*War* 1:5:656).

It was to this sick, miserable and psychopathic king that the Magi came, six to eight months after the birth of Jesus. The rumour of their enquiry would no doubt have spread quickly through the city. No wonder Matthew tells us, 'when King Herod heard this he was disturbed and all Jerusalem with him' (Matt 2:3). Pretenders to this king's throne had a habit of bringing down a curtain on more than just their own lives! Herod's impression on hearing their news was, needless to say, vastly different from the piety of the Magi. The barest possibility of the advent of *the* Messiah – the One to whom all Israel looked for deliverance – must have struck a special note of terror into his heart. The mere thought of a pretender with such claims would fill him with suspicion, fear, and rage. Perhaps Herod also feared meeting his Maker – a day that could not be far off – and the judgement that he would face at the hands of the Almighty. Then his attempted bribe of God and the people, in lavishly rebuilding the Jerusalem temple, would be shown for the sham it was!

Why had these Magi come? They told the king plainly —they had come to find the new King and 'to worship him'. We presume that the Magi did not know that the new King was of such obscure background. Their visit, as Paul Barnett suggests, may have been primarily a diplomatic gesture and their gifts designed to create a favourable impression upon the court of the new monarch. These gifts may also have been intended to express some form of worship to the new ruler. Acts of reverence towards kings were not unusual in the Eastern world at that time.[5]

Herod reacted cunningly: calling together his chief priests and teachers of the law and without telling them of the Magis' mission, he simply put before them the question of the Messiah's birthplace. Having received the answer – Bethlehem – Herod *secretly* called back the Magi, no doubt having already settled on the idea that he would have Bethlehem and its people carefully watched with a view to isolating and eliminating the infant pretender. He enquired from the Magi the *precise* time that the star had first attracted their attention. This information enabled him to judge how far back he would need to take his own investigations, since the birth of the pretender could be linked to the appearance of the sidereal phenomenon. As long as any male lived who was born in Bethlehem between the earliest appearance of the 'star' and the time of arrival of the Magi, Herod could not feel safe. The later conduct of Herod (Matt 2:16) leads us to believe that the Magi must have told Herod that their earliest observation of the star had taken place two years before their arrival in Jerusalem. Herod now directed the Magi to Bethlehem with the pious request that, as soon as they had located the babe, they should let him know, so that he too, might go and worship the Messiah.

As they left Jerusalem, the star which had attracted them at its 'rising' and which, the narrative seems to imply, they had not seen of late, now reappeared and led them towards Bethlehem. It seemed to move ahead of them until 'it stopped over the place where the child was' —this, we may assume, means Bethlehem, not the actual house where Jesus lived. The reappearance of the star must have been a confirmation to these wise men that they were near journey's end and mission's accomplishment, for they could certainly not have needed the star to *guide* them from Jerusalem to Bethlehem —the distance is only six miles. It cannot have been difficult in such a small town, scarcely larger than a village, to have located the Holy Family, around the birth of whose firstborn child some notable, and probably well-known, marvels had occurred.

The temporary shelter of the 'stable' had now been exchanged for the more permanent abode of a 'house' (Matt 2:11) where the Magi found the infant Jesus with his mother. (Joseph is not mentioned though it is likely he was there.) Only two things are recorded by Matthew of the visit of the wise men to Joseph and Mary's home: their humble eastern homage, bowing down and worshipping the boy, and the gifts they brought. Viewed as gifts, the incense and myrrh would have seemed strangely inappropriate. These offerings were no doubt intended by the Magi as specimens of the produce of their country and their presentation was, we may assume, similar to diplomatic practice in our own day, a simple mark of homage of their country to this new king. In this sense the wise men were true representatives of the Gentile world —their homage was the first and 'typical' of the homage that would soon be accorded to Jesus by those who had hitherto been 'far off'. Their offerings were symbolic, then, of the world's tribute to the Lord Jesus.

But there was a deeper symbolic significance to the gifts themselves, of which the Magi may not have been completely aware. The gold was a clear acknowledgement of Jesus' Kingship, the incense a symbol of prayer and of Christ's Divinity, and the myrrh was symbolic of His humanity and the fullest evidence of that humanity —for myrrh was used as an embalming spice. Christians through the ages have recognised in these gifts a Spirit-inspired theological statement. Firstly, Christ's position as King in their lives (for example, Luke 23:3; 1 Tim 1:17). Secondly, of the beauty of His life as a fragrant offering to God His Father (as indeed are our prayers a fragrant offering to God – Rev 5:8a), as well as His Divinity. Finally, the confirmation that He was fully man in His mortality: it should be added that myrrh was symbolic of the preservation of bodies from corruption, and that Jesus' own body would see no corruption (Acts 2:31 and 13:37). This latter fact is taken by Christians as the guarantee of the bodily resurrection from death of all those who are found in Jesus —see 1 Corinthians chapter 15 for the biblical explanation of the Christian's understanding of the resurrection from the dead.

It may also be that in the gold there was a practical value in the gift. Very shortly, probably within hours of the Magi's visit, Mary and Joseph were forced to flee with the infant Jesus to Egypt. Perhaps, in the gift of gold, God made provision for all the expenses that would inevitably be incurred in the escape and the subsequent period spent in exile. From Egypt, the family eventually returned to Nazareth where they began life afresh. These upheavals must have involved considerable expense and the gold would have provided the necessary means to ensure those expenses were met in full. Certainly God is, as one of His Old Testament titles suggests, *Jehovah jireh* —the Lord Who Provides.

The slaughter of the innocents
We pause for a moment to look at how the Lord Jesus' entry into this world was seen from the perspective of heaven. There is one biblical view of the Nativity that is never depicted on a Christmas card, and nor could it be. Found in the Revelation to John, the last book of our New Testament, "the revelation of Jesus Christ, which God gave him to show his servants what must soon take place. He made it known by sending his angel to John, who testifies to everything he saw" (Rev 1:1-2). John wrote his book to the churches of seven cities scattered across the Roman Province of Asia. In writing to the church across these widely dispersed cities, John, in effect, addressed the entire church of this Province. Revelation is the only part of the New Testament written to such a broad geographic area. It was written at a time when Christians were under severe and growing persecution for their faith in Jesus Christ as Lord, and consists of series of revelations presented in symbolic language that would have been understood by Christians of that day, but would have remained completely mysterious to all others. The themes of the book are presented repetitively through a series of visions and, although there are to this day differences

of opinion about the precise interpretation of the book, its central theme shines through clearly. Through the Lord Jesus, God will defeat all His enemies, saving his faithful people and creating a new heaven and a new earth when that victory is complete.

Revelation chapter 12 gives us a glimpse of the battle waged in the spiritual realms as the infant Jesus was born. It gives us a different and more accurate perspective on Herod's motivation in seeking the new born King —the real power and impetus behind Herod is the devil himself. The coded story is given in verses 1 through 6. It does not mention Herod, wise men or shepherds. Instead it tells of a red dragon engaged in a bitter struggle in heaven. A woman clothed with the sun, and wearing a crown of twelve stars cries out in pain as she is about to give birth. Then an enormous red dragon with seven heads and ten horns appears, and stands in front of the woman "so that he might devour her child the moment it was born" (Rev 12:4). But in the nick of time the child is snatched away, the dragon is foiled, and the woman flees into the desert "to a place prepared for her by God" (Rev 12:6).

So Revelation's perspective is a simultaneous view of events in heaven and on earth. As the Saviour is born a new and final phase of the heavenly battle begins. The devil's immediate counter to this invasion of his principality is to try to kill the new King. We take up the story again in Matthew's Gospel, just after the Magi have presented their gifts:

When they had gone, an angel of the Lord appeared to Joseph in a dream. "Get up," he said, "take the child and his mother and escape to Egypt. Stay there until I tell you, for Herod is going to search for the child to kill him." So he got up, took the child and his mother during the night and left for Egypt, where he stayed until the death of Herod. And so was fulfilled what was said through the prophet: "Out of Egypt I have called my son."

When Herod realised that he had been outwitted by the Magi, he was furious, and he gave orders to kill all the boys in Bethlehem and its vicinity who were two years old and under, in accordance with the time he had learned from the Magi. Then what was said through the prophet Jeremiah was fulfilled: "A voice is heard in Ramah, weeping and great mourning, Rachel weeping for her children and refusing to be comforted, because they are no more."

Matt 2:13-18

It is a recurrent feature in the gospel of Christ, that glory and suffering often sit side by side. In the glorious announcement of the Lord's birth was, for Mary, the pain of being thought an immoral woman —even by her betrothed. Now, in the glory of the worship of the Magi, there was a bitter aftertaste. From God's vantage point, it could certainly not be that these Magi, representatives of the world's adoration of the Christ, should become unwitting instruments in His murder. Nor could it be possible that the Christ child should fall victim to Herod's psychopathic jealousy and fear.

The Magi, having themselves been warned in a dream not to return to Herod, went back to their country 'by another route'. Frustrated in his hope of attaining his objective through the Magi, the evil tyrant sought to achieve it by an indiscriminate slaughter of all the infant boys in Bethlehem and its surrounding countryside. Allowing that Jesus was born in 6 BC and Herod died in 4 BC, and allowing that it was no fewer than six to eight months, possibly even longer, after the Nativity that the wise men brought their disturbing tidings to Herod's court, it must have been towards the very end of Herod's life that his infamous order to destroy the male infants of Bethlehem was given. With the palace-castle of Herodium only a few miles from Bethlehem, the evil deed could have been ordered and executed in the space of a few hours.

Bethlehem, a small town, would have had relatively few male children of the necessary age —scholars have calculated that the number was probably not more than twenty boys. Despite this relatively small number, the deed was no less atrocious and the Christian church has long regarded these hapless and in every way innocent children as 'protomartyrs' —the first martyrs for Christ. The slaughter was entirely in accordance with the character and former measures of Herod. Josephus, for example, tells us in Antiquities 15:8:4:290 of the slaughter of whole families that had defied the king. We should not be unduly surprised that the slaughter of the Bethlehem innocents remained unrecorded by Josephus, since on other occasions he omitted events which, to us, seem important. There are, in any case omissions, inconsistencies of narrative and chronology in and between the works of Josephus.[6] The murder of a few infants in an insignificant town might have seemed scarcely worth a mention in a reign steeped in so much blood. Besides, Josephus may have had an ulterior motive for silence; he carefully suppresses reference to Jesus as Christ, probably not only in accordance with his own religious beliefs, but because reference to a Messiah might have been dangerous and inconvenient in a work written by an intense self seeker, for a mainly Roman audience.

Anti-Christians have long sought to undermine the factual basis of the slaughter of the innocents. Before looking at their somewhat insubstantial objections, it is worth reminding ourselves of two powerful bodies of evidence which lend weight to the commonly held view that the account is true. Firstly, the Gospel writer affirms that it is so, and many serious and scholarly works have attested to reliability of the Gospel witnesses and the weight and age of manuscript evidence which gives us confidence in the modern Bible translations. Secondly, we have also seen the frankly disgusting personal history of Herod, and that life was held very cheap in those largely heathen times.

So what are these objections? Basically they revolve around the idea that the prophecy cited by Matthew in verse 18 of chapter 2, which is itself a quotation from Jeremiah 31:15, has been taken out of context and that Jeremiah was in fact referring to something quite different. So we read in Matthew: "A voice is heard in Ramah, weeping and great mourning, Rachel weeping for her children and refusing to be comforted, because they are no more." Readers with access to the modern internet may have picked up such objections in anti-Christian websites. They can be summarised as:

* Matthew (who was not, the critics say, a contemporary!) scoured the Scriptures looking for verses that might be seen as being prophecies about Jesus;

* Matthew exercised poetic and literary license in order to reconstruct from Scripture what he believed to be a biography of Jesus;

* The Jeremiah text refers to Jews who had been exiled abroad during the great Babylonian exile, not to events six hundred years later;

* The Jeremiah text refers to children who are not dead but who will return to Israel (as suggested in Jeremiah's next verse);

* The 'alleged' murders took place in Bethlehem and 'not twenty miles away in Ramah';

* Only Matthew wrote about the slaughter of the young boys;

* There is no account outside the Bible of this event;

* Even some Christians do not see Jeremiah 31:15 as a messianic prophecy.

We will quickly look at these objections in turn:

* *Matthew (who was not, the critics say rather sweepingly, a contemporary) scoured the Scriptures looking for verses that might be seen as being prophecies about Jesus.* Certainly Matthew, as other Gospel writers, drew on Scripture to demonstrate that Jesus was indeed the Messiah. We have already seen that something in excess of 450 Old Testament prophecies were viewed *in Jesus' own day* as being messianic. Various parts of Jeremiah 31 were so viewed —but not Jeremiah 31:15. The messianic application of this only became apparent to the Gospel writer after the event which, it might be argued, adds rather than detracts from its authenticity. Jeremiah 31:31ff is one of the most powerful messianic prophecies in the Old Testament. Critics who suggest that Matthew was not a contemporary would probably say the same for the other Gospel writers. Whilst the Gospel is not signed 'Matthew', scholars have long held that the disciple Matthew was by far the most likely author of this book.

* *Matthew exercised poetic and literary license in order to reconstruct from Scripture what he believed to be a biography of Jesus*. This is countered by the reliability of the Gospel witnesses, a subject that may be explored in many serious and scholarly books on the Holy Bible. See also Appendix 5 in this regard.

* *The Jeremiah text refers to Jews who had been exiled abroad during the great Babylonian exile, not to events six hundred years later*. Most assuredly, Jeremiah's book was principally a warning to the rebellious Jews that their sin against God would lead to national and religious disaster —and so it did. But it is obvious that all messianic prophecies are to be found embedded in narrative and contexts which refer firstly to a local audience contemporary to when the Scripture was written, and only indirectly, or secondarily to the Messiah of the future. Now that the Old Testament days have passed, their principal value lies in their foreshadowing of Jesus in many hundreds of messianic prophecies.

* *The Jeremiah text refers to children who are not dead but who will return to Israel (as suggested in Jeremiah's next verse)*. This may be true, although it has been suggested by some that there was bitter wailing in Israel at the prospect of parting for hopeless captivity and greater lament because those who might have encumbered the outward march were mercilessly slaughtered. Be this as it may, Matthew is evidently hearing the lamentations of Rachel as echoing those of the mothers of Bethlehem at the slaughter of the innocents.

* *The 'alleged' murders took place in Bethlehem and not twenty miles away in Ramah*. Here biblical critics betray lack of knowledge of the geography of Judaea. Their criticism runs along these lines: If Matthew is right, then the mother's lamentations and cries of grief were so loud that they could be heard in the village of Ramah, twenty miles from the scene of the crime in Bethlehem! This matter was dealt with completely by Jack Finegan in his valuable book *The Archaeology of the New Testament*, from which the following helpful explanation is taken:

Gen 35:19 and 48:7 state that the burial place of Rachel was "on the way to Ephrath (that is, Bethlehem)." The wording suggests that Ephrath or Ephrathah was an older village that was absorbed into Bethlehem and in Micah 5:2 the two names are put together, Bethlehem Ephrathah. 1 Samuel 10:2, however, places the tomb of Rachel in the territory of Benjamin, and the site of er-Ram five miles north of Jerusalem probably corresponds with a Ramah at this place. Indeed the Madaba map shows another Ramah, north and slightly east of Jerusalem. It was presumably to the Northern Ramah that Nebuzaradan in 588 BC took Jeremiah and the captives of Jerusalem and Judah who were being exiled to Babylon (Jer 40:1). Rachel was the mother of Joseph and Benjamin, and Joseph's son Ephraim became synonymous with northern Israel (Jer 31:9). So Jeremiah (31:15) hears a voice in Ramah and it is Rachel weeping for her children, perhaps with reference to the earlier deportation (722 BC) of the Northern Israelites by the Assyrians (2 Kings 18:11) as well as the present carrying into exile of the Babylonians. Between the two locations, Matthew is evidently thinking of Ramah and Rachel's tomb as near Bethlehem, and as he quotes Jer 31:15 he is hearing the ancient lamentation of Rachel echoing in that of the mothers of Bethlehem at the slaughter of the innocents by Herod (Matt 2:18).[7]

The location of Rachel's tomb is on the old Jerusalem–Bethlehem road, some two miles away from Bethlehem. Today a small building is constructed over the tomb, but the site has been venerated by Jews for over two thousand years. Apart from the fact that this Ramah is literally close enough for some sounds to be heard from two miles distant, we would speculate that Herod's slaughter almost certainly encompassed homes in the surrounding countryside.

* *Only Matthew wrote about the slaughter of the young boys.* This is not altogether surprising. None of the Gospels sets out to be a biography of Jesus in the modern sense, as we have seen earlier in these studies. Only two of the four Gospels give any detail of the Lord's birth in any case and, although tragic, in the larger scheme of Jesus' life, the event did not shape or cause any subsequent events.

* *There is no account outside the Bible of this event.* Again, in the

context of first century Judaea, such action by the ruler was not of sufficient importance to merit any comment. For various reasons it might have been politically more convenient to ignore it.

* *Even some Christians do not see Jeremiah 31:15 as a messianic prophecy.* Without knowing who such Christians are, or what their reasoning, no useful comment can be made. In a world faith the sheer size of Christianity we would expect there to be a spectrum of views.

We will let the matter rest with a perceptive comment from Alfred Edersheim on both the slaughter of the innocents and on the associated prophecy in Hosea concerning the Holy Family's flight into Egypt, to which we will turn in a moment: "To an inspired writer, nay, to a true Jewish reader of the Old Testament, the question in regard to any prophecy could not be: what did *the prophet* mean – but, what did *the prophecy* mean? And this could only be unfolded in the course of Israel's history. Similarly, those who ever saw in the past the prototype of the future, and recognised in events not only the principle but the very features of that which was to come, could not fail to perceive in the bitter wail of the mothers of Bethlehem over their slaughtered children, the full realisation of the prophetic description of the scene enacted in Jeremiah's days. Had not the prophet himself heard, in the lament of the captives to Babylon, the echoes of Rachel's voice in the past? In neither one nor the other case had the utterances of the prophets (Hosea and Jeremiah) been *predictions*; they were *prophetic*. In neither one nor the other case was the fulfilment literal; it was Scriptural, and that in the truest Old Testament sense."[8]

The flight into Egypt

When they had gone, an angel of the Lord appeared to Joseph in a dream. "Get up," he said, "take the child and his mother and escape to Egypt. Stay there until I tell you, for Herod is going to search for the child to kill him." So he got up, took the child and his mother during the night and left for Egypt, where he stayed until

the death of Herod. And so was fulfilled what was said through
the prophet: "Out of Egypt I have called my son."

Matthew 2:13-15

Having fled their own country, refugees will settle if possible,
somewhere where they will be among their own people. Anyone
taking an infant will prefer a place of safety close to the border.
On the road from Israel to Egypt, about six miles north of modern
Cairo, lies the village of Al-Matariyah, not far from the right bank
of the Nile. Here there is a church called 'Sanctae Familiae in
Aegypto Exuli', the Church of the Holy Family, originally built
by French Jesuits. Ancient tradition, and it must be emphasised
only tradition as far as can be proved, has attached Al-Matariyah
to the Holy Family's flight to Egypt.

In the middle ages there was a famous herbal garden at Al-
Matariyah which produced plants found nowhere else in Egypt.
"Slender little trees which are no higher than the belt of your riding
breeches and resemble the wood of the wild vine,"[9] wrote Sir John
Maundeville, who saw them during his travels in 1322. He was
describing balsam bushes —and how these valuable shrubs came
to Egypt is recounted by the Jewish historian Josephus.

After the murder of Caesar, Mark Antony came to Alexandria,
the important coastal city in Egypt, where the scheming queen
Cleopatra had a liaison with him. She was secretly planning
to recover some of Egypt's old spheres of influence, including
winning back the lands of Israel. Cleopatra visited Judaea several
times and even tried to ensnare Herod 'the Great' in a relationship
so as to win to her side this Roman client-king. Herod, no fool,
recognised that any involvement with Cleopatra or her schemes
would bring down on him the wrath of Antony, of whom Herod
was, in any case, a personal friend.

Herod's rejection of Cleopatra's advances nevertheless nearly
cost him his life. He had deeply wounded her feminine vanity
and so she schemed with Mark Antony against Herod. Cleopatra
arranged that the Jewish king should be summoned to Alexandria
to answer grave charges, but Herod, anticipating the 'lie of the

land' bribed Mark Antony at considerable expense. The scheming queen had lost this particular battle but did not come away completely empty handed. Herod was forced to cede the valuable coastal lands to Egypt, together with Jericho on the Jordan with its surrounding plantations. These contained large fragrant gardens of valuable herbs, said to have been reared from seeds presented by the Queen of Sheba to King Solomon some 800 years before. Among these plants were balsam bushes.

The new owner, Josephus, specifically tells us (*Antiquities* 15:4:2:96) took over these plantations and, it is believed, arranged for cuttings to be taken home to Egypt with her. These were planted on her instructions in the temple Gardens just outside Heliopolis (the 'On' of the Bible, Gen 41:50), a mile or so from today's Al-Matariyah.[10] Here, under the care of skilled Jewish gardeners from the Jordan valley, these rare shrubs thrived on the Nile —the 'herbal garden' of Al-Matariyah. Thirty years later Joseph, Mary and the infant Jesus are said to have found safe refuge among the Jewish gardeners in the fragrant balsam gardens of Al-Matariyah. The idea is certainly plausible, but there is no external evidence of the Holy Family's whereabouts whilst in Egypt.

The Gospel writer Matthew, as we have already noted, saw the flight to Egypt by the Holy Family as the fulfilment of the prophecy in Hosea 11:1, "out of Egypt I called my son". The context of the verse to Hosea's *original* audience refers quite clearly to the rescue of the Israelites from Egypt by Moses. Hosea was assumed by the ancient synagogue to have been himself alluding to Exodus 4:22. ("Israel is my firstborn son .... let my son go, so that he may worship me.") Exodus 4:22 *was* seen as being a messianic prophecy, e.g. in the Midrash interpretation of Psalm 2:7, so for Matthew to have interpreted the events of the flight into Egypt as the fulfilment of Hosea's prophecy was both reasonable and appropriate.

The Holy Family's stay in Egypt must have been of short duration. Since the flight probably took place no more than a few months prior to the tyrant Herod's death, we may presume that Joseph's thoughts quickly turned to making the return journey and to permanent settlement in Bethlehem. The period immediately before Herod's death in Judaea was, according to Josephus, frightening. Tormented by fears and prey to fits of remorse when he would shout out the name of his murdered wife Mariamme and her sons, even making attempts on his own life, Herod was on the verge of insanity. The most terrible diseases had affixed themselves to his body (see Josephus for the gruesome details) and he knew his final hour had come.

On return from his convalescence in Callirhoe and feeling death approaching, Herod summoned the nobles of Israel to Jericho and imprisoned them in the Hippodrome,[11] with orders to his sister Salome to slay them immediately upon his death, in the grim hope that the joy of the populace at his death would thus be changed to genuine mourning. (*Antiquities* 17:6:5:168 to 181). Five days before his death, Herod, on hearing that his son Antipater had tried to bribe his gaoler to release him, had him executed. Upon Herod's death, Salome released the noble Jews imprisoned in the Hippodrome, reckoning this would be a popular move and commence the new King Antipas' reign (Herod Antipas of the New Testament) on a positive note.

Herod 'the Great' had in fact divided his kingdom among several relatives. Archelaus, the elder brother of Antipas (both sons of Malthake, a Samaritan) was appointed to be king, Antipas tetrarch of Galilee and Peraea, and Philip (son of Cleopatra, of Jerusalem) tetrarch of the territory east of the Jordan. Herod made these dispositions dependent on the approval of emperor Augustus —by no means a foregone conclusion. Although the army proclaimed Archelaus king immediately, he prudently declined the title, pending the emperor's confirmation, but was quickly challenged to use his royal powers to quell a rising which had been simmering since the execution by Herod of two important rabbis over the golden eagle incident. Three thousand insurrectionists were killed in the ensuing troubles, mainly in the temple area (*Antiq* 17:9:3:218). Archelaus was summoned to Rome at the same time as his brother Antipas, so each could press his rights to the throne. The Herodian family at large (excepting Archelaus and his supporters) whilst each faction quietly pressed its own claims, were of the public opinion that they wanted direct rule from Rome but that, if they were forced to have a king, they preferred Antipas rather than Archelaus. Meanwhile fresh insurrections in Judaea were brutally put down. A Judaean deputation of fifty went to Rome and, supported by eight thousand Roman Jews, argued for deposing the entire Herodian clan, on account of their crimes.[12] Their plan was for Judaea and Galilee to be incorporated into Syria —no doubt hoping for semi-independence under Roman rule, with the Sadduces and Pharisees holding effective power.

Before Augustus had made his decision on Herod's will, there came yet more bad news from Judaea. In the absence of the Herodians, unrest surfaced again in Jerusalem. As a security measure a Roman legion was despatched to the city. In the midst of this turmoil arrived one of the hated Romans in the form of Sabinus, a tax collector. Disregarding warnings, he took up residence in Herod's palace and proceeded to audit the tribute of Judaea to Rome. Thousands of pilgrims were streaming into the city for the Feast of Weeks. Bloody clashes ensued, again focusing on the temple. Roman legionaries were pelted with stones and in reply fired the temple arcades. Sabinus himself took 400 talents from the temple treasury, after which he was forced to retreat to the palace and barricade himself in. Rebellion spread throughout Judaea, where royal palaces were plundered and torched. The governor of Syria, one Quintilius Varus, hastened to reinforce the Judaean garrison with a powerful army. The rebels fled when the Roman army appeared in sight of Jerusalem, but were captured in large numbers. Two thousand men were crucified.

Augustus decided to confirm the last testament of Herod with a few minor amendments. The most significant of these was that Archelaus would be given the title *Ethnarch*, which, if he performed the role well, would eventually be exchanged for that of king. His dominions would be Judaea, Idumaea, and Samaria. Alfred Edersheim takes up the sad story: "It is needless to follow the fortunes of the new Ethnarch. He began his rule by crushing all resistance by the wholesale slaughter of his opponents. Of the high priestly office he disposed after the manner of his father. But he far surpassed him in cruelty, oppression, luxury, the grossest egotism, and the lowest sensuality, and that without possessing the talent or energy of Herod. His brief reign ceased in the year 6 of our era, when the Emperor banished him, on account of his crimes, to Gaul."[13]

It was to this terrifying situation in Judaea that Joseph first thought to return. We gather from the expression in Matthew 2:22 "when he heard that Archelaus was reigning in Judaea" that, at the time Joseph and his family left Egypt, the emperor had not yet decided whether or not he would confirm Herod's succession plans. The first intention of Joseph seems to have been to settle in Bethlehem —we have already considered some reasons that may have encouraged him in this thought. But when, on reaching Judaea Joseph learned who Herod's successor was to be, and no doubt in what manner he had begun his reign and the troubles since, Joseph wisely decided to remove his son from the dominion of Archelaus. Matthew tells us, moreover, that Joseph was given a Divine direction not to enter the territory of Judaea, as we read in Matthew 2:22-23: "Having been warned in a dream, he withdrew to the district of Galilee, and he went and lived in a town called Nazareth. So was fulfilled what was said through the prophets.[14] 'He will be called a Nazarene.'" In this case we can presume that the Holy Family travelled along the Mediterranean coast almost entirely out of Judaean territory, until they passed through Samaria and into Galilee. Alternative but more complicated routes would also have been possible.

So the account of the Nativity of the Lord Jesus draws to a close. For the purposes of this book we drawn a line under the Gospel account with John's theological summary in John 1:10-14, "He was in the world and though the world was made through him, the world did not recognise him. He came to that which was his own, but his own did not receive him. Yet to all who received him, to those who believed in his name, he gave the right to become children of God – children born not of natural descent, nor of human decision or a husband's will, but born of God. The word became flesh and made his dwelling among us. We have seen his glory, the glory of the One and Only, who came from the Father, full of grace and truth."

John, of course, was right. Jesus' own did not receive Him, and in large measure have *still* not received Him. Similarly the world at large, that mass of humankind beyond God's chosen race, still fails to recognise Jesus and prefers the 'broad road' that leads away from Him. (Matt 7:13-14.) This is a sad and sober fact, especially considering that God loves to save, even *yearns* to save and paid such a high price to ensure that salvation is open to all. This chapter, with its oppressive reflection on the flight to Egypt and the slaughter of the innocents, helps us to see just how high that price truly was. Before looking at the controversies that have surrounded the biblical account of the Nativity, the final piece in our Christmas 'jigsaw' is the star over Bethlehem, the Natal star followed by the Eastern Magi. It is to this which we turn our attention in the next chapter.

Notes

[1] In titling the wise men 'kings', John Henry Hopkins (1820-91) may have had in mind the messianic prophecy of Psalm 72:9-11 where we read that kings from Tarshish, Sheba and Seba will bow down before the Messiah.

[2] The word 'magician' derives from the *magus*, an ancient Persian priest, and the cognate *maghdim*, a Chaldean term meaning wisdom and philosophy.

[3] There was a small Jewish community in Yemen as late as 1950.

[4] Paul Barnett *Bethlehem to Patmos* (Hodder and Stoughton, 1989), p. 25.

[5] *Ibid.* see p. 26

[6] See for examples *The Life and Times of Jesus the Messiah op. cit.* p. 149, footnote # 50.

[7] Jack Finegan *The Archaeology of the New Testament* Revised Edition (Princeton University Press, 1992), p. 38.

[8] *The Life and Times of Jesus the Messiah op. cit.* p. 150.

[9] Quoted in Werner Keller *The Bible As History* (Hodder and Stoughton, 1958), p. 338.

[10] Both sites are very close to today's Cairo (Almaza) Airport.

[11] A place for racing horses.

[12] These events may well have been the historical basis of the Lord Jesus' parable about the ten Minas, in Luke 19:12-27.

[13] *The Life and Times of Jesus the Messiah op. cit.* p. 153.

[14] Which prophecy Matthew had in mind is obscure. Nazirites were, among the ancient Hebrews, men who were consecrated to God, but this is unconnected with Matthew's comment. It seems that Matthew had in mind something in either Scripture or in the Talmud that in some way elevated the status of Nazareth. Nazareth, itself, seems to have been held in low esteem by some Judaean Jews. So we read the incredulous comment by the disciple Nathaniel in John 1:46 —"Nazareth! Can anything good come out of Nazareth?"

10

The Natal Star

After Jesus was born in Bethlehem in Judea, during the time of King Herod, Magi from the east came to Jerusalem and asked, "Where is the one who has been born king of the Jews? We saw his star in the east and have come to worship him."

Matt 2:1-2

A miraculous event?

The feature of a God-sent symbolic star in the biblical account of the Nativity of the Lord Jesus has caused some critics to claim a mythical element to the story. This, they say, is a straightforward embellishment to give the account added reverence to the credulous Christians. Others have expended considerable thought and energy in trying to locate a known stellar phenomenon that would 'fit' with the account we have in the Bible. As the possible 'explanations' of these phenomena are complex, it seems appropriate to treat the matter as a separate subject in its own right. Whilst it is not possible to 'prove' what the Natal Star (or stars) was, many scholars have been convinced for some 350 years that the biblical events coincide with known sidereal events and that this adds credibility to Matthew's account.

A strong possibility, given the nature of salvation history (previously examined in Chapter 2) is that the phenomenon was unprecedented. In other words it was a miraculous occurrence by being a direct intervention of God in the workings of 'nature' outside of normal human experience. So God would have ordained and caused a stellar phenomenon which has no precedent and which will not recur, as part of the altogether greater miracle of the Incarnation. Miracles, of course, have proved to be a stumbling block to belief for some who hold that God cannot 'do' such things. This is puzzling, especially where this view is expounded from time to time from within the church. It is unclear what sort of God these church-based doubters believe in. If God created the universe and ordered the laws that govern it, how can such 'doubters' proscribe acts of God within His universe? It seems illogical to believe that the God who established the 'laws of nature' would allow Himself to be limited from re-ordering and occasionally setting-aside those 'laws'.

It has been rightly pointed out that 'science' can say nothing conclusive about miracles, as the following quotation from an open letter by fourteen UK scientists to *The Times* newspaper succinctly argued:

"It is not logically valid to use science as an argument against miracles. To believe that miracles cannot happen is as much an act of faith as to believe that they can happen. We gladly accept the virgin birth and the resurrection of Christ as historical events. We know that we are representative of many other scientists who are also Christians standing in the historical tradition of the churches.

"Miracles are unprecedented events. Whatever the current fashions in philosophy or the revelations of opinion polls may suggest, it is important to affirm that science (based as it is upon the observation of precedents) can have nothing to say on the subject. Its "laws" are only generalisations of our experience. Faith rests on other grounds."[1]

It is possible, then, that the Natal Star was a miraculous, one-off event. Equally likely, however, it was a miraculous event or series of events linked to observable and recurring stellar phenomena. If so the miracle, in this sense, is that God who set the stars in their courses (Genesis 1:14; 1 Chronicles 16:26; Nehemiah 9:6, etc) should have so pre-ordained the timings of "natural" sidereal phenomena that they coincided precisely with the events which we now think of as the Nativity. It is this assumption which many today believe to be the most satisfactory 'explanation' of Matthew's account. Either way, the miraculous nature of the appearance is quite remarkable.

Sudden bright lights in the night sky, apart from shooting stars, are either comets or 'novae' (new stars). Origen, one of the early Christian church leaders, who lived in Alexandria about AD 200, wrote of the Natal star in terms of a new star which had nothing in common with other stellar activity. Other clerics and artists of the early church period thought of the Natal star as a comet and ancient illustrations of the star over Bethlehem will often depict it in this way, complete with a fiery tail.

Archaeological activity has discovered detailed information on ancient astronomical observations from the Greek, Roman, Babylonian, Egyptian and Chinese civilisations. It was normal among the ancients to think of unusual stellar activity as god-sent announcements of important events. Knowledge among the ancients of astronomical matters was extensive. Novae were witnessed and recorded but there were none recorded about the year 'zero'. We have already seen that Jesus was probably born in the year 6 BC, so it is about this time that we should be looking for unusual stellar activity.

Johannes Kepler

Born December 27, 1571, the Renaissance astronomer and astrologer Johannes Kepler is best known for his discovery of the three principles of planetary motion, by which he clarified the spatial organisation of the solar system. Kepler also founded modern optics by presenting the correct explanation of how human beings see. He was the first to deduce and explain what happens to light after it enters a telescope, and he developed a particular version of that instrument. His ideas provided a transition from the ancient geometrical description of the heavens to modern dynamical astronomy, into which he introduced the concept of physical force. Something of a child prodigy, although never in robust good health and small of stature, Kepler originally trained to be a Lutheran minister but, during his last year of training, he took up an opportunity to become a professor of mathematics in the Lutheran high school at Graz in Austria. Kepler was an admirer of the Polish astronomer Nicolaus Copernicus and his ground-breaking and controversial astronomical theories —the principal one being that the earth spins about its own axis and orbits the sun. Scientific and religious theory up to that time had held that the sun orbited the earth.

A week before Christmas, on December 17, AD 1603, Kepler, sitting through the night at an observatory near Prague, watched the conjunction of two planets, Saturn and Jupiter, which appeared on the same degree of longitude, in such a way that they appeared to be moving together to become a single larger and more brilliant star in the constellation of Pisces. On reference to his astronomy notes some short time later, Kepler recalled a piece in the writings of the rabbinic writer Abarbanel,[2] referring to the special influence which Jewish astologers were said to have attributed to the same constellation. This was that the Messiah would appear when there was a conjunction of Saturn and Jupiter in Pisces. The obvious question then was: could it have been the same conjunction at the time of the birth of Christ, which Kepler had witnessed in 1603?

Working through the necessary astronomical calculations, Kepler deduced that the same conjunction occurred in 6 BC. This was only one of a number of important scientific discoveries that Kepler made, but was for many years forgotten, in part because Kepler's own reputation dipped in his latter years as he became involved in mysticism and other controversies of his day. It was not until 1925 that the German scholar P. Schnabel deciphered the Neo-Babylonian cuneiform tablets belonging to the ancient School of Astrology in Sippar in Babylonia. Among many dates and astronomical observations, he came across a reference to the position of the planets in the constellation of Pisces, in which Jupiter and Saturn were carefully observed over a period of five months. Reckoned in our calendar, the year would be 7 BC! It is important to note that, whilst archaeologists and historians have to piece together their view of past ages with great diligence and effort, using monuments, documents, tablets and even broken fragments of artefacts, the task for the astronomer in reconstructing the historical celestial sky is, by comparison, much simplified. His task is essentially a mathematical one and he can turn back the 'cosmic clock' at will. In a 'virtual planetarium', the astronomer can arrange the stars and planets exactly as they were thousands of years ago, right down to their appearance on particular days.

We have already seen that the date of the Lord Jesus' birth is definitely between 6 and 4 BC, with most evidence pointing towards 6 BC. The biblical account indicates two sightings of the star, one before the Magi began their journey, probably from Persia or Babylonia, and the other near their journey's end, when, after their interview with King Herod, these Magi, "...went on their way, and the star they had seen in the east went ahead of them until it stopped over the place where the child was. When they saw the star they were overjoyed" (Matt 2:9-10). A celestial object near the horizon might well appear to an observer to point out a location on the surface of the earth below.

Stellar conjunctions

In the year 7 BC, Jupiter and Saturn met in Pisces and, as Kepler deduced, they met three times. Mathematical calculations established further that this threefold conjunction was particularly clearly visible in the Mediterranean area. The conjuctions probably took place in the following way. About the end of February 7 BC, Jupiter moved out of the constellation Aquarius towards Saturn in the constellation of Pisces. Since the sun at that time was also in the sign of Pisces its light covered the constellation and it was not until 12 April that both planets rose in Pisces heliacally (i.e. from the sun) with a difference of 8 degrees of longitude. On 29 May the first close encounter took place, visible for some two hours in the morning sky. The second encounter took place on 3 October and the third on 4 December. At the end of January in the year 6 BC, the planet Jupiter moved out of Pisces and into Aries. Werner Keller makes an interesting observation in his book *The Bible As History*: "'We have seen his star in the east,' (Matt 2: 2) said the wise men, according to the Authorised Version. Ingenious textual critics discovered that the words "in the east" are in the original *En te anatole* – the Greek singular – but that elsewhere "the east" is represented by *anatolai*, the Greek plural. The singular form *anatole* has, it is maintained, quite special astronomical significance, in that it implies the observation of the early rising of the star, the so-called heliacal rising. The translators of the Authorised Version could not have known this.'

As Werner Keller says, if this exposition of the text is accepted, the translation – in the jargon of these astronomical experts – would read: "We have seen his star appear in the first rays of dawn." That, observes Keller, would have corresponded exactly with the astronomical facts.[3] These calculations take us close to the presumed date of birth of the Lord Jesus in December of 6 BC. If He was born in the previous year, then the astronomical facts would accord almost exactly with the current understanding of the Lord's Nativity, i.e. late in the year after several observed stellar phenomena.

If a stellar phenomenon between 7 and 6 BC aroused the interest of first-century star-gazers in the middle east, and gives good reason why the Magi should have travelled West to seek out a new king, it may still be insufficient to explain the fact that by it they were able to locate *the house* where the infant Jesus was staying (Matt 2:9). Another intriguing possibility presents itself: the sidereal activity initiated the journey of the Magi, but a bright luminous angel led them for the last few miles to the precise point in Bethlehem where Jesus was to be found. Luke has told us separately in his account of the shepherds that, "An angel of the Lord appeared to them, and the glory of the Lord shone around them, and they were terrified" (Luke 2:9). Angels clearly have the ability to shine brilliantly, so this may well account for the "star" being able to lead them with precision the last few miles from Jerusalem to Bethlehem.

The significance of the stars to ancient astrologers

Many stars were thought to have special significance to ancient star-gazers. Whilst we cannot be completely certain as to the precise sidereal phenomena that announced the Lord's birth, if the 'Kepler' interpretation is correct, or only partly correct, then the stars concerned would have been thought to be the key to a God-sent message to the ancients. According to the Chaldeans, Pisces was the sign of the west (the Mediterranean countries) and in Jewish lore it was the sign of Israel. As Werner Keller points out, the constellation of Pisces stood at the end of the sun's old course and at the beginning of its new one. What would be more likely than that the Magi saw in it the sign of the end of an old age and the start of a new one?[4]

Jupiter was considered by most astrologers to be a 'lucky star' and a 'royal star'. According to Hebrew tradition, Saturn was the protector of Israel. Babylonian star-gazers thought the planet to be the special star of the neighbouring lands of Syria, Judaea, Samaria and Galilee. Ever since the time of King Nebuchadnezzar thousands of Jews had lived in Babylon. Some without doubt studied at the school of astrology in Sippar. The very obvious conjunction of Jupiter with Saturn in 7 BC, the 'guardian of Israel' with the 'constellation of the western countries', may have been greeted with considerable excitement by the Jewish community in Babylon at the time. It would certainly not have gone unnoticed by Jewish astrologers who lived in the Eastern lands. According to their analysis this might have been thought to indicate the appearance of a mighty king in the west countries, the land of their forefathers. Whether any of the Magi were of Jewish extraction we cannot know, but the event would have been interpreted as one of such significance that we can understand the Magi's desire to go and see the new king at first hand.

Having observed the first encounter on May 29th in 7 BC, possibly from the roof of the school of astrology in Sippar, the Magi would wisely delay their departure until later in the year, when the desert lands became cooler. Magi would have been able to predict the second conjunction on October 3rd and the fact that this day was the Jewish Day of Atonement may have been taken as a sign to commence their journey to the west at that point. Travel on the caravan trails, even on camels (the quickest means of travel), was a slow affair. Allowing that the journey would take perhaps six weeks, the earliest that the wise men would have arrived in Jerusalem would have been towards the end of November in 7 BC.

A more likely sequence of events, however, is that the "wise men" were intrigued by various stellar conjunctions over the early to middle of 7 BC and made their journey in the early part of 5 BC. The infant Jesus on our best estimate was born towards the very end of 6 BC. Allowing that the holy family, as we have seen, returned briefly to Nazareth before their intended permanent move to Bethlehem, then it may have been the middle of 5 BC when the Magi arrived in Jerusalem, Jesus now being at least six months old and living in a *house*, where gifts were presented to Him. Herod, on hearing from the Magi of stellar phenomena beginning eighteen months earlier, would then have settled on a two-year timeframe of infant suspects, and so issued the infamous order for the murder of boys up to two years old.

Did the first century Jews expect a stellar phenomenon to coincide with the advent of the Messiah?

Some critics have argued that first century Jews anticipated a sidereal phenomenon to be associated with the advent of the Messiah. This in turn, would have enabled or encouraged Matthew to invent a story to lend credibility to the Lord's birth. Further, if there were genuine sidereal phenomena at the time, these would provide a useful prop to hold up Matthew's story.

Was there an expectation of some stellar phenomena around the Messiah's birth? This is of particular interest to Christians, who are warned against astrology and divination in the Scriptures (e.g. Isaiah 47:13-15). If God Himself had ordained some stellar activity to coincide with Jesus' birth, would this in any way run counter to His clear commands on the subject? If the star was of purely supernatural origin, would this imply God condescended to the superstitious views of the Magi? If, on the other hand, the stellar activity was entirely predictable (and in that sense not miraculous) do Christians have any reason to call the event miraculous?

Regarding the question of Jewish expectancy of a star sign accompanying the Messiah's birth, some writers have indeed linked Jewish expectancy of the Messiah to the appearance of a star. One basis for this is the work of the Jewish commentator Abarbanel (mentioned earlier as a source of inspiration to Johannes Kepler) who, in his commentary on the Old Testament book of Daniel held that the conjunction of Jupiter and Saturn in the constellation of Pisces was a token of important events, especially in the life of Israel, for which he provided five mystic reasons. Abarbanel was of the opinion that such a conjunction took place three years before the birth of Moses which heralded the first great deliverance of Israel, and similarly that it would occur before the birth of the Messiah —the final deliverer of Israel. His argument failed to convince many, however, because his calculations were seen as inconclusive and even erroneous. It was also plainly absurd to assume the state of first-century Jewish belief regarding stellar phenomena based on the writings of a fifteenth century rabbi.

Reliable information about ancient Jewish belief in stellar activity announcing the Messiah is, however, available. One of the shorter *Midrashim*, translated and re-published in the middle of the nineteenth century, called the Messiah-Haggadah, opens with the following: "A star shall come out of Jacob. There in a Boriata in the name of the Rabbis: the heptad in which the son of David cometh – in the *first* year, there will not be sufficient nourishment; in the *second* year the arrows of famine are launched; in the *third* a great famine; in the *fourth*, neither famine nor plenty; in the *fifth*, great abundance, and the *star shall shine forth from the East, and this is the star of the Messiah*. And it will shine from the East for fifteen days, and if it be prolonged, it will be for the good of Israel; in the *sixth* sayings (voices) and announcements (hearings); in the *seventh* wars, and at the close of the seventh the Messiah is to be expected."[5] A similar teaching is given at the end of a collection of three Midrashim which are titled 'The Book of Elijah', 'Chapters about the Messiah', and 'The Mysteries of Rabbi Simon, the son of Jochai'. These tell us that a star in the East would appear two years before the birth of the Messiah —statements which are remarkable in the sense that, whether they originated in Judaism before or after the birth of Christ, they still bring us to circa 7 BC when, as we have seen, conjunctions of Jupiter and Saturn occurred three times, in May, October and December.

These conjunctions, whilst not meeting precisely the requirements of the stellar activity mentioned in Matthew's Gospel, nevertheless do explain the attention of the Magi being aroused and, even assuming they did not know of the Jewish community's expectation of their Messiah, it is certain that after due enquiry they would have ascertained that this was indeed their expectation. We may conjecture that the Saturn/Jupiter conjunction in 7 BC was the Magi's star seen *in its rising* and that a triple conjunction in early 6 BC of Mars, Jupiter and Saturn which stood at the points of a triangle might then have been the re-appearance at which the Magi rejoiced. Alternatively the reappearance might itself have been a separate stellar phenomenon occasioned directly by God.

No proof-positive of the 'how' of the Natal star is possible. It is clear only that there was exceptional stellar activity about the time that Christ was born. As suggested earlier, the real miracle in this is probably not what happened in the night sky, but rather the fact that God ordained His Son's birth as a human in a way that coincided with these heavenly phenomena, which is an impressive comment on the longevity and precision of His plan of salvation. Certainly God would not have done anything that would arouse an interest in astrology but He may in His wisdom and grace have decided to allow events to coincide with the expectation of the Magi, who would have seen guidance by a star as the fullest confirmation that they had been rightly directed to Bethlehem.

That some Jews, at least, *did* expect the appearance of a star to announce the Messiah's advent, seems beyond doubt.[6] But Matthew would have been unlikely to have latched upon this as a reason to invent a story about 'wise men' from the east. Nothing would have been more antipathetic to the notions of a Jewish readership, for which he principally wrote his Gospel. Rabbinism looked to a very different manner of the world's homage of their Messiah than the worship of a few superstitious non-Jewish Magi. Far from serving as an historical basis for the origin of a 'legend' by Matthew, the account of the Magi and their guidance by a star might have been calculated to have dissuaded many Jews as to Jesus' claim as Messiah! Again Christians look to the reliability of the original witnesses and remark that the Gospel accounts do not seek to suppress details that might otherwise be considered inconvenient.

Notes

[1] Letter to *The Times* by fourteen scientists, mainly university professors, headed by Professor R. J. Berry as President of the Linnean Society, dated 13 July 1984. Also quoted in *The Authentic Jesus* by John Stott, Marshall Morgan and Scott, 1985, p. 15.

[2] Born 1439, died 1508.

[3] See *op. cit.*, *The Bible As History* p. 332.

[4] *Ibid.* p. 333.

[5] Quoted in *op. cit.* p. 147.

[6] Ephrathah. In Numbers 24:17, Balaam's prediction of the star and sceptre is referred to as messianic in the Targum Onkelos and the Tagum Pseudo-Jonathan. Whilst Balaam's prophecy was of a king rising *like* a star, the fact that a rising star announced the Messiah's birth and guided the Magi to the King who they were to worship, may be seen as sufficient fulfilment of the prophecy.

11

The Two Genealogies and Mary's Davidic Credentials

Having followed the biblical account of the birth of the Lord Jesus via God's original plan of salvation in pre-history, through the events of the Nativity up to the return of Joseph and his family from brief exile in Egypt, there remain a number of controversies upon which it is helpful to have a clear view. Each in its way represents a 'battleground' over which, generation after generation, critics of the Bible and of Christianity have sought to undermine the credibility of the biblical accounts. For this reason, if for no other, it is valuable to understand the issues. Besides which, many will consider these controversies as being interesting in their own right.

It is clear, however, that the Bible accounts *taken in themselves* will never provide all the answers which some critics declare are necessary before they will accept the scriptural version of Jesus' birth. But it is equally clear, Christians will argue, that in natural and probable ways, using reasonable inference, the biblical accounts can be examined in detail and many 'difficulties' easily resolved. We will shortly review Mary's *Davidic credentials*, but we begin with what some consider to be a very intractable problem that defies easy resolution. This is the matter of the two genealogies which feature in the Gospels of Matthew and Luke. Genealogies leave most people uninspired and at first glance we may wonder why they are provided in the Gospel accounts at all. Do not the claims of Jesus stand up on their own? Why do we need lists of largely unknown people to help us draw close to the Prince of Peace? Actually, there are a number of important issues at stake, which is undoubtedly why these genealogies have proved to be a 'popular' area of controversy in the past —and no doubt always will.

The difference between the genealogies

See Appendix 1 for a listing of the names in the two genealogies. These differ in the following important respects:

In Extent

The genealogy given by Matthew goes back as far as Abraham; the list in Luke by contrast, traces the Lord's ancestry back to Adam.

* Matthew's list has 41 names, including Jesus.

* Luke's list has 74 names including Jesus.

* Matthew and Luke have 19 names in common, if Matthan and Matthat are the same person, 18 if they are not.

* Apart from the names common to both lists, Matthew has 23 and Luke 56 names. Luke's list has 19 names before Matthew's list begins.

* Luke's list has no artificial arrangement, as does Matthew's (which is divided into sub-lists of fourteen).

* Matthew's line is followed from David through Solomon, but Luke's is followed from David through Nathan. Both were sons of David.

In Names

The two genealogies are identical from Abraham to David, but at David the lines diverge, only briefly converging again at the time of Shealtiel and once again (probably) at Mattan. Most scholars are agreed that Matthew traces the family line of David down through Solomon and Luke through Solomon's younger brother, Nathan.

* *Rhesa* between 55 and 56 in Luke's list, is not a proper name, but a Chaldee title which means *prince*. Some early Jewish copyists[1]

mistook this for a name, whereas the title almost certainly should read Zerubbabel Rhesa —or Zerubbabel the prince.

* Matthew's list begins with Abraham, the father of the Jewish race, whereas Luke's begins with Adam, the father of the human race. Each of these is in keeping with the object and readers which the Gospel writers had in view —the one Jewish and the other Gentile.

* *Cainan*, between 12 and 13 in Luke's list, is an interpolation in some copies of the Septuagint occurring towards the end of the fourth century AD. Scholars are clear that it should not feature in the list.

* In Matthew's list Shealtiel (number 29) is said to be the son of Jeconiah, but in Luke's list Shealtiel is identified as the son of Neri. The likely explanation of this is as follows: In Jeremiah 22:24-30 it is predicted that King Jehoiachin (Hebrew Coniah or Jeconiah) would be childless and so he could not have been the father of Shealtiel. It is likely however that he adopted the sons of his relative Neri, the twentieth from David in the line traced through Nathan. In this regard we should bear in mind the so-called *Jehoiachin-Curse prophecy* and the *Zerubbabel-Blessing prophecy*, both of which are discussed below.

* In Matthew's list Joseph is identified as the son of Jacob, but in Luke as the son of Heli. Some confusion has arisen because of this. Matthew's genealogy is generally reckoned to be that of Joseph, whilst Luke's genealogy is generally thought to be Mary's. In Luke 3:23 we read "Jesus ..... was the son, so it was thought, of Joseph, the son of Heli." H. Brash Bonsall comments: "The Greek here simply reads 'Joseph of Heli'. In such a case as this a Greek would supply whatever word the context demanded, it might be son, son-in-law, father, sister, aunt, mother, grandparent. In this case it would be 'son in law'. Heli was Mary's father, and Joseph his son in law." (See *The Person of Christ, op. cit.* p. 42.)

Some sceptics have declared that at worst it is impossible to harmonise the genealogies, or that at best, they can only be harmonised by suppositions which are incapable of proof. We might quibble about what constitutes 'proof' but most reasonable people will accept that providing evidence is examined in natural and probable ways, using reasonable inference, then we are as close to 'proof' as we need to be. But why are there *two* genealogies? Three views have been put forward:

1. Both genealogies give the descent of Joseph: Matthew's the *real* and Luke's the *legal* descent.

2. Matthew gives Joseph's legal descent as successor to the throne of David and Luke gives the 'real' parentage.

3. Matthew gives the real descent of Joseph, and Luke the real descent of Mary.

In discussing these three hypotheses we need always to bear in mind the fact of the virgin conception. If both genealogies were Joseph's, as suggested in the first hypothesis, then there would be no evidence of Mary's Davidic descent, and such evidence is important bearing in mind that Joseph was not Jesus' natural father, only his adoptive (legal) father.

If it is argued that Luke's genealogy could not possibly be Mary's on account of the fact that genealogies of women were never given in the first century, we can refer to the fact that, contrary to this custom, Matthew includes in his genealogy the names of several women, each of whom would have been considered less than wholesome to the minds of a first century Pharisee. There was Tamar, involved in an unholy relationship with her father in law (Genesis chapter 38), Rahab the prostitute (Joshua 6:17; Heb 11:31), Ruth the foreigner and Bathsheba whose husband King David in effect murdered (by putting him into the front of the front line in an impending battle) in order to possess her. So Luke certainly broke with tradition in mentioning women in his genealogy —it might also be inferred that Jesus, the Saviour promised from pre-history, does not disdain those whom society thinks of as outcasts, for it was these very people to whom Jesus came first and foremost ("I have not come to call the righteous, but sinners" said Jesus —Matthew 9:13). In this sense, then, there is a 'gospel' in the genealogy itself, and a revelation of the gracious character of the Christian message!

The third hypothesis above seems, on the basis of our present understanding, the most likely. The Davidic descent of the Lord Jesus was never questioned in his own day —on the contrary, popular opinion was that He was indeed the Son of David (e.g. Matthew 12:23; 15:22; 20:30-31 and 21:9, 15). God, in His wisdom, has ensured that there is absolutely no doubt as to Jesus' Davidic credentials. Those who did not accept the virgin conception would nevertheless have to acknowledge that His title was determined by Joseph's line via 'legal' adoption. And those who did accept the virgin conception would have had good reason for believing that Mary was of Davidic descent, thus ensuring a 'blood' line, and not merely a legal line of descent.

It might be added that it is quite clear that the Lord Jesus saw Himself as *the* fulfilment of Davidic prophecy. So, in Matthew 4:12-17, when Jesus began His preaching ministry, he consciously chose to begin it in the territory of Zebulun and Naphtali, in fulfilment of Isaiah's prophecy (see Isaiah 9:1-7). The Gospel writer Matthew quotes the Isaiah 9:1–2 prophecy. If Jesus viewed beginning His preaching ministry in the Zebulun and Naphtali region as fulfilling the verses from Isaiah, then it follows that He also saw Himself as reigning on David's throne, as the New International Version puts it. Or more prosaically, as "King David's successor" (Isaiah 9:7, Good News Bible).

Prophecies concerning the genealogies

The Davidic covenant
Messianic prophecy, as we saw earlier in these studies, held that the Christ would come from the seed of David. God Himself spoke to David through the prophet Nathan when He said, "When your days are over and you rest with your fathers, I will raise up your offspring to succeed you, who will come from your own body, and I will establish his kingdom. He is the one who will build a house for my Name, and I will establish the throne of his kingdom for ever" (2 Samuel 7:12-13). This prediction looked beyond Solomon to Christ. Frequently in the Prophets, Christ is

said to spring from David (e.g. Isaiah 11:1, where David's father Jesse is described as the root from which a branch will spring; also Jeremiah 30:9; Ezekiel 34:23-4; 37:24 and Hosea 3:5 —in each case where Christ is referred to as 'David'). It was from the line of David that Mary came (Luke 3:31) and Nathan's prophecy was clear that the Messiah would come from David's own body. The blood line, it may be repeated, was from Mary, not Joseph.

The promise to David was fulfilled in the following way: his wife Queen Bathsheba, had two sons, Solomon and Nathan. Joseph was descended from Solomon (see Matthew 1:6) but Mary from Nathan (see Luke 3:31). So the angel was able to pronounce in Luke 1:32-3, "The Lord will give him the throne of his father David and he will reign over the house of Jacob forever."

The Jehoiachin-curse prophecy

Jehoiachin (in Hebrew Coniah or Jeconiah as we have it in the New International Version) the son of Jehoiakim, was the second to last king of the house of David to sit upon the throne in Judah. During his reign the prophet Jeremiah lived and pronounced God's word against him because of his rebellious ways: "As surely as I live" declares the Lord "even if you Jehoiachin son of Jehoiakim king of Judah, were a signet ring on my right hand, I would still pull you off. .... This is what the Lord says: "Record this man as childless, a man who will not prosper in his lifetime, for none of his offspring will sit on the throne of David or rule any more in Judah". (Jeremiah 22: 24 and 30). In spite of the fact that this was pronounced against Jehoiachin, almost straight afterwards we read one of the great messianic prophecies in Jeremiah 23: 5-6 when we are told yet again that God will raise up a righteous Branch for David. The malediction on Jehoiachin came to pass in that Solomon's line effectively died out and was supplanted by Nathan's line.

The Zerabbabel prophecy

The prophecy against Jehoiachin (or Jeconiah of Matthew's genealogy) is lifted in the case of his descendant, Zerubbabel, who rebuilt the temple at the command of the prophets Haggai and Zechariah. Haggai 2:23 reads almost as the reverse of Jeremiah's earlier prophecy: "'I will take you, my servant Zerubbabel son of Shealtiel ... and I will make you like my signet ring, for I have chosen you' declares the Lord." The signet ring on a Persian king's right hand when impressed on a wax seal affixed to an official document had the effect of giving it the force of law. God in effect gave Zerubbabel the power of attorney for Him. The blessing prophecy came to pass in that Zerubbabel's descendants became the ancestors of the Lord Jesus as Matthew 1:12 and Luke 3:27 both show.

Did Mary descend from David?

Recognising that Mary's Davidic descent is an important part of the fulfilment of Old Testament prophecy, we should not be surprised to find it under attack from anti-Christians. Most of the objections discussed in this study were read by the author on an anti-Christian internet website —a useful source of current, if often erroneous, debate. As suggested previously in this series of studies, we should bear in mind the credentials and motivation of biblical critics. How selective are they in the information they present? It is worth checking Bible references in full, to see that they are correct (some are not!) and also that they have not been taken out of context. The currently popular arguments are summarised as follows:

1. A man 'born of a virgin' can have no human father. As Jesus was therefore not the *biological* son of Joseph (who was a descendant of David) the birth could not have fulfilled the Davidic prophecy unless Mary was a descendant of David.

2. Inerrantists (that's atheist-speak for people who believe the Bible!) reject the 'obvious meaning' of Luke 3:23 – that Heli was Joseph's father – and insist that Mary was the daughter of Heli.

3. Inerrantists claim that as Jesus was not a son of Heli in the normal sense, that He must have been a 'son' in some other sense.

4. Since a virgin-born Jesus could not have had a paternal ancestor,

it follows that Heli must have been a maternal ancestor —this the critics say is an 'improbable interpretation' of Luke 3:23. Inerrantists 'pretend that Luke believed that his future readers would naturally and without difficulty work their way through this logic'.

5. If there had been any suggestion that Jesus traced His lineage back through Mary, the Bible writers would have been 'laughed out of town' because in Bible times women 'did not count in reckoning descent'.

6. If Luke had meant his readers to see Heli as Mary's father, he would have said so specifically. But he wouldn't do so because this would involve him in 'personal ridicule'.

7. Mary *may have been* a Levite, i.e. of the tribe of Levi, not of the tribe of Benjamin or Judah, which were the Davidic tribes. This is because her cousin, Elizabeth, was a descendant of Aaron (Luke 1:5).

Having examined earlier in this series of studies the reliability of the manuscript tradition and the Gospel writers as witnesses,[2] we need to keep in mind that the Gospel writers were honest men who, had they wanted to fabricate a story around the life of Jesus, could have found easier and less controversial ways of doing so. With this in mind it is worth considering these anti-Davidic arguments in turn.

1. A man 'born of a virgin' can have no human father. As Jesus was therefore not the biological son of Joseph (who was a descendant of David) the birth could not have fulfilled the Davidic prophecy unless Mary was a descendant of David.

This is not correct. Certainly a man born of a virgin can have no human father. But the idea that the birth could not have fulfilled the Davidic prophecy unless Mary was a descendant of David is only true in a biological sense. Joseph's direct line of descent and his marriage to Mary would enable him legally to confer the line of David through to his firstborn son, even without a biological link. Since the prophecy to David in 2 Samuel 12, however, was that David's messianic offspring would come from his own body, we are right in looking for a biological connection and this must logically come through Mary. It should be emphasised, however, that even were there no such link, the Lord Jesus would still be David's son.

We refer now to the earlier comment that 'proof' of these matters sufficient to satisfy some critics is simply not available. We cannot therefore prove that Mary was David's descendant but, given what we know of the Gospel witnesses, the fact that had they wanted to invent a story they surely would have done so in a less controversial manner, and the clear line in Matthew's Gospel to Joseph, it seems a perfectly reasonable inference that Heli was Mary's father and Joseph's *father in law*, as suggested earlier by H. Brash Bonsall. Furthermore, this seems quite consistent with the providence of God in ensuring both a biological and legal line of descent for His Son.

2. Inerrantists reject the 'obvious meaning' of Luke 3:23 – that Heli was Joseph's father – and insist that Mary was the daughter of Heli.

This has been dealt with above.

3. Inerrantists claim that as Jesus was not a son of Heli in the normal sense, that He must have been a 'son' in some other sense.

This has been dealt with above.

4. Since a virgin-born Jesus could not have had a paternal ancestor, it follows that Heli must have been a maternal ancestor —an 'improbable interpretation' of Luke 3:23. Inerrantists 'pretend that Luke believed that his future readers would naturally and without difficulty work their way through this logic.'

As set out above, the maternal ancestry seems both natural and probable, using reasonable inference. It may be that first century readers found this more straightforward, because we may assume that at 'short range', the background to Jesus' birth was better understood because it was so recent, and, as suggested by H. Brash Bonsall, the Greek understanding of Luke's genealogy would have supplied the necessary understanding of what the context required.

5. If there had been any suggestion that Jesus traced His lineage back through Mary, the Bible writers would have 'been laughed out of town' because in Bible times women 'did not count in reckoning descent.'

Good! That helps to 'prove' that the Bible writers knew what they were talking about and were willing to deal unashamedly with difficulties. We have already seen that several women were mentioned in Matthew's genealogy, and that in this we see a Gospel message! However, there is no evidence of any of the Gospel writers being 'laughed' out of anywhere.

6. If Luke had meant his readers to see Heli as Mary's father, he would have said so specifically. But he wouldn't do so because this would involve him in 'personal ridicule'.

This is partly dealt with in the foregoing. We do not know why Luke did not state specifically how Mary figured in the genealogy —it may be that for cultural or stylistic reasons this was not considered appropriate. We may also reflect that, as an inspired writer (not a dictating machine!) Luke gave out only what was given to him.

7. Mary may have been a Levite i.e. of the tribe of Levi, not of the tribe of Benjamin or Judah which were the Davidic tribes. This is because her cousin, Elizabeth, was a descendant of Aaron (Luke 1:5).

Here it appears that the Bible critics are 'straining mightily' to secure a point! The 'may' in 'Mary may be' seems a very large one. That Elizabeth was a cousin is without doubt. What sort of a cousin is not explained. Elizabeth is unlikely to have been a very close cousin in view of her age as against Mary's youth.

Davidic descent conferred by the genealogies

It should by now be apparent that the Lord Jesus has a double-claim to the throne of David —via Mary and Joseph. We may suggest the reason why God inspired two genealogies to be recorded was to demonstrate this double-claim adequately to His people. **Joseph** represents the regal-legal line through Solomon. Had it not been for the absolute and total decline of Israel as a nation, Joseph would have been king. The reason why Israel went into decline is beyond the scope of this book, but W. Graham Scroggie DD, in his book *A Guide to the Gospels*, suggests that one reason for Matthew dividing his genealogy into three is a comment on Israel's fortunes through its Old Testament history. Its form of government: Judges (theocracy), kings (monarchy) and priests (hierarchy); its fortunes over these periods being respectively growth, then decline, and finally ruin —at the lowest point of which the Saviour was born.

Bishop Paul Barnett comments on this very issue, questioning how Matthew and Luke could have thought of Jesus as the "son of David", since Joseph was not Jesus' biological father. A serious question, observes Barnett, the answer to which must be that Joseph was the legal father, if not the biological father. Joseph, Barnett notes, would have acted as the legal father at both the naming and registering of his son (Matt 1:20-21; Luke 2:1-5). Furthermore, the Jewish law of levirate marriage reminds us that biological paternity was not a prerequisite to legal fatherhood. So, according to Deuteronomy 25:5-10, if a man died without a son, his brother was to marry the man's wife. The first born son of that union was to bear the name of the deceased brother. This boy was truly the son of the deceased in Jewish law, albeit he was the biological offspring of someone else. The laws of levirate marriage help us to understand why neither Matthew nor Luke see any incompatibility between the Lord Jesus' virgin conception and his descent from David, through Joseph.[3]

Mary also had throne rights as a direct descendant of David. By the so called 'Daughters of Zelophehad Enactment' (Numbers 27:1-11) she could receive and transmit to her son inherited rights —and apart from the other reasons we have elsewhere suggested for Mary accompanying Joseph to answer the census call in Bethlehem, it might have been partly to assert or record the specific claims of her descent in the census registration (this would lend further weight to the view that Heli had no son).

Mary's Davidic credentials implied genetically

For this final line of thought the author acknowledges the work of Dr E K Victor Pearce in his helpful book *Prophecy*. He points out that modern science provides clues as to the authenticity of God's statement made to Satan (Genesis 3:15) that the offspring – or "seed" – of the woman would eventually crush Satan's head. Victor Pearce comments that the seed may be understood as the genetic code – the Mitochondrial DNA – passed from one generation to the next exclusively through females and without which human life would not be possible. This discovery has encouraged scientists to the view that the human race is descended from one woman. Victor Pearce writes: "this seed's essential constituency was passed down through the generations from Eve to Mary. It would also be the reason why, in Luke's account, it is Mary's kindred list which is given and not Joseph's .... in the Old Testament, the mother's names of the kings descending from David are always given, but in contrast they are not for the North Israel Kings .... This system of reference to the mother is consistently repeated. Only divine inspiration can explain this genetic anticipation, from Eve to Mary the virgin, through the mothers of David's line, through centuries of prophecy."[4] It is the woman's offspring – Jesus – who will eventually and finally defeat Satan.

The importance of the genealogies

We begin to see the importance of the genealogies. No orthodox Jew today would consider the claim of anyone to be the Messiah unless he could prove his pedigree through David. The genealogies given to us in the Bible demonstrate Jesus' lineage beyond reasonable doubt as the promised King of Israel who, as a direct descendant of David, will reign forever as promised in the many messianic prophecies of the Old Testament.

The preservation of the documents from which the genealogies were (presumably) copied by Matthew and Luke demonstrates both the sovereignty and the faithfulness of God. The records were kept in the temple archives in much the same way as the equivalent modern records are held in a municipal Register Office.

The precious temple archives survived the destruction of God's house at Shiloh (1 Samuel 4:11 ff) and the overthrow of Solomon's temple in Jerusalem in 586 BC. They survived the invasion of Alexander the Great in 330 BC, who came perilously close to destroying Jerusalem, and they survived the Jewish civil war ended in 63 BC by the Roman general Pompey. Some of the fighting in this war raged in the temple itself. The precious scrolls survived unharmed through the extraordinarily dangerous decades of the first century AD, until some time in the 'sixties' when Matthew and Luke made reference to them. Only a few years later, on 2 September AD 70, during what the Romans came to call the Jewish War, a Roman soldier hurled a burning torch through a window in the temple that started a conflagration in which the archives were destroyed forever. No imposter could attempt to prove his Davidic descent today.

Notes
[1] It is assumed that Matthew and Luke at different times consulted, or made arrangements for the consultation of, the temple archives in Jerusalem, where these details used to be lodged.
[2] See Appendices 4 and 5 to these studies.
[3] See Paul Barnett *Bethlehem to Patmos* (Hodder and Stoughton, 1989), p. 19.
[4] Dr E. K. Victor Pearce *Evidence for Truth* Volume 3: Prophecy (Eagle, 1998), pp. 61f.

12

The Virgin Conception

A battleground

We should perhaps begin with a simple definition of the 'problem'. Most people speak in terms of the virgin birth, as though there was something unusual in the Lord's physical manner of birth. This has never been a question —Jesus was born in an entirely normal manner. It was the conception that led to the birth that was supernatural and so we should correctly refer not to the 'virgin birth' but to the 'virgin conception' and this is the term normally used in this book. To be precise, therefore, the Lord Jesus was conceived by the operation of the Holy Spirit without the co-operation of a human father. It is this simple truth to which most in the church lay hold.

In the UK in the mid 1980s a bishop was consecrated in the Church of England's see of Durham who became for a short while a *cause celebre*, especially amongst segments of the press and media keen to undermine the authority of Scripture and exploit division within the church. He referred in a number of articles to what he considered to be the symbolic and mythological nature of the 'story of the virgin birth', opposing the views of those who were offended by his apparent denial of the straightforward biblical account —his own view being that many of the stories in the Bible are not literally true, but just inspired symbols of the activity of

God. He considered parts of the Bible to be of the literary genre called 'myth' which seeks to set truth in historical form *without claiming that it is historical*. This particular bishop is mentioned here only because he was a well-publicised apologist for the idea that the 'virgin birth' was allegorical, not literal.

The first question to be considered, therefore, is whether the Gospel writers Matthew and Luke were deliberately writing myth when they recounted the virgin conception, and intended their readers to see it as such. Let us remind ourselves what they wrote:

This is how the birth of Jesus Christ came about: His mother Mary was pledged to be married to Joseph, but before they came together, she was found to be with child through the Holy Spirit.

Matt 1:18

"How will this be," Mary asked the angel, "since I am a virgin?" The angel answered, "The Holy Spirit will come upon you, and the power of the Most High will overshadow you. So the holy one will be called the son of God. Even Elizabeth your relative is going to have a child in her old age, and she who was said to be barren is in her sixth month. For nothing is impossible with God."

Luke 1:34-35

Since the setting of both Matthew and Luke (and, for that matter, Mark and John as well) is quite clearly in a certain geographic place at a certain point in history, and since the Gospels in many places provide quite clear geo-political information, do we have any reason to assume that the authors weaved between two separate literary threads, one historic and the other 'myth' in order to present a synthesis that was to be accepted as 'truth' by their readers?

Critics who wish to pursue this line point towards the Jewish literary genre of *Midrash*, the method of biblical investigation in which oral tradition interprets and elaborates on scriptural text.

Midrash searched in particular for the spiritual truth contained in a biblical passage, rather than its literal interpretation. Critics have suggested that Matthew, especially, may have used this form of writing. There is no real evidence to support this view, however. Whilst Midrash *was* used in the first century AD, it did not reach its zenith of popularity until the second century. Midrash writers were embroidering the Old Testament with fiction, whereas Matthew was writing an account of the life of a contemporary man. There is no evidence that Matthew's readers understood him to be writing Midrash either at the time of writing or in the life of the early Christian church. On the contrary, the abundance of geo-political detail in the Gospels leads naturally to the conclusion that the writers were writing serious prose, not poetry.

Whilst much ink has been spilled on the battleground of the virgin conception, as opponents of the traditional view try to force in their favour the issue of 'myth' versus history, it must be said that the proponents of the myth theory muster no great weight of evidence to support their position. Indeed these critics might win more plaudits if they simply stated unequivocally that they cannot believe the biblical accounts because they do not believe in miracles —this would perhaps be a more honest approach to the question. Some who are (or claim to be) adherents of the Christian faith, maintain that the doctrine of the virgin conception is unimportant and that one can deny it and still be a mainstream Christian. In support of this they say that the virgin conception is only referred to in two New Testament Scriptures —Matt 1:18 and Luke 1:34-5, and only once in the Old Testament (Isaiah 7:14) and that therefore what the Bible deals with so scantily cannot be of great importance.

It is true that the virgin conception does not gain as much prominence in the New Testament as does Jesus' teaching, death and resurrection. But the account of the circumstances of Jesus' birth are not integral to the message of the New Testament in the way that His teaching, death and resurrection are. In the two Gospels where the virgin conception is mentioned, it is plainly taught, and the literal interpretation of the account has been the universal understanding of the Christian church over two millennia. Are we to believe that God left His church floundering in erroneous understanding for all that time? It is also entirely congruous that the one who was simultaneously God and man should enter and leave His world in a supernatural way. It would seem bizarre, to say the least, that a holy God should look down over His creation with all the options no doubt at His disposal to manage the physical entry of His son into the world, and decide upon an illegitimate birth to be that method!

So, the virgin conception is directly mentioned only twice in the New Testament. Why, we might ask, do Mark and John not refer to the fact and why is it not mentioned elsewhere in the New Testament —most importantly in the writings of Paul? We should first remember that in English law silence may be construed as consent! An argument from silence, however, is unreliable. As John Stott comments in his splendid short book *The Authentic Jesus*, neither Mark nor John tell us anything about the childhood of Jesus, but we do not conclude from this that He never had one![1] The fact that these writers do not refer to the virgin conception is actually quite irrelevant for the simple reason that neither Gospel writer chose to include anything about the Lord Jesus' birth and childhood; both, instead, begin their account with John the Baptiser. It is significant, conversely, that the two Gospel writers who *did* choose to write an account of Jesus' birth were both quite clear that he was born of a virgin.

John Stott, in *The Authentic Jesus*, highlights three important factors to be taken into account in weighing the evidence for the virgin conception:

1. *The authenticity of the atmosphere*

The early chapters of Matthew and Luke present to us the last days of the Old Testament. Here we meet Zechariah and Elizabeth, Joseph and Mary, Simeon and Anna —devout Old Testament believers, waiting with patience for the kingdom of God. The context is one of Old Testament piety, and the written style, language and structure is thoroughly Hebraic. Far from being later inventions, these accounts give the strong impression that they were written very early in the Christian era. The narrative unfolds with simplicity and discretion. Certainly there were pagan myths of "gods" having sexual relations with human women, but in place of such crude and fantastic legends the Gospel writers are reticent, treating the sacred intimacies of the conception of Jesus with the utmost delicacy.[2]

2. *The origin of the account of the virgin birth*

Matthew and Luke share the same essentials: both attribute Mary's pregnancy to the action of Holy Spirit and both refer to the perplexities and problems which were caused by her virginity. The two accounts are independent, there being no serious evidence of collusion, yet complementary in content. Luke writes of the annunciation to Mary and of her concern at how she could be a mother when she was not yet married. Matthew, by contrast, writes of Joseph's bewilderment on being told of Mary's pregnancy, his difficult decision to quietly divorce Mary, and of the dream in which God instructs Joseph to take Mary home as his wife. It might be said, then, that Matthew tells Joseph's story whilst Luke tells Mary's.

3. *The rumours of Jesus' illegitimacy*

That the Lord Jesus was not the biological son of Joseph and Mary seems to be the prime indisputable fact about his birth. Had it been so, if in wedlock, then Jesus would have been born distinctly of the line of David both from His mother and His father, and this would have saved any controversy. If out of wedlock, the Gospel writers could easily have said, had they been false witnesses, that the marriage pre-dated the conception and no one would have been any the wiser, thus obtaining the benefits of an in-wedlock birth. Why should they have invented an otherwise remarkable story and so made themselves 'hostage to fortune'? They obviously believed the facts they were given and so the only choice before us, as readers of their accounts, is between the virgin birth and an illegitimate birth.

We have already alluded to the seemingly incongruous idea that God should choose a birth out of wedlock (i.e. a circumstance of birth that runs counter to His will, to the teaching of the Old Testament and an action on the part of the parents that would therefore have been sinful) to be the manner in which to bring His sinless Son into the world. John Stott clinically reviews the evidence that deliberate slurs were being made about Jesus' birth during His own lifetime. For example, when Jesus declared that certain disbelieving Jews did not have Abraham as their father but rather the devil, they responded, 'we are not illegitimate children' —which appears to be an innuendo that He was (John 8:41). On another occasion, this time in Nazareth – His own home town – when the people were offended by His teaching, they asked contemptuously, 'Isn't this Mary's son?' (Mark 6:3). As Stott says, in a patriarchal society this was a deliberate insult; the insinuation could not have been missed. On a third occasion, whilst interrogating the man born blind, whom Jesus had healed, his interrogators shouted at him: 'We know that God spoke to Moses, but as for this fellow, we don't even know where he comes from' (John 9:29).

Rumours about the circumstances of Jesus' birth carried on long after the death of all the apostles. In the Jewish Talmud these rumours became explicit. The Christian scholar Origen in the third century had to respond to a jibe by the critic Celsus that Joseph had turned Mary out of his home because she had committed adultery with a soldier named Panthera. Stott asks how these hints and slanders could have arisen unless it was common knowledge that Mary was pregnant at the time when Joseph married her. However distasteful this gossip is, there can be no doubt it is corroborative evidence of the virgin conception.[3]

The importance of the virgin conception

We have already seen that some argue that what the Bible treats so scantily, we need not be too concerned about. Most Christians would reply that the doctrine of the virgin conception is indeed of fundamental importance because only in this way can we begin to understand how God the second person in the Trinity, could become man and take human nature into *eternal union* with His divine nature. If the virgin conception is false we have much less ground on which to base another central reality of Christ, that of His sinlessness and of course the legitimacy of His birth, as we have seen, then comes into question. The virgin conception is important, then, because it helps to explain the rather greater miracle of the Incarnation.

The correct placing of the verses which tell of the virgin conception in the original texts (Matthew 1:18 and Luke 1:34-35) has never been seriously doubted. Practically every ancient manuscript includes them, except a mutilated copy of a manuscript of the Ebionites (a Jewish/Christian sect that denied Christ's deity and which deleted many other things that also referred to His deity), and one Syriac reading of Matt 1:18 which is certainly wrong, but which critics sometimes claim may have predated other manuscripts: it says that Joseph begat Jesus – but then goes on to narrate the virgin birth – something the critics are less willing to own up to!

The Gospel writer Luke was, as we know, a physician and therefore an educated man, who accompanied the apostle Paul on his missionary journeys. These journeys encompassed many of the locations where the Gospel events took place. Whilst Paul was in prison in Caesarea, undergoing some protracted investigations by the Roman procurators Felix and Festus (see Acts 24 and 25) Luke may well have had time to travel within Judaea, Samaria and Galilee to interview surviving witnesses —as he wrote, "I myself have carefully investigated everything from the beginning" (Luke 1:3).

These witnesses may have included Mary herself. Allowing that Mary was no more than eighteen years old in 6 to 5 BC when Jesus was probably born, and knowing as we do that Luke accompanied Paul on his second missionary journey, AD 49-52, then Mary would have been in her late sixties at the time when Luke had an opportunity to meet her. Obviously this is supposition, but irrespective of this there would, without doubt, have been plenty of eyewitnesses still alive at the time. It is simply not possible that the apostle Paul, of whom Luke was a close companion over a number of years (see Col 4:14; 2 Tim 4:11; Philemon 24), was unaware of the virgin conception, yet nowhere in his writings does he seek to deny it. If anything he confirms it, as he writes to the Galatians (Gal 4:4), "when the time had fully come, God sent His son, *born of a woman*, born under law...." It is difficult to see why Paul would otherwise have made this statement unless it was to affirm that the Lord's conception was undertaken in a supernatural manner.

The doctrine of the virgin conception is important because it is clearly implied throughout the New Testament. In this respect it is similar to the doctrine of the Trinity which is also everywhere implied in the Bible but nowhere expressly stated. (The passage in 1 John 5:7 is not found in any reliable Greek manuscript and is rightly omitted from modern versions —though the questionable rendering is provided as an interesting footnote in the New International Version of the Bible). Paul, for example, believes in the real human birth of the Lord Jesus and in His deity. So in Romans 1:3-4 he says that Christ, "as to his human nature was a descendant of David," yet, "through the Spirit of holiness was declared with power to be the Son of God by his resurrection from the dead". In Galatians 4:4 we read that, "God sent his son, born of a woman, born under law." In 2 Timothy 2:8 Paul reiterates his doctrinal position: "Remember Jesus Christ, raised from the dead, descended from David. This is my gospel ......" The writer of Hebrews affirms the same thing: "since the children have flesh and blood, he too shared in their humanity" (2:14).

The virgin conception is also implied in the Gospel and epistles of John. Although no direct reference to the virgin conception is made as we have seen, it is also true that John omits to mention the temptations and the transfiguration —two other important facets of Jesus' life and ministry. John does not repeat facts already well known, nor details supplied by the other three evangelists who wrote before him. He implies his readers already know about baptism and even his doctrine of the Logos —the Word. John adds detail only to those aspects that illustrate his thesis that "Jesus is the Christ, the Son of God, and that by believing you may have life in his name" (John 20:31). John nevertheless places emphasis on the fact of Christ's genuine humanity and His absolute deity —both implying one common foundation, that of His virgin birth. The following verses from John's writings illustrate the point:

The Word became flesh and made his dwelling among us. We have seen his glory, the glory of the One and Only, who came from the Father, full of grace and truth.

John 1:14

The life appeared; we have seen it and testify to it, and we proclaim to you the eternal life, which was with the Father and has appeared to us.

1 John 1:2

This is how you can recognise the Spirit of God: Every spirit that acknowledges that Jesus Christ has come in the flesh is from God, but every spirit that does not acknowledge Jesus is not from God.

1 John 4:2-3

This is the one who came by water and blood —Jesus Christ. He did not come by water only, but by water and blood. And it is the Spirit who testifies, because the Spirit is the truth.

1 John 5:6

The creeds of the early Christian church refer plainly to Christ as 'conceived by the Holy Spirit and born of the Virgin Mary' which shows that the doctrine was an integral belief of the early Roman church and part of its baptismal confession of faith. The fact that the creed was used as part of the baptism rite suggests that it had already become an essential part of accepted doctrine. A creed is simply crystallised belief and crystallisation takes time.

As Justin Martyr and Ignatius quote the creed in their writings, and the latter died no later than AD 117, we may reasonably conjecture that the creed was in use by AD 100. Note also that the apostles' creed contains only the barest necessities, so we may assume that the virgin conception was from early times reckoned to be among the essentials of the Christian faith. Finally, since the Roman church was at this time the centre of Christianity, we may reckon that belief in the virgin conception was held by the entire church at that time.

The scriptures concerning the Virgin Mary

Let us look again at the three main Scriptures concerning the virgin conception. The words in parentheses are added by the author to assist explanation:

Matt 1:18-25   Joseph's dream and decision

This is how the birth of Jesus Christ came about: His mother Mary was pledged to be married to Joseph, but before they came together, she was found to be with child through the Holy Spirit. Because Joseph her husband was a righteous man and did not want to expose her to public disgrace, he had in mind to divorce her quietly. But after he had considered this, an angel of the Lord appeared to him in a dream and said, "Joseph son of David, do not be afraid to take Mary home as your wife, because what is conceived in her is from the Holy Spirit. She will give birth to a son, and you are to give him the name Jesus, because he will save his people from their sins."

All this took place to fulfil what the Lord had said through the prophet: "The virgin [Greek *parthenos* Ed] will be with child and will give birth to a son, and they will call him Immanuel —which means "God with us."

When Joseph woke up, he did what the angel of the Lord had commanded him and took Mary home as his wife. But he had no union with her until she gave birth to a son. And he gave him the name Jesus.

Luke 1:26-37   Annunciation of birth of Jesus Christ, Mary, Elizabeth, Mary's song

In the sixth month, God sent the angel Gabriel to Nazareth, a town in Galilee, to a virgin pledged to be married to a man named Joseph, a descendent of David. The virgin's name was Mary. The angel went to her and said, "Greetings, you who are highly favoured! The Lord is with you." Mary was greatly troubled at his words and wondered what kind of greeting this might be.

But the angel said to her, "Do not be afraid, Mary, you have found favour with God. You will be with child and give birth to a son, and you are to give him the name Jesus. He will be great and will be called the son of the Most High. The Lord will give him the throne of his father David, and he will reign over the house of Jacob for ever; his kingdom will never end."

How will this be," Mary asked the angel, "since I am a virgin?" The angel answered, "The Holy Spirit will come upon you, and the power of the Most High will overshadow you. So the holy one will be called the son of God. Even Elizabeth your relative is going to have a child in her old age, and she who was said to be barren is in her sixth month. For nothing is impossible with God."

Isaiah 7:10-17

Again the Lord spoke to Ahaz, "Ask the Lord your God for a sign, whether in the deepest depths or the highest heights." But Ahaz said, "I will not ask; I will not put the Lord to the test."

Then Isaiah said, "Hear now, you house of David! Is it not enough to try the patience of men? Will you try the patience of my God also? Therefore the Lord himself will give you a sign: The Virgin [*Ed.* Hebrew *almah*] will be with child and will give birth to a son, and will call him Immanuel. He will eat curds and honey when he knows enough to reject the wrong and choose the right. But before the boy knows enough to reject the wrong and choose the right, the land of the two kings you dread will be laid waste. The Lord will bring on you and your people and on the house of your father a time unlike any since Ephraim broke away from Judah —he will bring the king of Assyria.

The historical situation presented in the book of Isaiah concerns the fortunes of Israel, then divided into two opposed kingdoms of Israel in the north and Judah in the south. Isaiah, as God's prophet, has been told by God to meet King Ahaz of Judah just outside the city of Jerusalem at the spring he was planning to divert and seal up against an attack by his enemies, the axis formed by the coalition of Israel and Syria. To repel this invasion, king Ahaz of Judah contemplated calling Assyria to his aid, something which God opposed. It was as if to defend himself against two fierce little puppies that a man should summon a wolf —something he obviously would not be able to control, and which would have dire long term consequences for Judah.

God accordingly told Ahaz through the prophet Isaiah not to ally himself with Assyria but that instead He, God, would save Judah. He promised that, to strengthen Ahaz's weak faith, He would grant any sign Ahaz asked for. Ahaz refused because he was determined not to trust God. Isaiah then said that God Himself would give Ahaz a sign. A virgin (Hebrew *almah*) would bear a son and before he was old enough to know the difference between right and wrong (presumably three years) the Israel/Syria coalition would be overthrown by Assyria.

We read in Isaiah chapter 8 how a child, not necessarily the same one, was to be called Maher-Shalal-Hash-Baz (Hebrew *quick to the plunder, swift to the spoil*) and how he was born to a prophetess (Isa 8:1-3). Twice the name Immanuel is used in chapter 8 (in verses 8 and 10) in the context of the thwarting of Ahaz's rebellious plans. Thus there was a double-fulfilment of this prophecy – as so often is the case with such messianic prophecies – one in the near term, answering the disbelief and rebellion of king Ahaz and one eight hundred years later when the name Immanuel would be understood in all its glory. As always, the scholar Alfred Edersheim has a perceptive comment on the real meaning of these prophecies. Referring to Joseph's dream and decision (in Matthew, above) he writes: "Viewing events, not as isolated, but as links welded in the golden chain of the history of the kingdom of God, 'all this' not only the birth of Jesus from a Virgin, not even His symbolic name with its import, but also the unrestful questioning of Joseph, 'happened' in fulfilment of what had been prefigured (Isa 7:14). The promise of a virgin-born son as a sign of the firmness of God's covenant of old with David and his house; the now unfolded meaning of the former symbolic name of *Immanuel*; even the unbelief of Ahaz, with its counterpart in the questioning of Joseph —'all this' could now be read in the light of the breaking day. Never had the house of David sunk morally lower than when, in the words of Ahaz, it seemed to renounce the very foundation of its claim to continuance; never had the fortunes of the house of David fallen lower, than when a Herod sat on its throne, and its lineal representative was a humble village carpenter, from whose heart doubts of the Virgin-Mother had to be Divinely chased..........But as nevertheless, the stability of the Davidic house was ensured by the future advent of *Immanuel* —and with such certainty that, before such a child could even discern between the choice of good and evil, the land would be freed of its dangers; so now all that had been prefigured was to become literally true, and Israel would be saved from its real danger by the advent of Jesus, Immanuel. And so it had all been intended."[4]

Critics, in attacking the biblical account of the virgin conception, often argue that the Greek word *parthenos* in the New Testament translated 'virgin' actually means 'young girl'. This is disingenuous. Both the word and the context make it quite obvious that in Luke 1:34, in her exchange with the angel, Mary was referring to the fact that she had had no physical relationship with a man.

Furthermore, the word *parthenos* always and unequivocally means virgin. It is interesting, in this regard, that the Hebrew word translated virgin in the messianic prophecy of Isaiah 7:14 is *almah*. The word *almah* usually, though not invariably, signifies a virgin. It was translated in the Greek Septuagint by the uncompromising word *parthenos*, which has only one meaning. The Septuagint was the Hellenist Jews' standard translation of the Hebrew Scriptures into Greek until the first century AD. As Christians used the word *parthenos* to defend the virgin conception of the Lord Jesus and made the Septuagint generally the Christian Bible, and as the Hebrew text was in any case undergoing revision in the first century, the Jews ceased to use the Septuagint and prepared a succession of other Greek translations, in which *almah* was translated not by *parthenos* but by *neanis* —a young woman, presumably (but not inevitably) unmarried.[5]

The significance of the Annunciation

The words of the conversation between Mary and the angel Gabriel that are recorded in Luke are heavy with scriptural and spiritual significance. The economy of the conversation – there are a little over one hundred and sixty words between them in an English translation – but the extraordinary spiritual scope that these few words convey, bear testimony to the inspired nature of the conversation itself, and the record that we have of it. This, in turn, adds weight to the normal Christian view that the account of the virgin conception we have is both accurate and truthful. Let us look again at the verbal exchange: the angel's disclosure to Mary of God's purpose was in two stages. The first emphasised her child's continuity with the past, because *she* would bear Him. The second laid emphasis on His discontinuity, His uniqueness, because the Holy Spirit would overshadow Mary.

In the first stage (verses 30-34), the angel told Mary that she would conceive and bear a son. The child, to be named 'Jesus', would be 'great', and would be called 'the son of the Most High'. This was a reference to His messianic ministry as Saviour. The angel said that Jesus would occupy the throne of His father David (verse 32) and would reign over the house of Jacob forever. In this way we can deduce that Jesus would inherit from His mother His humanity *and* title to the royal throne. Certainly this appears to be the implication, and the apostle Paul was later to underline this view when he wrote, "as to his human nature he was a descendant of David" (Rom 1:3). We already know that Joseph was also a descendant of David (Matt 1:20) and by accepting Jesus as his son Joseph gave Him all the legal rights of legitimate sonship (see below the legal basis on which this was achieved).

In the second stage (verse 35) the angel continued by explaining that the Holy Spirit would come upon Mary and that the *power* of the Most High – and in this we understand His *creative* power – would overshadow her. The deduction from this is that the 'holy one' (a reference to the Lord's sinlessness) will be called the 'son of God' and in this we perceive a deeper meaning than simply His messianic title. John Stott in *The Authentic Jesus* points out that what was announced to Mary was that her son's humanity and messiahship would be derived from her. She would conceive and bear Jesus, whilst his deity and sinlessness would be derived from the Holy Spirit who would powerfully overshadow her. Jesus' continuity with humanity would be traced from his natural birth via Mary, but his newness or discontinuity was via his supernatural conception by the Holy Spirit.

Jesus would be descended from Adam by his birth, but was also the second Adam – the head of a new humanity – by his conception by the Holy Spirit. As a result of the virgin conception the Lord Jesus was at one and the same time Mary's son and God's Son, human and divine. He was the Messiah descended from David and the sinless Saviour of sinners. As John Stott concludes, God is both sovereign and free in the choices He makes. He could perhaps have achieved all this in some other way, but the New Testament evidence remains clear that he chose to bring his Son into the world through a normal birth via a virgin conception. It is not difficult to understand its reasonableness and the appropriateness of this course.[6]

Compatibility of the virgin conception and the Messiah's descent from David

We consider once again that, had the Gospel writers wanted to falsely present Jesus as Messiah, they could quite simply have secured all the necessary Jewish and scriptural credentials for Him by referring to His ancestry via Joseph and Mary, and presenting to the world a 'normal' birth. Prima facie the virgin conception appears to deny His descent from David —so why should the Gospel writers introduce such a difficulty? The answer is surely that they did so because they believed it was true and, in honouring Jesus who was Himself 'the truth' (John 14:6) they unashamedly present this truth, irrespective of the difficulties it introduces.

The virgin conception, as should now be abundantly clear, removes Joseph's biological role in the procreative process which means that *in a physical sense*, Jesus was arguably not the 'son of David'. How do the Gospel writers then think of Jesus as 'son of David'? As noted in the previous chapter Bishop Paul Barnett has commented with precision on this very issue: how could the Gospel writers Matthew and Luke have thought of Jesus as the "son of David", when Joseph was not Jesus' biological father? A serious question, the answer to which must be that Joseph was the legal father, if not the biological father. Joseph transmits to Christ his 'crown rights' as Joseph represented, in himself, the regal-legal line. Being a direct descendant of David through Solomon he possessed the crown rights. "But for the misfortune of his race" writes H. Brash Bonsall, "he would have been known not as the carpenter of Nazareth but as King Joseph I and, by Jewish law, he could pass on these rights to his foster son, Jesus the Christ."[8] We see then, that there is no legal incompatibility between the virgin conception and the Lord Jesus' descent from King David.

Modern attacks on the Virgin Birth

Attacks upon the 'virgin birth' are almost as old as Christianity. What we tend to see is a repetition of arguments that have been heard and answered in the past, but which, to each new generation, may appear to be genuine new arguments. It also needs to be said that because of widespread and significant ignorance of what the Bible *actually* says and how attacks upon the Bible have been answered in the past, these common forms of attack may appear to casual observers to be quite compelling. Sadly, many churchgoing Christians have not much troubled themselves to look in detail at this key area of the virgin conception and consider it to be the responsibility of theologians to sort out! This is a great pity, as it means that they are themselves often ill-prepared to meet challenges to their own faith. It may confidently be predicted that many of the arguments we are about to consider will be heard again in the future. So the virgin conception, along with the resurrection, the creation, and the authority of the Bible will always be battlegrounds for Christians. Each new generation will find itself fighting the same old battles!

Attempts to brush off the historicity of the biblical records need to be treated with some scepticism. As we look at the arguments of the sceptics we need to ask ourselves: exactly who are these 'scholars' —if indeed they claim to be such? What are their qualifications? Do they have a hidden agenda? If they claim text-tampering on the part of the church, precisely *what* records indicate there were later changes? What is the weight to be attached firstly to 'evidence' they are able to present and secondly to the existing and widely accepted manuscript evidence? Bear in mind, it is easy for ANYONE to 'rubbish' the biblical (or any historical) account —but exactly where are these people coming from? What is their own agenda?

The current attack on Mary coalesces around the following propositions:

1. The virgin birth was not prophesied.
2. The prophecy in Isaiah 7:14 is a false translation.
3. The name Immanuel appears only once in Matthew and is a quotation of a false translation of Isaiah.
4. Immanuel was born at the time of Isaiah and not later.
5. Immanuel was not perfect.
6. The word *almah* normally means 'young woman' and not 'virgin'.
7. A number of other ancient stories involve 'virgin births'.

We will examine these propositions in turn:

1. 'The virgin birth was not prophesied'

Critics seek to undermine the prophecy in Isaiah 7: 14 ("Therefore the Lord himself will give you a sign: the virgin will be with child and will give birth to a son, and will call him Immanuel" – NIV). We saw in an earlier study that there was in fact an historic context in which Isaiah gave this message from God to king Ahaz. But the first thing to observe about the passage is that it is at the beginning of a fairly lengthy series of chapters, not just verses, which are almost totally messianic in content. These take us through to Isaiah chapter 11 (although there are messianic prophecies throughout Isaiah; readers interested to see the full scope of these are referred to Appendix 9 of Alfred Edersheim's *The Life and Times of Jesus*) but the particular verse in question was *not* seen by first century Jews as being messianic. This fact undermines any view that Matthew was trying to 'fit' Jesus' life into a pattern of known messianic prophecies. It was only in retrospect that the Gospel writers saw the connection, referred to above, between the Lord Jesus and Isaiah's verse concerning Immanuel.

Critics argue that the infant referred to in Isaiah 7 is the child born in Isaiah chapter 8. This is possible, but unlikely. Even if it was the same child, this does not undermine the fact that the prophecy had both a near-term and a long-term outworking. It should be noted that the child in chapter 8 was given an entirely different name, at God's instruction, being Maher-Shalal-Hash-Baz - a name with a meaning connected to the defeat of the Israel/Syria axis which was then poised against Judah. To most Christians, the linkage of the verse in Isaiah 7 to the beginning of a series of messianic prophecies, and the fact that Matthew recognised it as such, seems entirely reasonable.

2. 'The prophecy in Isaiah 7:14 is a false translation'

This is connected with objection 6 below, so the two are dealt with together. We have already seen the normal meaning of *almah* is a virgin. The fact that later Jewish translations of the word in the key verse in Isaiah changed it from *almah* to *neanis* – a young woman – speaks volumes. The normal meaning of the word and the context make the normative Christian interpretation beyond reasonable dispute.

3. 'The name Immanuel appears only once in Matthew and is a quotation of a false translation of Isaiah'

Immanuel – *God with us* – is used only once in the New Testament and twice in the Old —both times in Isaiah. The fact that Jesus is *only* referred to as Immanuel in the context of the fulfilment of Isaiah's prophecy is by no means extraordinary. More than fifty titles are applied to the Lord Jesus in the pages of the New Testament, and most are used only once or twice. But Jesus' deity – the fact that He *is* God with us – is referred to everywhere in the New Testament, both directly and by implication.

By the sovereign action of God, a virgin was able to conceive and give birth —no human father was involved. Why is this significant? The *name* Immanuel tells us: *God* with us —there is, realistically, no other way for this to be true other than by a virgin birth. God *with* us —born of a human mother. One hundred per cent human and one hundred per cent God.

4. 'Immanuel was born at the time of Isaiah and not later'

This was dealt with in (1) above.

5. 'Immanuel was not perfect'

The reasoning here is that in Isaiah 7:16 the prophet refers to the child Immanuel not knowing the difference between right and wrong. Since Jesus was born as a human being and had in every sense a normal childhood except that He did not sin, we may assume that, as a normal baby, infant and child, there were times when He did not fully know the difference between right and wrong. The Bible's claim is only that He did not sin, not that He had supernatural understanding from his first day of life! Furthermore, allowing that the child referred to as Immanuel in King Ahaz's day was not Jesus (and nobody thinks that he was!) we might conjecture that this child, as he grew up, also had to make choices between right and wrong and sometimes, as a result, he sinned! Never lose sight of the fact that the first outworking of the prophecy, in the life of King Ahaz, was simply that before 'Immanuel' was fully able to discern the difference between right and wrong, Judah's enemies would be defeated. And indeed they were.

6. 'The word almah normally means "young woman" and not "virgin"' This was dealt with in (2) above.

7. 'A number of other ancient stories involve "virgin births"'
They do. However these stories were fantastic, not to mention in some cases extremely crude. They were myth and no doubt understood as such. Those who quote such stories (especially on the internet) may make themselves sound very knowledgeable but a quick check against even non-specialist publications such as the Encyclopaedia Britannica, reveal serious misquotes and wrong dates attributed to these stories. The big difference we need to keep in mind is that these myths developed and evolved over (in some cases) many centuries. There is no equivalence with the Bible's near contemporary eyewitness reports and an acknowledged and carefully guarded canon of scripture.

Conclusion
That non-Christians should have difficulty with the virgin conception is not, at first sight, surprising. It is hoped that in this chapter, as elsewhere in this book, the reliability of the Gospel witnesses and the appropriateness of the action of God in bringing His Son into the world in this way, has been demonstrated. The disbelief of those – and in fact it is only a very few – who claim to be adherents of the Christian faith is rather more surprising, in particular because it calls into question just what sort of a 'god' they actually believe in. Critics of the biblical account of the virgin conception need to answer some serious questions:
* Why should the gospel writers invent a fable, knowing it would invite adverse comment, even ridicule?

* Why did a doctor such as Luke, an educated man, risk his reputation by reporting the story —and reporting it as fact?
* Why was the account of Jesus' birth not omitted by the early church from its creeds? By this time it was indeed drawing unfavourable comment.
* Why has the church always treated Mary with the utmost reverence, if she was no more than a loose woman?

It was a blessed duty and honour for Mary to bear the Christ child. We have already seen in Chapter 7, that the virgin conception has always been a battleground for Christians and their critics, and a truth of great importance to defend. We may recognise in some Bible-detractors unbelief borne first and foremost from a lack of personal knowledge and experience of God. But we should not forget that all attacks on truth *ultimately* have one source: "He was a murderer from the beginning, not holding to the truth, for there is no truth in him. When he lies, he speaks his native language, for he is a liar and the father of lies" (John 8:44). We should perhaps spend a few moments reflecting on what Jesus Himself said about the devil and 'the devil's children'. This is found in John 8:42-47 (italics added):

Jesus said to them, "If God were your Father, you would love me, for I came from God and now am here. I have not come on my own; but he sent me. Why is my language not clear to you? *Because you are unable to hear what I say.* You belong to your father, the devil, and you want to carry out your father's desire. He was a murderer from the beginning, not holding to the truth, for there is no truth in him. When he lies, he speaks his native language, for he is a liar and the father of lies. Yet because I tell the truth, you do not believe me! Can any of you prove me guilty of sin? If I am telling the truth, why don't you believe me? He who belongs to God hears what God says. *The reason you do not hear is that you do not belong to God.*"

This stark and simple statement by the Lord Jesus helps us to understand from where all untruth originates and why those who are not *born again*, to use Jesus' own term, cannot fully understand spiritual truth (see also 1 Cor 2:14; 2 Cor 4: 4; Rom 8:5-8). Reading this we might panic and ask, as the disciples did, "who then can be saved?" (Matt 19:25). Jesus' answer to them is an encouragement to all people, everywhere. Look it up and see for yourself! We need to keep in mind that for truth such as the virgin conception to be fully understood, as opposed to partly understood, the Father must 'draw' us to enable us to come to Him. (John 6:44f.)

We have referred several times in this chapter to John Stott's excellent short book *The Authentic Jesus*, which includes a chapter on the virgin conception. In relation to the so-called 'liberal' wing of the church, which tends to disbelieve the biblical account of Christ's birth, Stott's concluding remarks are telling. He comments that as Christians we need the humility of Mary who so completely accepted God's purpose for her life in that simple response, 'May it be to me as you have said.' There is a common tendency today to reject the virgin conception because it does not mesh neatly with our modern prejudices. Many reject miracles in general and the virgin conception in particular, because they believe the universe to be a closed system and fail to see the anomaly of dictating to our Creator God what he is permitted to do in His own creation. It would certainly be more modest to imitate Mary's faithful response of submissiveness to God's revelation.

Mary had great courage: she was so willing for God to fulfil his purposes that she was prepared to risk the social stigma of being an unmarried mother, thought an adulteress and being seen as having borne an illegitimate child. She surrendered her reputation to God's will. Perhaps the major cause of theological liberalism is that some scholars care rather more for their own reputation than for God's revelation. It is frankly hard to be ridiculed for being credulous enough to believe in miracles and some theologians are undoubtedly tempted to sacrifice the biblical account of Christ's birth on the altar of their own respectability. Theologian John Stott acknowledges how strong this temptation can be, but concludes that ultimately it is more important that we allow God to be God and to do things His way, even if by so doing we share with Mary the risk of losing our own reputation.[9]

Notes

[1] John Stott *The Authentic Jesus* (Marshall Morgan and Scott, 1985), p. 59.

[2] *Ibid.* p. 60.

[3] *Ibid.* p. 62.

[4] *Op. cit. The Life and Times of Jesus the Messiah*, p. 110.

[5] This again shows how early the fact of the virgin conception had become an issue between Christians and Jews.

[6] *Op. cit. The Authentic Jesus*, p. 65.

[7] See Paul Barnett *Bethlehem to Patmos* (Hodder and Stoughton, 1989), p. 19.

[8] H. Brash Bonsall *The Person of Christ* Volume 1: The Doctrine (CLC, 1967), p. 44.

[9] *Op. cit. The Authentic Jesus*, pp. 66f.

13

25th December? Was the Bethlehem Birth Prophesied?

The dangers of precision

The Bible does not give the date of birth of the Lord Jesus. We may question, in any case, whether any real importance attaches to the actual date. It may be that God, in His wisdom, ensured that the precise date shall remain a mystery simply to prevent too much superstition surrounding it, and the birth of Jesus becoming too prominent in the minds of Christians. Whilst the birth of the Lord Jesus is an historic fact, He did not come into the world in order to give us an annual jamboree. He came to achieve the purpose of God to make available the possibility of a right relationship between man and God, a relationship summarised in one word —salvation. We might also reflect on the fact that the celebration called 'Christmas' in the Western world today has, to a large extent, been hijacked by secular and commercial interests —something we may assume that God foresaw. So, if 'Christmas' had become even more prominent in the minds of Christians, by virtue of a known historic date, this could do more harm than good to non-believers as they see the true meaning of the celebration being thoroughly subordinated to other interests. Perhaps God has guarded against this by keeping the precise date a mystery.

Some Christians have distanced themselves from an excessive focus on Christmas as a celebration. Non-Christian cults, such as the Jehovah's Witnesses, refuse to have anything to do with Christmas because, they say, it is idolatrous. These cults deny the deity and Lordship of Jesus. Other religions, for example the Muslim faith, deny that Jesus is God's Son (though they defend the virgin-conception) and deny the death and resurrection of Jesus. Yet other religions, such as the Hindu faith, view Christ as just one of many 'gods' and are to that extent willing to tolerate Christmas as a celebration.

For Christians, and by this term is meant believing and renewed followers of the Lord Jesus in the sense of John 3:16, there is a difficult dividing line between genuine rejoicing at the birth of the Lord Jesus and becoming part of a false and often very ugly habit of excess which coincides with the Christmas season. Without, then, wishing to arouse undue emphasis on what is very much a secondary matter, the actual date of Christ's birth, Christians need to be aware of the conflicting views of the time of year that the Lord Jesus was born. This is especially important as there is a case made that Christians simply grafted "Christmas" onto pre-existing pagan winter celebrations. We will look at the arguments.

Mithras

Some hold the view that the 'Christmas' celebration was part of the early church's response to the growing threat of an Eastern religion known as Mithraism. Mithra, or Mithras, was in ancient Indo-Persian mythology, the god of light. According to legend, Mithra was born bearing a torch and armed with a knife, beside a sacred stream and under a sacred tree, a child of the earth itself. He soon rode and later killed a cosmic bull, whose blood fertilises all vegetation. Mithra's slaying of the bull became a popular subject in Hellenic art and became the forerunner of bull-slaying fertility rituals in the Mithraic cult, which may in turn be the origin of modern bull fighting. It is interesting to contrast the fantastic ideas about Mithras with the quiet and restrained record of the birth of the Lord Jesus.

The first written record of the Vedic 'Mitra' dates to 1,400 BC. Mitra worship spread from India to Persia and, after Alexander the Great's victory over the Persians, spread throughout the Hellenic world, although it never became popular with the Greeks because they identified the religion with their age-old enemies, the Persians. The cult spread from India in the east as far west as Spain, Germany and Britain so that in the third and fourth centuries AD the Mithras cult was the greatest rival to the steadily growing Christian faith. The sudden burgeoning of interest in Mithras in the Roman empire suggests that Roman Mithraism was to all intents and purposes a new creation, possibly brought about by some long-forgotten religious guru who may have lived as late as AD 100. Christians conjecture that the cult owed its rapid rise in popularity to a well-timed Satanic counter-attack upon Christianity.

Roman Mithraism was a religion of loyalty to the king and was carried and supported by the Roman military class. There was little notice of the religion in Rome until the beginning of the second century AD but from the year 136 onwards, archaeologists have discovered hundreds of dedicatory inscriptions to Mithras. The cult seems to have been encouraged by successive Roman emperors, in particular Commodus (180-182), Septimuis Severus (193-211) and Caracalla (211-217). Most adherents known to modern scholars were high and low ranking soldiers and other Roman officials. It seems that adherence to Mithras may have been seen as a way to social and professional advancement.

Within a few generations, the Roman world had completely assimilated this Persian god amongst their pantheon of deities and when the emperor Diocletian attempted a renewal of the Roman state and religion, he did not forget Mithra. In AD 307 in a dedication near Vienna, Diocletian dedicated an altar to Mithra as patron of the empire. However in AD 312 Constantine won the battle at the Milvian Bridge under the sign of a cross and the Roman empire quickly turned towards Christianity. Worship of Mithras seems to have collapsed with the change in adherence by the emperor although some noble families opposed to the emperor continued the old religion, but only to worship Mithras alongside other traditional Roman deities.

Origin of a December celebration of Christmas

The argument is sometimes heard that the date of 25 December was chosen by the early church fathers to coincide with the pagan celebration of Mithras. It is said that Jesus' birth is more likely to have occurred in spring than in winter, because Luke tells us that shepherds were "living out in the fields nearby" and that shepherds guarded their flocks by night as well as day *only* at lambing time, whereas in the winter the animals were kept in barn yards, unwatched. Precise evidence for ancient near-eastern shepherding practice is unclear, but the theory seems to be exactly that— a theory.

The idea of celebrating Christmas on December 25th, the theory continues, was first suggested in the early fourth century, a clever move upon the part of the church fathers, who wished to eclipse the December 25 festivities associated with Mithras. Roman patricians and plebians alike enjoyed festivals of a protracted nature, so the church felt it needed a December celebration of its own. In order to offer converts a celebratory occasion in which to take pride, the church officially recognised Christ's birth which, up to that time, had received no interest among Christians. To offer head-on competition with the Mithras feast, the date of December 25 was chosen, and after Constantine was converted to Christianity the 'Christmas' celebration became an official Roman feast some time in the mid 300s. A neat theory and attractive because it simultaneously relieves Christians of any necessity to defend December 25th as being in any way special, whilst explaining how we reached our present situation as regards Christmas. However, the theory may be wrong, as we shall see.

The Great Paschal period — BC and AD

Before we attempt to review the conflicting evidence for the date of Christ's birth, we need to consider the year. We have already looked at how the year of Christ's birth was deduced and how most scholars consider 6 BC to be the most likely year —but why is this not 0 BC or even AD 1? In ancient times a number of different major calendar systems were in use across the globe and it was not until the fifth century that the modern calendar was developed. In AD 463 Victorius of Aquitaine, who had been appointed by Pope Hilarius to undertake calendar revision, devised the Great Paschal (i.e. Passover) period. In the sixth century one Dionysius Exiguus (Dionysius the Little), a Scythian monk in Rome, in computing the date of Easter, took the year now called AD 532 as the first year of the Great Paschal period and the year now designated 1 BC as the beginning of the previous cycle. Dionysius fixed the date of the Christian era by working backwards. Among biblical data Dionysius had to work with was the following:

* Luke 3:1 —Jesus was baptised in the fifteenth year of the reign of Emperor Tiberius.

* Luke 3:23 —Jesus was baptised about 30 years of age, at the beginning of his ministry

Dionysius Exiguus, however, made several mistakes and miscalculations. He forgot the year zero which should have been inserted between 1 BC and AD 1. He also overlooked the four years when the Emperor Augustus had reigned under his own name Octavian. So, in the sixth century it was generally believed that AD 1 was the year of the birth of Christ and Dionysius introduced the idea of numbering years consecutively throughout the Christian era. The Dionysius method was used by some scholars but did not become widespread until it was popularised by the Venerable Bede of Jarrow (673-735) whose reputation as a scholar was extremely high in Western Christendom in the eighth century. This system of BC/AD threw into sharp relief the different systems then in use for reckoning the *beginning* of each year.

Pope Gregory XIII (1502-1585) noting that, for a variety of reasons, the calendar year was thirteen days behind the solar year, directed that ten days in 1582 should be dropped, the day of 4 October becoming 15 October. This so called Gregorian calendar was not universally accepted at the time, and was not adopted in Britain until 1752 when 03 to 13 September were dropped. Apparently protests were held in the streets demanding the "return" of the missing eleven days!

When the Gregorian calendar firmly established 1 January as

the beginning of each year, it was widely referred to as the New Style calendar, with the Julian calendar referred to as the Old Style calendar. In Britain, under the Julian calendar, the year had originally been computed as running from 25 December but later, from the fourteenth century, it was computed as beginning on 25 March. It was some hundreds of years before all of Western Europe (and the Americas) adopted the same calendar. Allowing that these different systems were in use, it can be recognised that computing the year of Christ's birth, let alone the actual date, would never be a straightforward matter.

The date of Christ's birth

In contrast with the primary Christian feasts of Easter (celebrating the resurrection) and the Lord's day as the weekly remembrance of the resurrection, there was, as far as is known, no early interest in the date of the Lord's birth nor indeed any annual remembrance of it. The Christian theologian Origen (b. c. 185, d. c. 254), who was the most important biblical scholar of the early Greek church, although he almost certainly visited the Bethlehem cave of the Nativity seems to have considered a birthday observance as a pagan ritual, and he claimed that only such persons as Pharaoh and Herod had their birthdays celebrated.

The earliest known statement of Christ's birth date was made by Origen's predecessor, Clement of Alexandria, writing in his *Stromata* in about AD 194. He cites a number of different dates and years then in vogue and goes on to give his own definitive statement: "Our Lord was born in the twenty eighth year ... in the reign of Augustus .... From the birth of Christ .... to the death of Commodus are, in all, a hundred and ninety four years, one month, thirteen days" (*Stromata* I 21, 145).[1] The reign of Augustus in Egypt, to which Clement would naturally refer, began in August of the year 30 BC, so the indicated year is 3/2 BC. The murder of the emperor Commodus took place on December 31 AD 192, so the precisely indicated date is 18 November in 3 BC Now this date is certainly wrong, because Jesus was certainly born before the death of Herod 'the great', and Herod died in the spring of 4

BC. We have already seen that the probable year of Christ's birth is 6 BC. Clement's assessment, however, is interesting – being the earliest – in that it places Christ's birth in mid-winter, as do a number of other ancient documents.

December 25 first appears in the year AD 354 as the officially accepted date in the Roman city calendar (an almanac for the use of Christians) edited by one Furius Dionysius Filocalus and based on a list probably drawn up in AD 336. Here the date of Christ's birth is the same as the date then accepted as the winter solstice, and sun worship was then widespread in the Roman Empire. Earlier, in AD 274, the emperor Aurelian had declared the 'unconquered sun' the official deity of the Roman Empire and set the deity's birthday celebration as December 25. It should be noted that at this time sun worship and Mithras worship were almost indistinguishable.

Ultimately, as Jack Finegan points out in *The Archaeology of the New Testament* (reference below), the full equation with the solar year was completed by the belief that the crucifixion as well as the conception took place on 25 March and the Lord's birth on 25 December. Thus Augustine (354-430) writing *On the Trinity* says, "For he is believed to have been conceived on the twenty-fifth of March, upon which day he also suffered .... But he was born, according to tradition, upon December the twenty fifth." From the west the 25 December date spread to the east. Finegan points out that the seal upon the acceptance of 25 December as Christ's birthday was the sermons of a famous early church leader John Chrysostom (c. 347-407) who from his pulpit preached that Christ's birthday was the holiest day of the year because without it, Christ could not have been baptised, crucified or risen. Chrysostom elsewhere says this date was known earlier in the west, but was known among the Antioch Christians for only some ten years. Since this date was so new to his hearers, Chrysostom offered three proofs that the date was the correct one:

1. Remembering what Gamaliel had said (Acts 5:38-39) about failure or success of the apostolic cause, he argued that the new

date would not have won such wide acceptance unless it was the right one.

2. The date is confirmed by the census (Luke 2:1-7) of which there was public record in Rome (to which record Justin, *Apology* I 34 and Tertullion, *Against Marcion* IV 7, also refer).

3. Exegesis of Scripture also confirms the date. The announcement of the birth of John the Baptiser to Zechariah came when it was Zechariah's turn to enter the temple and burn incense. Chrysostom assumes, incorrectly, that Zechariah was high priest and the occasion of the announcement was therefore the Day of Atonement —the one day of the year when the high priest entered the Holy of Holies in the temple. By a careful process of extrapolation, too complex to enter into here, Chrysostom calculates the date of Christ's birth to be 25 December. Jack Finegan comments: 'Although some of Chrysostom's assumptions were no doubt incorrect, some modern studies have followed somewhat similar lines by trying to establish when Zechariah's priestly division was on duty, and counting from there. In the organisation of the Priesthood there were twenty-four divisions or courses, of which the first was that of Jehoiarib and the eighth was that of Abijah, to which Zechariah belonged (Lev 24:7-18). Each course served one week at a time beginning on the sabbath (Josephus *Antiquities* 7:14:7:365) and if the sequence were followed through twice it would make forty-eight weeks, but it is not known how the remaining weeks of a fifty two week year were covered.... Some think that the courses followed each other in unbroken succession without regard to the beginning and ending of years, others that the sequence began afresh at the first month of Nissan or the seventh month of Tishri.

In the Talmud (*Ta'anith* 29a SBT 9, p. 154) it is stated that the first temple was destroyed on the ninth day of Ab (July/August) and the course of Jehoiarib was on duty at the time, and it was the same with the second temple (destroyed AD 70). Counting backward from this point one study finds that in the year 6 BC, before the birth of Jesus the course of Abijah would have been on duty during the week of October 2-9. From this point, fifteen months (six for Elizabeth and nine for Mary) would come toward the end of December (and quite reasonably on December 25) in the following year (5 BC) .... and this reckoning is not far from that by Chrysostom...... approximation is safer than exact dates in some conclusions, nevertheless there are several pointers in the foregoing toward the midwinter for the season of the birth of Jesus, and it may be thought not impossible that there was authentic tradition to that effect at least, while in respect of the later ministry of Jesus as well as to his birth, astronomical and calendrical data may allow greater exactitude.'[2]

And the shepherds in the fields?

It is often said that Jesus' birth is more likely to have occurred in spring than in winter, because Luke tells us that shepherds were "living out in the fields nearby" and that shepherds guarded their flocks by night as well as day *only* at lambing time, whereas in the winter animals were kept in barn yards, unwatched. We saw in chapter 8 that there is good reason to suppose that the shepherds referred to in Luke chapter 2 were not ordinary shepherds and that their lambs were not ordinary lambs. To recap, we refer once again to the helpful work of Alfred Edersheim. He points out that a passage in the Mishnah (Shek 7: 4) leads to the conclusion that the flocks which pastured at Migdal Eder were destined for temple sacrifices. The Mishna, says Edersheim, "...expressly forbids the keeping of flocks throughout the land of Israel except in the wilderness —and the only flocks otherwise kept, would be those for the temple-services........ accordingly, the shepherds who watched over them, were not ordinary shepherds. The latter were under the ban of Rabbinism, on account of their necessary isolation from religious ordinances and their manner of life, which rendered strict legal observance unlikely, if not absolutely impossible. The same Mishnic passage also leads us to infer that these flocks lay out *all the year round*, since they are spoken of as in the fields thirty days before passover —that is, in the month of February, when in Palestine the average rainfall is nearly greatest. Thus, Jewish tradition in some dim manner apprehended the first revelation of the Messiah from that *Migdal Eder*, where shepherds watched the temple flocks all the year round."[3]

There is a clear inference that these shepherds were watching over their flocks during the winter. This again lends support to the idea of a midwinter birth of the Lord Jesus. In conclusion, we simply cannot be dogmatic about the date of birth of our Lord and nor should we be. We can say, however, that the evidences for a midwinter birth are as strong as the evidence for a birth at any other time of the year. Whilst critics like to sneer and say that 'Christmas' is simply Christianity competing with pagan religions, we might conjecture that, in the realm of spiritual warfare, the reality may actually be the reverse: satanically inspired pagan religions may have adopted winter feasts to introduce an element of doubt as to the timing of the Lord's birth. This author's view, for what it is worth, is that it is more, rather than less likely that the Lord Jesus was born on 25 December.

Was the birth in Bethlehem prophesied?

The most breathtakingly absurd view to have emerged in recent years is that Bethlehem was not a place but a person. We will look at the 'logic' of this shortly. But it is worth reflecting on the vigour with which critics seek to 'rubbish' what the Bible says. Aside from the obvious realm of spiritual warfare in which Christians are always engaged (Ephesians 6:12), would it be too simplistic to suggest that those who expend most effort in attacking the Bible are those who, in reality, are most afraid that its claims are true and so live with the nagging fear of the logical conclusion that this truth demands a personal response? The response can only be of faith and surrender or rejection and attack.

In attacking the biblical account of the Nativity, anti-Christians will sometimes go to considerable lengths to question any and every aspect of the account. The position of Bethlehem in the narrative has accordingly come under scrutiny. In Chapter 10 we looked briefly at Bethlehem and its connection with the Nativity. Of most significance is the fact that Bethlehem was well known, to first century Jews, as being the place where the Messiah would be born. King Herod "the Great" turned to his chief priests and teachers of the law who gave the emphatic "in Bethlehem in Judaea" to answer his question about where the Christ would be born (Matt 2:5). It is, therefore, an uncomfortable and unwelcome fact to atheists that Jesus was born there. If this awkward and unwelcome fact can be denied, so much the better!

We should always carefully weigh biblical criticism, from whatever source, but especially where it attacks what the Bible says. A common trick is to alter punctuation in strategic places and to run verses into each other to alter the apparent meaning. Another is to paraphrase groups of verses but to present them as though, on a cursory inspection, they are *the actual verses verbatim*. Yet another is to quote from different versions of the Bible when 'investigating' the meaning of verses *in conjunction with each other*. These tricks are all used in the modern attack on the position of Bethlehem in the Gospel narratives and the Old Testament prophecies which refer to the Bethlehem birth.

The author came across the following 'scholarship' in anti-Christian sites on the internet. The basic premise is that the first century Gospel writers, believing the Old Testament to be the word of God, thought they had to 'fit' the 'Jesus story' into what was prophesied of old. It is worth asking ourselves again, what real benefit could the Gospel writers have achieved by deliberately falsifying their accounts. If they knew the accounts were lies, would they have risked their lives, liberties and reputations for them? Surely there were more congenial ways of spending time in first century Judaea?

The prophet Micah

Critics say that the words used in Matthew 2:6 ("But you, Bethlehem, in the land of Judah, are by no means least among the rulers of Judah; for out of you will come a ruler who will be the shepherd of my people Israel"), which are themselves a quotation of the prophet Micah in chapter 5 and verse 2 of the book which bears his name, refer not to Bethlehem the place but Bethlehem a person. So, they say, he is referred to as a 'ruler'. These critics point out, rightly, that the words in Micah are actually 'Bethlehem Ephrathah' but go on to say that this was a person. In support of this they run Micah 5:5 into one sentence which they roughly portray as "this man shall be the peace, when the Assyrian shall come into the land". It is not known what translation, if any, is used in this rendering, but all modern translations known to this author recognise a break in verse 5, where the prophecy concludes with the statement that the man born in Bethlehem will be the peace of the world (full stop!) and then goes on to refer to deliverance from the Assyrian invader.

In support of the view that Bethlehem was a person, critics then quote from 1 Chronicles 2:50 where, in a very long list of descendants of the clans of Caleb, there is referred to Salma, the father of Bethlehem and Hareph the father of Beth Gader. It is again unclear which translation is being used in this rendering, but modern translations known to the author render this Salma the *founder* of Bethlehem and Hareph the *founder* of Beth Gader. Be this as it may, it is unclear what possible connection there may be between a supposed person called 'Bethlehem' referred to in Chronicles and Micah's alleged person called Bethlehem, being a peacemaker for Judah at the time of the Assyrian troubles in king Hezekiah's reign (720-693 BC).

Muddying the waters still more, we are then presented with a conjecture that 'Bethlehem Ephrathah' of Micah was a proper name, referring back to Bethlehem son of Salma who was a grandson of someone called Ephrathah —who is indeed referred to in 1 Chronicles chapter 2. All this strikes one as being a fairly ragged attempt to link together random names which actually have no logical linkage. If the modern Bible translations are right, then Salma was founder of Bethlehem rather than a father of someone by that name. But Jack Finegan has a more scholarly approach to Bethlehem Ephrathah as he refers to Rachel's burial place: "Gen 35:19 and 48:7 state that the burial place of Rachel was, 'on the way to Ephrath' (that is Bethlehem). The wording suggests that Ephrath or Ephrathah was an older village that was absorbed into Bethlehem and in Micah 5:2 the two names are put together."[4]

Before leaving Micah, we should stop and look at the full prophecy. The debate above is over individual words taken out of the context in which they are written. If we read the entire book of Micah, who was a contemporary of Isaiah, we see that the book is a warning to the people of Israel that destruction from external invaders awaits them unless they repent and turn back to the Lord. But as so often with the writings of prophets, there is a strong allusion to the future Saviour. So, in Micah chapter 5 and verses 2 to 5 inclusive, we see a number of key evidences that the Saviour referred to is indeed the Lord Jesus. So, the Saviour comes out of Bethlehem, he comes from ancient times (or 'from days of eternity'), he will shepherd his flock and his greatness will reach the ends of the earth. Jesus was born in Bethlehem and the Bible tells us he comes from ancient times ("Before Abraham was, I am!" said Jesus —John 8: 58). He was the good shepherd who lays down his life for the sheep (John 10:11) and, beyond any dispute, His greatness today reaches to the ends of the earth, and has done so for at least the last fifty years. Jesus, we might remember, commanded that His message should be taken by His disciples to all nations, teaching them to obey all He had commanded the disciples (Matthew 28:19-20 —often called 'the great commission'). So far, Micah seems to have a pretty good success rate in terms of prophecy!

Notes

[1] Jack Finegan, quoted in *The Archaeology of the New Testament* Revised Edition (Princeton University Press, 1992), p. xliii. Readers who want to follow the full account of the development of the early Christian church's festivals should consult Finegan's chapter on the subject.

[2] *Ibid.* p. xlviii.

[3] Alfred Edersheim *The Life and Times of Jesus the Messiah* (Hendrickson Publishers Inc. 1993), pp. 131-132.

[4] *Op. cit. The Archaeology of the New Testament* (p. 38).

APPENDIX 1
THE TWO GENEALOGIES – MATTHEW AND LUKE

MATTHEW	BOTH		LUKE
-		-	1 Adam
-		-	2 Seth
-		-	3 Enosh
-		-	4 Kenan
-		-	5 Mahalalel
-		-	6 Jared
-		-	7 Enoch
-		-	8 Methuselah
-		-	9 Lamech
-		-	10 Noah
-		-	11 Shem
-		-	12 Arphaxad
-			*Cainan*
-		-	13 Shelah
-		-	14 Eber
-		-	15 Peleg
-		-	16 Reu
-		-	17 Serug
-		-	18 Nahor
-		-	19 Terah
-	(1) Abraham	20	-
-	(2) Isaac	21	-
-	(3) Jacob	22	-
-	(4) Judah	23	-
-	(5) Perez	24	-
-	(6) Hezron	25	-
-	(7) Ram	26	-
-	(8) Amminadab	27	-
-	(9) Nahshon	28	-
-	(10) Salmon	29	-
-	(11) Boaz	30	-
-	(12) Obed	31	-
-	(13) Jesse	32	-
-	(14) David	33	-

MATTHEW	BOTH	LUKE
(15) Solomon	-	34 Nathan
(16) Rehoboam	-	35 Mattatha
(17) Abijah	-	36 Menna
(18) Asa	-	37 Melea
(19) Jehoshaphat	-	38 Eliakim
(20) Jehoram	-	39 Jonam
(21) Uzziah	-	40 Joseph
(22) Joatham	-	41 Judah
(23) Ahaz	-	42 Simeon
(24) Hezekiah	-	43 Levi
(25) Manasseh	-	44 Matthat
(26) Amon	-	45 Jorim
(27) Josiah	-	46 Eliezer
(28) Jeconiah	-	47 Joshua
-	-	48 Er
-	-	49 Elmadam
-	-	50 Cosam
-	-	51 Addi
-	-	52 Melki
-	-	53 Neri
-	(29) Shealtiel	54
-	(30) Zerubbabel	55
(31) Abiud	-	*Rhesa*
(32) Eliakim	-	56 Joanan
(33) Azor	-	57 Joda
(34) Zadoc	-	58 Josech
(35) Akim	-	59 Semein
(36) Eliud	-	60 Mattathias
(37) Eleazar	-	61 Maath
-	-	62 Naggai
-	-	63 Esli
-	-	64 Nahum
-	-	65 Amos
-	-	66 Mattathias
-	-	67 Joseph

MATTHEW	BOTH	LUKE
-	-	68 Jannai
-	-	69 Melki
-	-	70 Levi
(38) Matthan	(38) Matta(n)(t) 71	71 Matthat
	[Mattan and Mattat may be the same]	
(39) Jacob		72 Heli
	(40) Joseph 73	
	(41) JESUS 74	

This is a comparison of the genealogies found in Matthew and Luke. For the purpose of comparison, the order of Luke is reversed. The following points emerge:

1. Matthew's list has 41 names, including Jesus.

2. Luke's list has 74 names, including Jesus.

3. Matthew and Luke have 19 names in common, if Matthan and Matthat are the same person.

4. Apart from the names common to both lists, Matthew has 23 and Luke 56 names. Luke's list has 19 names before Matthew's list begins.

5. *Rhesa* between 55 and 56 in Luke's list, is not a proper name, but a Chaldee title meaning *prince*. Some early Jewish copyists[1] mistook this for a name, whereas the title almost certainly should read Zerubbabel Rhesa —or Zerubbabel the prince.

6. Luke's list has no artificial arrangement, as does Matthew's (which is divided into sub-lists of fourteen).

7. Matthew's list begins with Abraham, the father of the Jewish race, whereas Luke's begins with Adam, the father of the human race. Each of these is in keeping with the object and readers which the Gospel writers had in view —the one Jewish and the other Gentile.

8. Matthew's line is followed from David through Solomon, but Luke's is followed from David through Nathan. Both were sons of David.

9. *Cainan*, between 12 and 13 in Luke's list, is an interpolation in some copies of the Septuagint occurring towards the end of the

fourth century AD. Scholars are clear that it should not feature in the list.

10. In Matthew's list Shealtiel (number 29) is said to be the son of Jeconiah, but in Luke's list Shealtiel is identified as the son of Neri. The likely explanation of this is as follows: In Jeremiah 22:24-30 it is predicted that King Jehoiachin (Hebrew Coniah or Jeconiah) would be childless and so he could not have been the father of Shealtiel. It is likely however that he adopted the sons of his relative Neri, the twentieth from David in the line traced through Nathan. In this regard we should bear in mind the so-called *Jehoiachin-Curse prophecy* and the *Zerubbabel-Blessing prophecy*, both of which are discussed in Chapter 11.

11. In Matthew's list Joseph is identified as the son of Jacob, but in Luke the son of Heli. Some confusion has arisen because of this. Matthew's genealogy is generally reckoned to be that of Joseph, whilst Luke's genealogy is generally thought to be Mary's. In Luke 3:23 we read, "Jesus ..... was the son, so it was thought, of Joseph, the son of Heli." H. Brash Bonsall comments on this: "The Greek here simply reads 'Joseph of Heli'. In such a case as this a Greek would supply whatever word the context demanded, it might be son, son-in-law, father, sister, aunt, mother or grand-parent. In this case it would be 'son-in-law'. Heli was Mary's father, and Joseph his son-in-law." (See H. Brash Bonsall *The Person of Christ* CLC, 1967, p. 42).

Notes

[1] It is assumed that Matthew and Luke at different times consulted (or made arrangements for the consultation of) the temple archives in Jerusalem, where these details used to be lodged.

APPENDIX 2 – FLAVIUS JOSEPHUS
(born AD 37/38, Jerusalem — died AD 100, Rome)

Born Joseph Ben Matthias, Josephus was a Jewish priest and scholar, most famous for writing the definitive account of the Jewish revolt against Rome (AD 66-70) as well as earlier Jewish history. His major works were *History of the Jewish War, the Antiquities of the Jews* and *Against Apion.*

Josephus was by his own account, born into an aristocratic, priestly family in Jerusalem. In his early twenties he became a Pharisee —an intensely religious Jew adhering to a strict (though in many ways non-literal) observance of the Torah. Politically the Pharisees had little sympathy for the freedom-fighting Zealots and instead were content to submit to Rome —providing they could maintain their religious independence.

In his mid thirties Josephus travelled to Rome and was greatly impressed by its culture, sophistication and military might. He returned to Jerusalem on the eve of the general rebellion against Rome which began in AD 66. A rebel government was established in Jerusalem and Josephus, in common with the Pharisees, counselled compromise, but was drawn reluctantly into the rebellion. Josephus, in spite of his conciliatory stance, was appointed military commander of Galilee. He fortified the towns of the north in anticipation of the Roman counter-offensive.

The Romans, under the command of the future emperor Vespasian, entered Galilee in AD 67 and speedily defeated the Northern Jewish resistance. Josephus held the fortress at Jotapata for 47 days, but after the fall of the city he fled and, after spending a short period 'on the run', surrendered to the Romans. Led in chains before Vespasian, Josephus foretold that Vespasian would soon become emperor. This favourable prediction saved his life and for two years he remained a prisoner of the Roman army. In AD 69 Vespasian indeed became emperor and Josephus was given his freedom.

Josephus then became loyal to Rome, adopting the name Flavius (Vespasian's family name) and accompanying Vespasian's son (the future emperor Titus) to the siege of Jerusalem in AD 70. Josephus attempted to act as a mediator between Rome and the

237

rebels, but, hated by the Jews for his treasonable switch in loyalties and considered untrustworthy to Rome as a Jew, he accomplished little. After the fall of Jerusalem and the destruction of the temple, Josephus went to live in Rome, where he devoted the remainder of his life to being a sort of ambassador of Judaism under imperial patronage. This was partly (it seems) to redeem his reputation before the Jews as an unforgiven traitor, and partly because he wanted to represent the puzzling Jews to their Roman overlord —helping them as they continued to govern Galilee and Judea.

Josephus' works provide independent corroborative evidence of the early church. We gain most of our detailed knowledge of the life of Herod "the Great" from *The Antiquities of the Jews* (commonly shortened to 'Antiquities'), a work completed in AD 93, which traces the history of the Hebrews from the Creation to the period immediately preceding the Jewish revolt. Because of his intimate first-hand knowledge of the Jewish rebellion he was able to give a detailed account of that troubled time in *History of The Jewish War*, which was an official Roman history completed in AD 79, towards the end of Vespasian's reign.

From the viewpoint of the biblical account of Christ's birth, the immediate interest in Josephus' works are in *Antiquities* "Books" 15 and 16 which contain a long account of the awful reign of Herod, and Book 17 where we learn that Archelaus was as bad as his father and was later banished to Vienna on account of his crimes by Rome. There is a fascinating summary of father and son in *Antiquities* 17.11.2 —which underscores the detail given by the Gospel according to Matthew in Chapter 2 where we read of the treachery of Herod with the Magi and Joseph's concern on hearing that Archelaus had succeeded his father (Matt 2:22).

Other points of interest in Josephus, which corroborate the detail in the New Testament, are the mention of the Lord Jesus (18.3.3), of John the Baptist (18.5.2), and of James the brother of Jesus (20.9.1). The mention of Jesus is the most interesting in many respects and (of course) has led to controversy: it has been claimed that this reference may have been a later addition, or that it was edited by a later Christian copyist. The reference to Christ in somewhat glowing terms may however be some form of scorn or sarcasm, or even had some political undertone we cannot now recognise —Josephus was, after all, a very complex character. And it is just possible that, as a Jewish apostate, Josephus indeed recognised Jesus as the Messiah, even if he failed to understand the importance of that recognition.

THE BIRTH OF CHRIST

APPENDIX 3 (see notes on pp. 242-243)

EVENT	DIRECT PROPHECY
A John 1:1-5 The Word	Note 3
B Matt 1:1–17 the genealogy cp. Luke 3:23–38	Ps 132:17 2 Sam 7:8-17, Isa 11:1-11 Jer 33 (esp vv. 14-17)
C Luke 1:5-25 John the Baptist birth announced	Isaiah 40:3 (see John 1:23)
D Luke 1:26-56 – annunciation of birth of Jesus Christ, Mary, Elizabeth, Mary's song	Isa 7:14 Isa 9:1-7
E Luke 1:57-66 –the birth of John the Baptist	Isa 40:3 and 9-11
F Luke 1:67-80 –Zechariah's prophecy about John the Baptist (cp. John 1:6-9)	–
G Matt 1:18-25 –Joseph's dream and decision	Isa 7:14
H Luke 2:1-20 –the birth of Jesus Christ, the visit of the shepherds	Micah 5:2-4
I Luke 2:21-38 –the baby Jesus presented in the temple in Jerusalem	Re Lk 2:30-32 cp. Isa 11:10, 42:6, 60:3 Re Lk 2:38 cp. Isa 52:9 (note all of Isa 52 and Isa 53 are seen as messianic prophecy)
J Matt 2:1-12 –the visit of the wise men	Note 4
K Matt 2:13-18 –the flight into Egypt and the slaughter of the innocents	Hosea 11:1 Jeremiah 31:15
L John 1:10-14 –to all who received Him	–

INDIRECT PROPHECY (Note 2)

Gen1:1, Isa 42:1–7, Prov 8:27–31, Ps 33:8-9, Ps 45:18-19, Ps 51:4-6

Zech 3:8 (see also Matt 21:1-11), Gen 22:18, Isa 9:2, 6-7, Ezek 34 (esp vv. 23f)

Mal 3:1 [Jews traditionally apply this to Elijah, who they believe will return to herald the Messiah. John the baptist saw himself in this role (see Lk chapter 3) and so did Jesus (see Lk 7:24-28)].

The miraculous birth of a son to an old woman, as Elizabeth, is prefigured in the similar circumstance of Hannah and the birth of her son Samuel (1 Sam 1). Mary's song is prefigured in Hannah's prayer (1 Sam 2:1-10).

Mal 4:5-6 noteworthy as the last words of the OT. The heart of the father turned to his child could be Zechariah (Lk 1:7). Compare to the first 2 verses of Mark's Gospel, the first Gospel to be written.

In Jewish tradition, as in others, the birth of a child is the cause of celebration (see Prov 23:24f).

Eastern people, including the Jews had a great regard for dreams. On numerous occasions God used dreams to reveal some important message to his people, although Joseph's dream is not specifically prefigured.

Ezek ch.34 (Note: the primary reference to 'shepherds' is to the false religious leaders of Israel, but the secondary reference is to the Messiah (e.g. v.11). It is significant that the first visitors to the baby Jesus were shepherds, as Jesus himself would in a few years shepherd the lost sheep of Israel (see John 10:11).

Exodus 13:2 consecration of first born males
Leviticus 12:8 mother's offering on the birth of a child

Psalm 72:9-11 all kings will bow down before Him

Ex 4:22 has been applied historically in Judaism as a messianic prophecy but does not appear to modern commentators to be a true messianic prophecy

Joel 2:28-32a   Note 5

Note 1

The schedule above assembles the accounts of the nativity of the Lord Jesus from the Gospels of John, Matthew and Luke into chronological order of the events described, commencing in pre-history (A) and concluding in the theological statement (L) that to all who receive Him, to those who believe in His name, He gives the right to become children of God. The Schedule, whilst by no means exhaustive, presents those Old Testament texts generally accepted as fulfilled in the New Testament narrative of the Incarnation of the Lord Jesus.

Note 2

Within Old Testament prophecies there was often a two-fold purpose —a message to hearers at the time the prophecy was given (direct prophecy) and a partially concealed message giving insights into God's overall scheme of salvation (indirect prophecy). This is sometimes referred to as "salvation history" and, as one biblical commentator has pointed out, all history is ultimately His-story!

Note 3

The Old Testament does not make a direct prophecy of the Messiah being "the Word". The indirect references illustrate that God has revealed through the Scriptures that His servant is inextricably linked to the creation process. When God created the world, as described in Genesis chapter 1, it is notable that the narrative describes this process eight times with the prefix "and God said". Whether this is accepted as literal or allegorical, the underlying code in the text is inescapable —the creation process was carried out by the Word of God.

Note 4

The visit of the Magi, or wise men, is not directly prophesied. Some commentators, perhaps with mischievous motives, have suggested that Numbers 24:17, Isaiah 8:4 and Isaiah 60:6 point towards the Magi. Others have consequently seized upon this as "evidence" that the narrative concerning the Magi is rooted in myth as Christians seek texts to 'support' the New Testament account. However, Psalm 72 was considered by the ancient synagogue to be messianic throughout. It is in Psalm 72:9-11 that we read of desert tribes bowing before Him, and the kings of Tarshish, Sheba and Seba presenting Him with gifts. In this passage we have some support for the idea there may have been three Magi bearing gifts for the infant Jesus.

Note 5

Most Christian commentators see the gospel of Jesus Christ as the fulfilment of all Old Testament prophecy. Whilst the Jewish nation was chosen by God to be His own people (the 'old covenant' —Genesis 17:7-9), the nation's continued rebellion throughout the Old Testament period led to the promise of a 'new covenant' (Jeremiah 31:31-34) which was clarified in God's covenant with King David to 'build him a house' and to 'establish his throne' forever (2 Samuel 7:8-17). But it was always God's intention that the covenant should eventually extend to all nations (Isaiah 42:6).

APPENDIX 3A

CHRONOLOGICAL BIBLICAL READINGS
CONCERNING THE BIRTH OF CHRIST

A. John 1:1-5 The Word
B. Matt 1:1-17 The Genealogy (cp. Luke 3:23-38)
C. Luke 1:5-25 John the Baptist's birth announced
D. Luke 1:26-56 Annunciation of birth of Jesus Christ;
    Mary; Elizabeth; Mary's song
E. Luke 1:57-66 The birth of John the Baptist
F. Luke 1:67-80 Zechariah's prophecy about John
    the Baptist (cp. John 1:6-9)
G. Matt 1:18-25 Joseph's dream and decision
H. Luke 2:1-20 The birth of Jesus Christ;
    the visit of the shepherds
I. Luke 2:21-38 The baby Jesus presented in the temple
    in Jerusalem
J. Matt 2:1-12 The visit of the wise men
K. Matt 2:13-18 The flight into Egypt and the slaughter
    of the innocents
L. John 1:10-14 To all who received Him....

APPENDIX 4

BIBLICAL SOURCES

How did we get our Bible?

As essential background to our detailed review of the account of the Nativity of the Lord Jesus, it is valuable to pause to look broadly at the documents from which we obtain virtually all our information about this event —at the Holy Bible itself. Why is this collection of books referred to as 'holy' by Christians? The answer is simply that the 66 separate books that make up the Bible as we have it are recognised as being a unique revelation by God of His dealings with mankind. The various Bible writers were, it is generally accepted in believing Christian circles (and, in relation to the Old Testament alone, accepted also in believing Jewish circles) inspired to write words that are from God and in that sense, *set apart* from all other writings of any sort. The word "holy" means variously, sacred, free from sin, set apart for God and pure. Most believing Christians, in spite of some difficulties with the Bible, would claim all these virtues for it.

John Stott, author of many books about the Holy Bible, writes in his excellent standard work *Understanding the Bible* that Christianity is essentially a historical religion, in the sense that God's unique revelation of Himself was given in an unfolding historical situation, first through the Jewish nation and later through Jesus Christ. Stott points out that, although there is much history in the Bible, it does not claim to be an objective history book. He writes:

"A historian today is supposed to give a full and objective account of all the facts of his period. The biblical historians, however, made no such claim. On the contrary, they were regarded as the 'former prophets', for they were writing 'sacred history', the story of God's dealings with a particular people, for a particular purpose.... So their record is more a testimony than a history. They were writing down their own confession of faith.

Therefore they were selective in their choice of material and (the secular historian would add) unbalanced in their presentation

245

of it. For example, ancient Babylonia, Persia, Egypt, Greece and Rome – each a mighty empire and a rich civilisation – are only included as they impinge on the fortunes of Israel and Judah, two tiny buffer states on the edge of the Arabian desert, which hardly anybody had heard of. The great thinkers of Greece like Aristotle, Socrates and Plato are not so much as mentioned, nor are national heroes like Alexander the Great (except obliquely) and Julius Caesar. Instead, the scriptural record concentrates on men like Abraham, Moses, David, Isaiah and the prophets to whom the word of God came, and on Jesus Christ, God's Word made flesh. For the concern of Scripture is not with the wisdom, wealth or might of the world, but with the salvation of God. Biblical history is ..... the story of salvation."[1]

The Old Testament is a collection of 39 books. The order in which they appear is not related necessarily to the date of writing or the date of subject matter, but is related to their literary genre. The three types of literature that dominate the Old Testament are history, prophecy and poetry. John Stott continues:

"Christians divide history into BC and AD, indicating the periods before and after Christ, believing that Jesus Christ's coming into the world is the watershed of history. So too it is the life of Jesus Christ which divides the Bible into half, the Old Testament looking forward to his arrival and preparing for it, the New Testament telling the story of his life, death and resurrection and drawing out its implications as they begin to emerge in the infant church and will one day reach fruition."

Origins

Even an atheist will probably concede that if God exists He will logically have made some arrangements for making Himself known to those He has created. Christians believe that God has revealed Himself uniquely to humans, first to the Jewish nation, whom He chose to be His covenant (or promise) people and then in the person of the Lord Jesus through whom all humans may have a personal relationship with God, as their Father.

The events described in the early chapters of the Bible, as God began to make Himself known through Abraham and to embark upon His plan of salvation, started some time after 2,000 BC, probably between 2,000 and 1,800 BC. The question naturally arises, at what point did God begin to make provision for His revelation to be committed to writing? Some historians believe that there may have been God-*inspired* writings before the days of Moses (who lived circa 1,300 BC) but there are three principal objections to such a view:

Firstly, there is **no record** of any *inspired* writings before the time of Moses. Of the inspired writings in the Bible there are some clear records as to authorship, thus: "Moses then wrote down everything the Lord had said" (Ex 24: 4). Whilst there were undoubtedly holy men in those early days, such as Noah, Abraham and Joseph, with whom God had frequent communication, we nowhere read that any of them were inspired to write down what He said to them.

Secondly, there is **no reference** to such writings. From the days of Moses onwards, the inspired writings of the Bible were referred to constantly by prophets, priests and rulers as the final court of appeal (e.g. Ex 32: 8; Joshua 1: 8). The Lord Jesus Himself frequently referred to the Old Testament Scriptures in the familiar words: "it is written". A natural inference would be that had there been any sacred writings in the days of Noah or Abraham, they would have referred to them.

Thirdly, there are **no remains** of any such writings. Had there been any such writings, it is unlikely they would have been allowed to disappear but, as divinely-inspired writings, would have found their way into the accepted canon of Scripture. As stated in Isaiah 40:8, "the word of our God stands forever."

In spite of the fact that some words used in the Pentateuch (the first five books of the Bible) have been identified by scholars as being not of Hebrew origin, but borrowed from an earlier language, it seems safe to conclude that there were no *inspired* writings prior to those we have in our Bible. This is perhaps surprising, even so, as there were uninspired writings of various kinds that pre-date the Bible, specimens of which have been discovered in Egypt and Babylonia, in the form of clay tablets with signs or letters impressed upon them. One of these is the remarkable pillar of black stone discovered in 1901 by Jacques de Morgan which contains the 'code of Hammurabi of Babylon' written in cuneiform writing. These laws bear some resemblance to Mosaic laws, but the writing dates back some 500 to 600 years before Moses, probably to the time of Abraham.

In the early days of God's revelation to mankind, it appears He chose to make known His will verbally, in a direct and personal manner to individuals such as Adam (Gen 2:16), Cain (Gen 4:6), Noah (Gen 6:13), Abram (Gen 12:1), Abimelech (Gen 20:3), Isaac (Gen 26:2) and Job (Job 38:1). It is reasonable to assume that, in this way, God first instructed humans in the laws which were later embodied in the Pentateuch. For example, we read that, "Abel brought fat portions from some of the firstborn of his flock" before God as an offering —suggesting that God had already given clear instructions for the use of offerings. So we see that from the earliest times, humankind possessed, even without the Scriptures, some knowledge of God and His laws. This primitive knowledge, although dimmed and polluted over the course of time, has never completely died out, so that, everywhere on the face of this planet, even where no Bible has ever been seen, the worship of a Supreme Being, sometimes accompanied with sacrifice, is still practised.

With or without the Bible, there have always been two distinct and independent clues to the existence of God. First, the 'natural' world (see Psalm 19:1-3) and second the inbuilt knowledge of right and wrong, which we call conscience (see Rom 2:14-15). Whilst the 'natural' world strongly suggests that there is a creator-God who has created what we easily recognise as order, beauty and splendour, conscience can be so much abused as to render it practically inoperative. Hence there is a need for a separate written revelation of God as contained in the Bible, one which is trustworthy and able to be understood by all people. Christians believe, with very good reason, that this is what God has provided for us in the Bible.

On the question of the inspiration of the human authors of the Bible, John Stott again has some helpful insights:

"The process of inspiration was not a mechanical one. God did not treat the authors of Scripture as dictating machines or tape recorders, but as living and responsible persons. Sometimes he spoke to them in dreams and visions, sometimes by an audible voice, sometimes by angels. At other times we are not told how the word of God came to them. They may well not have been conscious of it at all. Thus in the case of Luke the evangelist, divine inspiration was certainly not incompatible with human research, for he tells us in the preface to his Gospel about the painstaking enquiries he had pursued. Whatever means of communication God employed in speaking to men, it never obliterated their own personality. On the contrary, as they wrote, their literary style and vocabulary were their own. So too – more important still – was their theme. It is not an accident that Amos was the prophet of God's justice, Hosea of his love and Isaiah of his kingly sovereignty, nor that Paul was the apostle of faith and grace, James of works, John of love, and Peter of hope. The internal evidence, gathered from reading the biblical text, is that God made full use of the personality, temperament, background and experience of the biblical authors, in order to convey through each an appropriate and distinctive message."[2]

The birth of the Bible

Man, when acting under conscience, failed God and continued to rebel against Him. This is amply shown in the whole episode of the Flood and Noah's escape from it. Man's sin is intolerable to a holy God. So God, in developing His plan of salvation, now brought mankind under LAW. It was some time shortly after 2,000 BC that God called Abram out of the idol-ridden surroundings of his native home (Gen 12:1; Joshua 24:2, 15), changed his name to Abraham and constituted him as head of a people (Gen 12:2; Gen 15:5) known as the Hebrews (or Jews). These God chose as his 'treasured possession' (Deut 14:2). God specially equipped the Hebrews over many hundreds of years, through many trials and tribulations, so that they should in due course become a clear example to the rest of mankind and, significantly, the trustee of a revelation committed to writing (Rom 3:2). They were to be separated from all other peoples so that they might themselves first learn to "follow all the words of this law" (Deut 29:29) before spreading the blessings of their special heritage among all other nations (Mark 16:15; Luke 24:47; Acts 1:8).

About 500 years after the call of Abram (c. 1300 BC) the time came for the first part of God's revelation to be committed to writing. This would encompass a history spanning at least the preceding 3,000 years and includes the necessary account of Creation. For this purpose Moses, who had been prepared in a very remarkable way and at some real personal cost (see Heb 11:24-28) for this supremely important work, was chosen to begin these sacred writings. The first reference to such writing in the Bible is Exodus 17:14 where God commanded Moses to "write on a scroll" the story of the battle with the Amalekites. Here it was, then, possibly on Mount Sinai, that the Holy Bible was begun. These writings were continued by other holy men – prophets and apostles – as they were guided by the Holy Spirit from time to time (2 Peter 1:21) until the revelation of God was complete and a library of 66 books had been secured —the history of salvation.

Original manuscripts

It is a fact that of all the sacred writings there are no *original* manuscripts, so far as is known. With regard to the Old Testament manuscripts in particular, as they became old and worn, they were reverently buried by the Hebrew priests, who ensured that reliable copies were made to use as replacements. Original manuscripts were undoubtedly lost during the frequent wars and persecutions to which the people of God were subjected. Even the New Testament original manuscripts are not available, so the Bible we have today is translated from Hebrew copies, and copies of Greek translations of early Hebrew documents. Whilst this raises obvious questions about the reliability of copies and of translations, we might *first* reflect on the possibility that, in ensuring that there are no original documents left, we see the providential hand of God. Had any original documents bearing the handwriting of Moses, David, Isaiah, Daniel, Paul or John survived, then men and women might easily have been swayed by superstition and begun to worship the writings as a sort of idol, instead of the God who first provided them. This would have run counter to one of God's first priorities, to lead mankind away from idols

There are in existence today some 25,000 Hebrew and Greek manuscripts of the Old and New Testament Scriptures (which compares with some 643 manuscripts of the next most numerous ancient work, Homer's *Iliad*) which have been copied periodically from other manuscipts. These are the 'original' manuscripts to which scholars now refer. They are preserved in the great public libraries of the world as well as in some private collections. These manuscripts can be sub-divided as follows:

* Hebrew manuscripts of the Old Testament —the earliest of which date back to about 800 AD.

* Greek manuscripts of the New Testament —the earliest of these date back to the early second century AD.

* Greek manuscripts of the Old Testament (known as the Septuagint) translated from Hebrew manuscripts themselves dated about 277 BC —the earliest surviving copies of these date back to the third century A.D.

Ancient Jewish scribes, as they made copies of the Scriptures which are the precious heritage of today's church, exercised the greatest possible care in this work – even to the point of superstition – counting not only the words but also every letter, noting how many times each letter occurred and destroying immediately any sheet on which a mistake was detected. All this, in their anxiety not to introduce any error into the sacred Scriptures. Each new copy had to be made from an approved manuscript, written with a special kind of ink, upon sheets made from the skin of ritually "clean" animals. The writers also had to pronounce aloud each word before writing it and on no account was any word to be written from memory. The scribes were reverently to wipe their pen before writing the name of God and to wash their whole body before writing the sacred word which we now render as 'Jehovah', lest that holy word should be tainted even in the writing. The new copy was then exhaustively compared with the original. It is said that if only one incorrect letter was discovered, the whole copy was rejected! Such was the quality control of those entrusted with copying the Scriptures!

Even so, mistakes did occasionally creep in, such as the age of Ahaziah when he began to reign as King of Judah, which in 2 Kings 8:26 is given as twenty two years whilst 2 Chronicles 22:2, in some versions, says he was forty-two years old. The early documents available do not help to resolve this, indicating the discrepancy is due to an error of a very early copyist. The suggestion is that this copyist, in trying to avoid introducing a new error whilst correcting an earlier one, decided to perpetuate the earlier one! The mistake was understandable, however, as the Hebrews used letters to express numbers and the ancient letter for forty was so similar to that for twenty that the they might easily be confused. The age of twenty-two given in 2 Kings is the correct one, and no doubt that was the number originally written by the inspired writers, because the age of forty-two would mean that Ahaziah was born two years before his father who died at the age of forty (2 Kings 8:17.)[3]

Since many thousands of ancient manuscripts have survived (and in this fact Christians again see the providential hand of God) whether in whole or in part, it is plain to see that a copyist's mistake in one is easily detectable by reference to the correct reading of the same passage in other manuscripts. We can confidently say, then, that although the manuscripts are only copies, scholars are able to arrive at the exact words of the Scriptures, as originally inspired by God. It might be added that this is backed up by numerous quotations from the Scriptures in non-biblical writings through which further verification can be gained.

Language

It is assumed by many scholars that when Abram left Ur of the Chaldees and came at God's direction to the land of Canaan (Gen 12:1-5) he adopted the language of the Canaanites among whom he had come to live and whose land he was ultimately to possess (Gen 12:7). Similarly, the exiled Jews during their captivity in Babylon discarded their own pure Hebrew and adopted the Chaldean or Aramaic language, which continued to be the common tongue until the time of Christ. If the assumption that Abram adopted the Canaanite language is correct, then the language he adopted would eventually have become what was later thought of as Hebrew. Indeed in Isaiah 19:18 there is a strong suggestion that the language of the Hebrews was actually called "the language of Canaan" for a time.

The name "Hebrew" probably came from Heber, a descendant of Shem and ancestor of Abraham. The name is mentioned in the genealogy of the Lord Jesus in Luke 3:35, where it is actually rendered 'Eber' in the more modern translations but 'Heber' in, for example, the Authorised King James Version of the Bible. Heber means 'crosser' as in crossing from one place to another. An equivalent modern word might be emigrant —a characteristic which has clung to the Jewish people through the ages. In Genesis 48:15, when Jacob blessed Joseph, he referred to 'the God before whom my fathers Abraham and Isaac walked'. Here, the word walked could be rendered 'walked about' or 'wandered'. Certainly the word Hebrew became associated with Abraham and his descendants. As noted earlier, the Hebrew language was used by the Jewish nation until the captivity in Babylon, when Aramaic was adopted. Obviously, then, most of the Old Testament, and all of the earlier parts of it, was originally written in Hebrew.

Not so, the New Testament. Jews in the time of Christ spoke mainly Aramaic, but the Greek language – the common administrative and trading language of the Roman world – became more and more used as time went on so that, when the New Testament was written, it was written without exception, in Greek.[4] The Greek of the New Testament, however, differs from the Greek of the classical writers. It is the commonest dialect which spread over the Near East as a result of the conquests of Alexander the Great, some 300 years before Christ. New Testament Greek was spoken by the *Hellenists*, or Greek-speaking Jews, who for business and other reasons made their homes in the area. It could be easily understood by persons acquainted with the classical language, but more importantly, could easily be understood as the everyday common language of the people. This is, perhaps, the strongest justification today for the periodic updating of the Bible into the language of ordinary people —to be as easily understood by the modern 'man in the street' as were the original Gospels and epistles to ordinary people of New Testament times. Such translation, of course, must remain true to the original text. All modern mainstream translations of the Holy Bible contain a detailed statement of the manner of translation and source texts used, normally as a 'preface' to the Bible itself.

Translations

The Holy Bible we have today is the result of the work of devout and dedicated teams of translators who have worked tirelessly and often at great personal risk or discomfort to themselves. The earliest translators had the advantage of undertaking their work using very early documents which have since been lost. More recent translators have had the advantage of using more numerous documents discovered even as late as the twentieth century, such as the *Dead Sea scrolls*, which were not available to their predecessors. (Again, most Christians would see the providential hand of God in making available fresh corroborative manuscripts down through the passage of history, thus ensuring that the Bible itself can continue to be subjected, and successfully subjected, to the most rigorous literary and scholastic criticism)

The Septuagint (or LXX)

About 270 BC, a little over 100 years after the close of the Old Testament canon, a Greek translation of the Old Testament Scriptures was made. Scholars know that this was complete by

221 BC, as a reference to the document is made the apocryphal 'Wisdom of Jesus the son of Serach' where the translation is stated as being complete during the reign of an Egyptian king known to be alive at that time.[5] The translation was probably made for those Jews who had been scattered abroad by the dispersion and had adopted the Greek language in place of Hebrew which by this time amongst the Jews of the dispersion had been almost completely forgotten. The Septuagint was a poor translation —in fact, so poor that the Gospel and other New Testament writers when quoting from the Old Testament, did not use it, preferring (it appears) to use the Hebrew versions available at the time.

The text of the Septuagint is contained in a number of early manuscripts. The most important of these are the Codex Vaticanus (B) and the Codex Sinaiticus (S) both dating from the fourth century AD, and the Codex Alexandrinus (A) from the fifth century. There are also many earlier papyrus fragments and numerous later manuscripts. Christians see the providence of God at work again in the fact that the three main versions (B), (S), and (A) have been lodged among the three great traditions of the professing Christian church, viz the Vaticanus version as its name suggests is in the Vatican, the seat of the Roman Catholic Church, where it has been for over five hundred years; the Sinaiticus is in the possession of the Greek Church, and the Alexandrinus is in the British Museum, London, an important centre of the Protestant tradition. The first printed copy of the Septuagint was in the Complutensian Polyglot (1514-22).

The importance of the Greek language Septuagint, insofar as the early Christian writers used Greek, was that in the Septuagint translation these Christians located the Old Testament prophecies which pointed to the birth, life, death and resurrection of the Lord Jesus. Jews considered this to be, as many still do, a misuse of Scripture and so ceased to use the Septuagint. Its subsequent history and use lay with the Christian church. The Septuagint also provides some measure of independent verification of the older Hebrew Old Testament texts and subsequent translations of it.

The Vulgate

In the second century AD Latin superseded Greek and remained for many centuries the diplomatic language of Europe. In 382 AD Pope Damascus commissioned Jerome,[6] the leading biblical scholar of his day, to produce a Latin version of the Bible from the various translations then in use. Jerome moved to Palestine to make a first-hand study, and his revised Latin version of the Gospels appeared in about 383. Jerome initially used the Septuagint for the Old Testament parts of the Bible but later translated the entire Old Testament from original Hebrew versions, a process completed after some twenty years about 405 to 410. From the mid-sixth century the complete Bible, contained between two covers, came into common use. It is known still as the Vulgate, from the Latin word meaning "to make common or public" and from which the English derive their word "vulgar".

In 1546 the Roman Catholic Council of Trent decreed that the Vulgate was to be the exclusive Latin authority for the Bible and the Vulgate was republished in 1592, removing some earlier errors.

Anglo-Saxon and English translations

During what has become known as the Dark Ages, access to the Holy Bible was restricted first by language, as Latin was the preserve of scholars and the ruling class, and second by simple non-availability. In spite of this, Christianity made headway in Europe and paganism slowly died out. In the seventh century a man in England named Caedmon wrote a paraphrase of parts of the Bible, but it was not until the eighth century that the Venerable Bede of Jarrow (b. c. 673; d. c. 735), a significant literary figure in England at the time, translated the Psalms and the Gospels into Anglo-Saxon. He died before he could translate the rest of the Bible. In AD 871 Alfred the Great was crowned King of the West Saxons, and in 893 nominally King of all England. He instituted a translation of the Bible into Anglo-Saxon but, like Bede, died before the work was completed.

About the year 1330 was born John Wycliffe, an important

early reformer of the English Church. He was the first to translate the whole Bible into the English language – a task that took some twenty-two years – and made his translation from the Latin Vulgate, as Hebrew and Greek originals at this time were virtually unobtainable. The translator was much opposed by the Catholic Church and there began a long period of violent opposition to the translation of the Bible into the common tongue. Wycliffe himself died peacefully, however, in 1384.

Printing was invented by Johannes Gutenberg in Mainz (now in Germany) in 1450 and was introduced to England by William Caxton in 1476, about which time parts of the Old Testament were printed in Hebrew. In 1516 Desiderius Erasmus, a learned Greek scholar, published in Basel a Greek New Testament translated direct from ancient manuscripts. This edition was to be of great value to future translators, as for some centuries the only 'original' documents available had been Latin translations.

In 1525 William Tyndale, one of the great Protestant reformers, prepared a fresh English translation from Erasmus's Greek translation. Tyndale is distinguished for being the first to publish in print an English New Testament. He went on to translate the Pentateuch and Jonah into English as well. All this work was accomplished at immense personal difficulty owing to opposition from the Roman authorities in England, and was largely carried out in exile and virtual poverty, initially in Cologne and later at Worms. Thousands of his translations were smuggled into England, but in 1536, having returned to England, Tyndale was executed by being burned at the stake. Ironically, in the same year King Henry VIII, although at this time still a Roman Catholic, granted a royal licence for the issue of a Bible in the English language and this became available a year later.

Bible in chapter and verse divisions
In 1250 Cardinal Hugo became the first to divide the Bible into chapters. His occasionally arbitrary divisions have been followed ever since. The sub-division into verses was not accomplished for another three hundred years, however. It was in 1551 in England

that Sir Robert Stephens divided a new translation of the Greek New Testament into verses. The 1550s were violent times in England during the reign of Mary Queen of Scots and many Protestant reformers were executed. As part of the attempt to crush the Protestant church in England, the printing, importation and circulation of the Bible was prohibited. One version of the New Testament was, however, published during the reign of Mary —and this was the first English edition divided into verses, as arranged by Sir Robert Stephens.

In 1558 Queen Elizabeth I ascended the English throne and the Protestant church became again ascendant. Two years later, in 1560, the *Geneva Bible* was published in England, so named because it had been prepared by the Protestant reformers in Geneva, where many had fled during the persecutions under Queen Mary. This version, as it happens, was the first Bible in which *italics* were used to indicate words not in the original, it was the first in which the whole Bible was divided into verses and it was the first to omit the apocryphal books since their introduction into the Septuagint in the fourth century.

The Douay-Rhemish Bible and the English Authorised Bible
In 1610 the Roman Catholic authorities issued the Douay-Rhemish Bible, being a revised translation from the Latin Vulgate originally translated by Jerome. Its name was derived from the fact that the Old Testament was translated at Douay and the New Testament at Rheims. In the Catholic fashion it also included the apocryphal books which were now considered to be part of the Roman Catholic canon of Scripture.

By the beginning of the seventeenth century there were a number of good – but old – Bible translations in use in England. The English language was changing and evolving and there was an evident and growing need for a fresh translation. Under the patronage of King James I of England, fifty-four translators were assembled to undertake this project. These scholars, using Greek originals and other ancient documents for reference, in a period of five years translated and then published (in 1611) what is still published as the Authorised King James Version. In this version, marginal notes were adopted, which have proved so helpful to Bible readers and students alike. Whilst this *was* a scholarly translation and is still loved by readers today, a dispassionate observer would note that it was based on Greek texts (essentially the Greek text of the New Testament edited by Beza in 1589, who closely followed that published by Erasmus 1516-1535) which themselves contained errors. The earliest and best of the manuscripts used by Erasmus was from the tenth century and, whilst Beza had access to good manuscripts from the fifth and sixth centuries, he made little use of them because they differed from the text translated by Erasmus! Nevertheless, the Authorised Version was in its time a good translation. For two and a half centuries no further authorised translations were made into the English language.

Recent translations
Of course, in Bible history 'recent' is a relative word. The survey above considers the major versions of the Holy Bible through the first millennium and into the first half of the second millennium. As language changed and developed, and as fresh and often older source documents in the form of original manuscripts became available, and with the Bible itself being at the heart of the teaching of a number of the Protestant denominations, the need for a newer revision of the Bible was evident in the mid nineteenth century.

During the Victorian era in Britain, many fresh manuscripts became available to scholars and the task of revision was undertaken with the authority of the Church of England in 1870. The English Revised Version was published between 1881-85 and the American Standard Version, embodying some preferences of American scholars, was published in 1901.

Because of difficulties caused by unauthorised publications over the last two decades of the nineteenth century, especially tampering with the English Revised Version to the requirements of various cults that were emerging at the time, the American Standard Version was copyrighted in 1901 to protect the text from unauthorised amendment. In 1928 this copyright was acquired by the International Council of Religious Education and thereby into the 'ownership' of American and Canadian churches which were associated with the Council. The Council appointed a committee of scholars to make enquiry as to whether further revision was necessary, and in 1937 such a revision was authorised by a vote of the Council. This directed that the resulting translation should "embody the best results of modern scholarship as to the meaning of the Scriptures, and express this meaning in English diction which is designed for use in public and private worship..."

Translation was undertaken by an appointed Committee, working in two groups, one responsible for the Old Testament and one for the New Testament. Each group submitted its work to the scrutiny of the other and the charter of the Committee required that all changes must have a two-thirds vote of the total membership of the Committee. In this way, a very good measure of 'quality control' was ensured. The Revised Standard Version of the New Testament was published in 1946 and the whole Bible in 1951.

In the latter part of the twentieth century one version of the Bible has won a very wide measure of acceptance throughout the world and can now be described as the yardstick by which other translations are measured. The *New International Version* was a completely new translation made by over one hundred scholars working directly from the best available Hebrew, Aramaic and Greek manuscripts. In 1965, following several years of exploratory discussions by committees from the Christian Reformed Church and the National Association of Evangelicals in the USA, a group of Scholars gathered at Palos Heights, Illinois, and agreed the need for a new translation in contemporary English. In the words of the Preface to the New International Version:

"Responsibility for the new version was delegated by the Palos Heights group to a self-governing body of fifteen, the Committee on Bible Translation, composed for the most part of biblical scholars from colleges, universities and seminaries. In 1967 the New York Bible Society (now the International Bible Society) generously undertook the financial sponsorship of the project

—a sponsorship that made it possible to enlist the help of many distinguished scholars. The fact that participants from the United States, Great Britain, Canada, Australia and New Zealand worked together gave the project its international scope. That they were from many denominations – including Anglican, Assemblies of God, Baptist, Brethren, Christian Reformed, Church of Christ, Evangelical Free, Lutheran, Mennonite, Methodist, Nazarene, Presbyterian, Wesleyan and other churches – helped to safeguard the translation from sectarian bias.

The translation of each book was assigned to a team of scholars. Next, one of the Intermediate Editorial Committees revised the initial translation, with constant reference to the Hebrew, Aramaic or Greek. Their work then went to one of the General Editorial Committees, which checked it in detail and made another thorough revision. The revision in turn was carefully reviewed by the committee on Bible Translation, which made further changes and then released the final version for publication. In this way the entire Bible underwent three revisions, during each of which the translation was examined for its faithfulness to the original languages and for its English style."

The New International Version explains in some detail how the work was undertaken and the Preface is well worth reading in its own right! Towards the latter end of the twentieth century a large number of 'contemporary' versions of the Bible were published. Some, it is true, fulfilled a real need in a society where for many, the Holy Bible is completely unknown and reading skills are in decline. Others err towards various types of 'political correctness' or are market-driven and are to that extent poor translations which will not pass the test of time. Yet others, issued by non-Christian cults, are designed to deceive. Bible readers should check on the translation they are using and use only well recognised versions. The biblical quotations and extracts used in the series of studies on the birth of Christ are from the New International Version.

Conclusion

Since we obtain virtually all our information about the Lord Jesus from the pages of the Holy Bible, it is valuable to have a clear idea of how we obtained the Bible we currently use, as the brief survey in this appendix has sought to do. Critics of Christianity generally look to discredit the Bible as the source of information about Jesus, and consequently methods of translation and source material often come under scrutiny. It must be said that much of the detail in the attack upon the Bible emerges from either poor scholarship (or no scholarship!) and/or present only information that supports a particular viewpoint. To the uninitiated, so-called biblical criticism may at first sight appear to be persuasive. Christians argue that much of this literary, historic and scholastic criticism is in fact pretty weak stuff, and many Christians have taken pains to present the correct and truthful biblical answer to all of the criticisms from time to time put forward. Not everyone, it must be said, is prepared to look at the Christian viewpoint —not with any real openness of mind, at any rate.

This is sad, but not something that should unduly perturb Christians. Allowing that the Bible is truth, and Jesus, in His own words, "the way, the truth and the life" (John 14:6), it should not be surprising that such truth should come under constant attack. Such attack may come from the lips (or the pens!) of men, but ultimately it originates always with the devil. As the Lord Jesus said, "He was a murderer from the beginning, not holding to the truth, for there is no truth in him. When he lies, he speaks his native language, for he is a liar and the father of lies" (John 8:44).

The Holy Bible has come under greater 'scholastic' criticism and investigation than any other book in history, but has not been found wanting. The very fact of its continued existence is testimony to its Divine inspiration and the Divine intervention at many points in history to ensure its existence and continued availability. The Nazis burned Bibles in public places, yet the 'Third Reich' which was supposed to last for a thousand years lasted just twelve. The Bible, which they tried to destroy, traces its history back four thousand years. It might be observed that

Communism, which sought to crush the Bible and create an atheist state, lasted just seventy years and the final vestiges of the Communist religion are likely to die out in the early part of the third millennium. The *father of lies* may well have prepared something to replace Communism and Fascism, and it seems certain that the Bible and those who live by it will continue to face pressure in the years ahead.

Allowing that the Bible we have today is a true representation of the (inspired) words originally given through the prophets and apostles, there remains one last major area of legitimate concern. Were those words truly inspired? Were *all* those words inspired? Just *how* reliable were the original witnesses? This is particularly important in terms of the New Testament and the subject of this series of studies —the Nativity of the Lord Jesus. It is to this subject we turn our attention in Appendix 5.

Notes
[1] John Stott *Understanding The Bible* Revised Edition (Hodder & Stoughton, 1972), p. 45.
[2] *Ibid.* p. 140.
[3] The New International Version corrects this in the text of 2 Chronicles 22:2, but includes a footnote stating that some early manuscripts use the figure of forty two.
[4] Although some scholars have suggested that the original of Matthew's Gospel may have been written first in Hebrew and subsequently translated into Greek.
[5] A full discussion of the Septuagint is found in *The Life and Times of Jesus the Messiah. Op. cit.* Book 1, Chapter 2
[6] Sometimes known as "Saint Jerome" (b. c. 347 d c. 419/420) whose Latin name was EUSEBIUS HIERONYMOUS.

THE RELIABILITY OF THE BIBLICAL SOURCES

Jesus the Christ's provision for the New Testament

In this Appendix we look at the reliability of the biblical sources, and especially the reliability of the New Testament writers. Christians believe that the Old Testament was given to prophets —men chosen and inspired by God to bring His message at particular times to address particular circumstances facing His chosen people. Often however, their writings also contain a hidden message, which today we might call a 'source code' that points towards Jesus the Messiah. Elsewhere in this book about the birth of Christ we have considered in detail some of the Old Testament prophecies which point directly or obliquely to the birth of Jesus. But for now we look principally at the New Testament record. Could it be argued that the New Testament writers had a particular message that they wanted to convey, and that they were so enthusiastic about this man Jesus whom they followed, that their writings must be treated with caution as a sort of well-meaning propaganda? Could it be argued that their writings were therefore not inspired by God?

Bible believing Christians do not fear biblical criticism or honest and open questioning. Indeed, such questioning can in itself lead to a fuller understanding of biblical truth both for the questioner and those who seek to answer the question! Before looking at the New Testament witnesses, it is instructive to look at the Lord Jesus' own attitude to the 'Bible' of His day, what we now call the Old Testament. John Stott's excellent standard reference work *Understanding the Bible* contains a full discussion of the authority of the Bible (see especially chapter 6). Stott makes, in some detail, a number of points about the Lord Jesus' own submission to the Scriptures, summarised here:

1. **Jesus submitted to the Old Testament in his personal conduct**: He countered the temptations of the devil when He was in the wilderness with an appropriate biblical quotation,

2. **Jesus submitted to the Old Testament in the fulfilment of his mission**: Jesus seems to have drawn much of his understanding

of His role as Messiah from the Scriptures and saw himself as the Son of David, the Son of Man and Isaiah's suffering servant.

3. **Jesus submitted to the Old Testament in his controversies**: "He found himself engaged in continuous debate with the religious leaders of his day. Whenever there was a difference of opinion between them, he regarded Scripture as the only court of appeal. 'What is written in the Law?' he would ask. 'How do you read it?' (Luke 10:26). Again, 'Haven't you read this in Scripture...' (Mark 12:10). One of his chief criticisms of his contemporaries concerned their disrespect for Scripture. The Pharisees added to it and the Sadducees subtracted from it."[1]

4. **There is no example of Christ contradicting the divine origin of the Scriptures.**

As John Stott concludes "All the available evidence confirms that Jesus Christ assented in his mind and submitted in his life to the authority of Old Testament Scripture. Is it not inconceivable that his followers should have a lower view of it than he?"

The Lord Jesus' way of 'endorsing' the New Testament was entirely different from his way of endorsing the Old. After all, none of the New Testament books had been written by the time of Christ's death and resurrection. John Stott again tackles the question in detail, with a number of clear points emerging. Jesus foresaw the need for New Testament Scriptures corresponding to the Old. He therefore provided authoritative scribes of Christ's redemption and judgement of the world. The Lord Jesus carefully chose, appointed, trained and authorised twelve apostles to be his ultimate witnesses (see Luke 6:12-13). These apostles had a fourfold uniqueness:

1. They had a *personal call* and authorisation by Jesus (e.g. Gal 1:1).

2. They had an *eyewitness experience* of Christ (e.g. John 15:27; 2 Peter 1:16-21).

3. They had an *extraordinary inspiration* by the Holy Spirit. Whilst the gift of the Holy Spirit is given to every child of God, the ministry of the Holy Spirit which the Lord promised his apostles was unique:

"All this I have spoken while still with you. But the Counsellor, the Holy Spirit, whom the Father will send in my name, will teach you all things and will remind you of everything I have said to you.... I have much more to say to you, more than you can now bear. When he, the Spirit of Truth, comes, he will guide you in all truth..." (John 14:25-26 and John 16:12-13).

4. They had the *power to work miracles*, one purpose of which was to authenticate their apostolic commission and message (e.g. Heb 2:3-4).

As Stott notes: "When in the fourth century the church came finally to settle which books should be included in the canon of Scripture and which excluded, the test they applied was whether a book came from the apostles. That is, was it written by an apostle? If not, did it nevertheless emanate from the circle of the apostles and carry the endorsement of their authority? It is important to add this, for not every New Testament book was written by an apostle."[2]

The time delay from the events to the written records

We have already seen in Appendix 4 that the translations we have today are extremely accurate, based as they are on early documents. But has the New Testament been tampered with in the succeeding centuries? Scholars are in a much better position to evaluate the reliability of the New Testament documents than they are with any other ancient book. The interval between Thucydides' writing of his *History* and the earliest manuscripts we have of it is some 1,500 years. In the case of the Roman historian Tacitus it is 800 years. These time gaps do not unduly worry classical scholars, who accept the manuscript tradition as being broadly reliable. The reason why the question is of far greater importance with regard to the early Christian documents is because of the issues at stake. As Michael Green says in his excellent book *World on the Run*, "The Christian material is so challenging and disturbing that it would be very convenient if we could write off the reliability of the text. But that is just what we cannot do."[3]

In complete contrast to the comparatively few manuscripts

available from the first century classical authors, there are literally hundreds of the New Testament, written in a variety of languages and found all over the ancient world. There are, it is true, a number of variants in the documents available, but, as Michael Green points out, two things can be stated with absolute certainty:

1. There is no single point of Christian doctrine which depends on a disputed reading.

2. The text is so certain that that anybody who tried to make 'conjectural emendations' – a common practice when dealing with ancient manuscripts – would, in Green's words, "be laughed out of court".

It might be added that our available manuscripts are not separated by gaps of hundreds of years as are many other trusted ancient works. Certainly, all four Gospels are available in papyrus records written before AD 200, little over a century after the originals. There is a fragment of the Gospel of John discovered in Egypt which has been dated as early as AD 125. A document known as *The Unknown Gospel* and written before AD 150 and drawing heavily on the four canonical Gospels, indicates the position which those four Gospels had already achieved by that date. An early heretic, Valentinus, whose *Gospel of Truth* is thought to have been written about AD 130, quoted the New Testament writings extensively. As Michael Green notes: "...you need to quote the acknowledged stuff if, like Valentinus, you are keen to insert your own heresy!"

The most recent research at the time of preparing these studies places the Gospel of Matthew even earlier. In December 1994 Carsten Thiede, a German theological scholar who as deputy director of research at the Centre of the German Institute for Education and Knowledge in Paderborn, undertook fresh work on the 'Jesus Papyri' at Magdalen College (part of Oxford University) and, on the basis of exhaustive papyrology (study and dating of papyrus), comparative handwriting analysis and laser scanning microscopy, has dated the Jesus Papyri to 60 AD - 30 AD. The Jesus Papyri contain parts of Matthew Chapter 26 —the story of the anointing of Jesus with alabaster perfume by the woman in

Simon's home, the betrayal by Judas Iscariot, and part of the last supper. Part of Carsten Thiede's thesis rests on the fact that in cave 4 at Qumran (where the 'Dead Sea Scrolls' were discovered) the handwriting in one document found there closely resembles that of the Jesus Papyrus. Since Qumran was overrun by the Romans in 68 AD, this suggests that the Jesus Papyrus was written before 68 AD.

A full explanation of Carsten Thiede's work is beyond the scope of this Appendix but his work, if correct, is of considerable importance. It means that Matthew's Gospel is clearly an eyewitness account —in other words an account written by someone who was a first-hand eyewitness of what he wrote about. This in turn means that the view held by some scholars that, for example, the sermon on the mount is only a compilation of 'the essence' of Jesus' teachings, is almost certainly wrong. The sermon on the mount is much more likely to be an accurate, verbatim report of the sermon as preached by Jesus.

Certainly, then, by the end of the first century, the New Testament was written and well on the way to being collected. From the beginning it was considered to be authoritative —so much so that early heretics knew they must quote it extensively in order to persuade people with their teachings. (In this we might find two modern equivalents: the cult of the Russellites, better known as the Jehovas Witnesses, and the cult of Joseph Smith, better known as the Church of Jesus Christ of the Latter Day Saints (or Mormons). Both these cults use heavily amended versions of the Bible in addition to their own 'inspired' writings). Of much more importance, at the end of the first century the Christians began to quote the New Testament with the same reverence that they gave to the Old Testament Scriptures.

The time delay between the dates of the original writing of the New Testament books and the earliest available copies of them are so small as to be, in terms of ancient documents, negligible. It might be objected, however, that although the time lag in documentary terms is insignificant, in human terms it is rather more significant. Could the witnesses have remembered the details with the necessary precision to give us a reliable record? Apart from the possibility that Jesus may well have taught his disciples in the manner of a Jewish rabbi, perhaps involving them in memorising certain parts of His teaching, it should be said that His use of parables and other memorable formulations would have assisted a tenacious oriental memory, used to the oral tradition of teaching, to remember precisely the words used. Furthermore, He promised that the Holy Spirit would stimulate the apostles' memory (John 14:25-26). The documents we have, it can be said with great confidence, are substantially as they were written —and in this, once again, Christians see the providential hand of God at work.

The reliability of the New Testament witnesses

In preparing this section, the author has again drawn upon the work of John Stott. His book *The Authentic Jesus* contains an excellent and clearly argued chapter about the reliability of the Gospel and other New Testament writers.[4] Our knowledge of Jesus comes almost exclusively from the New Testament, although there are a few independent references to him in Roman and Jewish literature (e.g. see Appendix 2 on Josephus, the Jewish historian). It is obviously important, therefore, that we can have confidence in the New Testament writers. Stott makes a number of valuable points:

1. **The Gospel writers had a serious purpose, namely to be** *witnesses*: The New Testament Scriptures contain the record and interpretation of Jesus given by the apostolic eyewitnesses and those associated with them in the early church. The apostle John's statement about his Gospel is equally applicable to all the rest of the New Testament. He said that the words and works of Jesus were recorded so, "you may believe that Jesus is the Christ, the Son of God, and that by believing you may have life in his name" (John 20:31).

2. **The Gospel writers had an objective of 'evangelising'**: It was not their intention to write a comprehensive history or biography of Jesus in the modern sense. Instead, they were setting forth the

good news of Jesus Christ, with a view to inducing their readers to believe in him.

Michael Green emphasises the same point: "the great thing to remember" he says of the Gospels "is that they are an entirely new *genre*. Clearly, they are not biographies of Jesus in the conventional sense. What biography would fail to tell us of any of the physical features or personal details of its hero, pass over thirty of his thirty three (?) years without mention, and concentrate up to half of its account on his death? Equally obviously, they are not histories either, in the normally accepted sense of the word. The evangelists cheerfully bring God and his actions into the story —which would look odd in a history book. On the whole they are singularly lacking both in chronology and in references to what is going on in the secular world."[5]

3. **The Gospel writers *were* historians of *salvation history***: God is the God of creation, of the covenant, the God of Abraham, Isaac, Jacob and Moses, He is the God of the Exodus from Egypt, the God of the Judges and Kings, of the prophets and wise men. But above all He is the God and Father of our Lord Jesus, whose most mighty act was performed through the birth, life, death and resurrection of the Lord Jesus, culminating in the gift of His Spirit and the birth of His church. As Stott notes "The history it [the Scripture] records is 'salvation history' and the salvation it proclaims was achieved by means of historical events".[6]

4. **Among the Gospel writers, Luke outlines his purpose in writing his Gospel most explicitly** (See Luke 1:1-4): Luke speaks of things that have been 'fulfilled', a clear reference to the fulfilment of Old Testament prophecies, especially in the terms of the birth of Jesus. Luke refers to the fact that he himself had carefully 'investigated everything from the beginning' from 'eyewitness' reports, in order to write 'an orderly account', so that the reader will 'know the certainty' of the events.

Stott comments on these introductory four verses from Luke: "....the tradition which emanated from the original eyewitnesses did not remain oral. No, 'many' had undertaken to 'draw up an account' of what had happened. So Luke followed suit. He clearly states his qualification, namely that he had 'carefully investigated everything from the beginning.' That is, he had not taken everything on trust from the apostolic eyewitnesses; he had personally checked what had been handed down to him. When and how he did this we do not know, but we can make a guess. He tells us (by one of his unobtrusive 'we' sections in the Acts [which Luke also wrote]) that he arrived in Judaea with Paul after the third missionary journey (Acts 21:15) and that about two-and-a-half years later he left with Paul on their journey to Rome (Acts 27:1). During most of the interim period Paul was in prison in Caesarea (Acts 24:27). But Luke was a free man. He does not tell us how he occupied his time, but the strong probability is that he travelled the length and breadth of the Holy Land, visiting the sacred sites associated with the ministry of Jesus, and interviewing the people who had known and heard him."[7]

5. **The language of Luke was not that of a man writing unhistorical myths**: Luke's claim is entirely different and clear. He has personally and carefully investigated what the eyewitnesses had passed on. He wrote an orderly account of what his investigations had revealed.

6. **The early witnesses were reliable because they were Christians**: As Stott says: "Most of us, before we buy or read a book, want to know something about its author, about his character and about his qualifications for writing it. Is he trustworthy? .... whatever uncertainty there may be about the identity of the four Gospel writers, there is no uncertainty about the fact that they were all dedicated followers of the Lord Jesus. And the Lord Jesus they followed (according to one of them) said he had come to bear witness to the truth, claimed even to be himself the truth ....we can assert without fear of contradiction, therefore, that the evangelists were themselves honest men."[8]

7. **The Gospel writers' impartiality**: This is shown by the fact that they include mysterious sayings of Jesus which, for fear of misinterpretation, they might have preferred to omit. They also include incidents about themselves which, as leaders of the church, they would doubtless rather forget, such as the selfish request of

James and John for the most honourable seats in the kingdom, and Peter's shameful threefold denial of the Lord. The writers make no attempt to hide their earlier failings, again demonstrating their commitment to truth.

8. **Can we believe that God, who sent the Lord Jesus into the world to usher in a new age, something decisive for the salvation of mankind, should allow this message to be lost in the mists of antiquity**? Stott: "Such a contradiction is impossible. Instead, it is reasonable in itself, and congruous with the Old Testament pattern, to affirm that the God who spoke and acted uniquely through Jesus would also make provision for his revelation and redemption to be written down by reliable witnesses, so that future generations throughout the world might partake of their benefits too."[9]

The reliability of the Gospels
The word "gospel" means "good tidings". It comes from two Anglo-Saxon words: "god" = good, and "spell" = news. The Greek word "evangelion" really means "good message" and is translated "gospel" in the New Testament. The gospel is the good news entrusted to Christ's followers to tell the world that salvation is available to all people who truly repent (or turn away from) their rebellion against God (or from sin), and turn in faith to the Lord Jesus. The gospel offers this salvation and tells how it may be had. As one missionary, J.E. Church, once wrote, the gospel can be summarised in the verse John 3:16 (which many would cite as the single most important verse in the whole Bible) in the following memorable way:

God so loved the world, that He gave His
Only begotten
Son, that whoso believeth on Him should not
Perish, but have
Everlasting
Life ......"

The Gospels in the Bible are the four accounts of the life of Jesus —Matthew, Mark, Luke and John. A full treatise on the authorship of the Gospels is outside the scope of this book. Instead, we concentrate on the message which the Gospels bring. The Gospels are essentially the proclamation of this good news about Jesus, who the writers present as God's way of rescue (or salvation) for all people. Salvation from what? Salvation to what? The Gospel writers are clear that salvation is from the power and grip of sin, and to a place in the family of God:

Matthew: (1: 21) "... you are to give him the name Jesus, because he will save his people from their sins."
Mark: (1: 15) "The kingdom of God is near. Repent and believe the good news!"
Luke: (1:77) "... to give his people the knowledge of salvation through the forgiveness of their sins."
John: (1:12) "... to all who received him, he gave the right to become children of God ..."

The apostles may not have written their Gospels until thirty or forty years after the events they record, although as noted above good scholarship at the end of the twentieth century suggested a much earlier dating is very likely. The apostles were heavily engaged in preaching this good news and they apparently believed, in any case, that the return of the Lord Jesus in His glory was imminent (i.e. likely to happen in their own lifetimes). They probably saw no need for a detailed written record. Writing was a difficult and expensive process in the days before the invention of printing, and was not valued as much as the spoken word. So, for between twenty and forty years the Gospels were not written, although during these years many of the epistles (or letters) which form half of the New Testament and which develop the theology of Christ's sacrifice for the forgiveness of sin, were written. The time came, however, as eyewitnesses became fewer and fewer, for their testimony to be preserved in writing for future generations.

The objection might be raised, if they were written so "late", can the Gospels be reliable? In a modern legal sense, the answer is certainly yes, they would be acceptable as evidence in a modern court of law. In 1999 there was a legal case in the UK to try an alleged war criminal from the second world war. Written and oral evidence from witnesses was gathered more than fifty years after the events.[10] When considering the New Testament as a whole, the same preaching about Jesus can be found across the various books that go to make up the New Testament. There is, therefore, little doubt that this unplanned homogeneity faithfully represents the Christian message. Whilst there was no human editor-in-chief of the books (they were, after all, written by different people at different times and for different audiences) Christians see a divine Editor who inspires the whole.

The survival of eyewitnesses to the time the books were written provides considerable confidence in their truthfulness. Bearing in mind the possible time delay on writing the Gospels, it is also noticeable that what we might presume were pressing concerns and controversies of the early church (such as the Holy Spirit, circumcision, the lordship of Jesus, meat offered to idols, etc) are completely absent in the Gospels —another factor suggesting their truthfulness. After all, there would have been, for any leader with dishonest motives for writing the Gospels, an overwhelming temptation to have used these same Gospels to put forward their own partisan viewpoints in these controversies.

Consider, also, the amazing and timeless teaching provided by the parables. Are these the genuine teachings of Jesus? Without serious question, the answer is yes, these are the authentic teachings of Jesus. Why would the Gospel writers have pretended He taught in this remarkable way if He did not? Who could have been the genius who devised them if it was not Jesus? "One thing is clear," writes Michael Green, "Nobody in Judaism before him taught in parables like that. And nobody after him was able to continue it. The early church did not preach in parables: but they knew Jesus had done so."[11]

The reliability of the Gospels is attested in themselves. We have already seen how, in the opening four verses of Luke, the writer gives a clear statement of the fact that he has carefully studied the reports of the 'things that have been fulfilled among us' as they were 'handed down to us by those who from the first were eyewitnesses', and that he has 'carefully investigated everything' so as to write 'an orderly account' leading to his readers knowing 'the certainty of the things you have been taught'. Matthew gives a hint as to his reason for writing his Gospel in the closing verses (28:19), where he records the Lord Jesus' final commission: "Go and make disciples of all nations, baptising them in the name of the Father and of the Son and of the Holy Spirit, and teaching them to obey everything I have commanded you." Matthew's lasting response to this great commission was in writing his Gospel account.

Mark, like Luke, gives a clue as to his reason for writing in the first few verses of his Gospel: "The beginning of the gospel about Jesus Christ, the Son of God. It is written in Isaiah the prophet...." Mark sees in Jesus the fulfilment of Scripture, and that Jesus' authority is demonstrated in His teaching, in His power over demons and in forgiving people's sins. Mark presents the story of Jesus in a straightforward, vigorous way, with emphasis on what Jesus did rather than what he taught.

The Gospel according to John presents Jesus as the eternal *word* of God, who became a human being and lived among us. As the book itself says, it was written so that, "you may believe that Jesus is the Christ, the Son of God, and that by believing you might have life in his name" (John 20:31). After an introduction that identifies the eternal Word of God with Jesus, the first part of the Gospel presents various miracles which show Jesus as the promised Saviour, the Son of God.

It might be said, therefore, that the Gospel writers have a serious purpose in writing their accounts of the life and work of Jesus, and that they present Him as Lord, in whom they want their readers to put their faith and trust. These books present themselves as truth, and anyone who thinks that these accounts are partly mythological (or completely mythological, as used to be taught by the Communists), needs to answer this question: why should the

Gospel writers, four different men writing at different intervals, two of whom were definitely eyewitnesses of the events they describe, seek to deceive their readers? What benefit would they achieve thereby? Had they sought money, there might have been some reason —but they lived, by all accounts, as their Lord had predicted they would, with nowhere to lie down and rest (Luke 9:58), taking no money with them (e.g. Matt 6:19, 24 and Luke 9:3). Had they sought an easy life, there might have been some reason, but the anecdotal evidence is that many of the disciples paid gruesomely, even with their lives, for their allegiance to Jesus as their Lord. The evidence is that they lived, as Jesus had said His followers must, forgetting self, carrying their own cross and following Him (Mark 8:34).

If, perchance, one of the Gospel writers was deranged, the mathematical chances of four of them being so deranged are extremely remote. And had one or all of them been so deranged, it is unlikely they could have written such self-consistent (and mutually consistent) accounts. Nor is it likely that thousands of sane people would have followed their teaching about Jesus, a course that, in the first century, led them almost inevitably into conflict with the all-pervading and desperately cruel Roman empire.

To what extent did the Gospel writers depend on each other?

The Gospels describe the same basic events around the life of the Lord Jesus, but they tell them differently. The first three Gospels (Matthew, Mark and Luke) are usually referred to as synoptic, in that they provide a similar account of the events. Matthew and Luke appear to have referred to Mark's Gospel, which was almost certainly the first to be written, and indeed to have included most of it in theirs. They share, in addition, some other common material which Scholars refer to as 'Q' (from the German word 'Quell' - a source. Some scholars believe that 'Q' was a very early document containing some of Jesus' teachings. Most recent scholarly work has, however, questioned whether, in fact, 'Q' existed). Matthew and Luke each contain independent material. It is less clear to what extent, if at all, that John used the other Gospels.

The apostle Peter referred to Mark as his 'son', obviously in a spiritual sense (1 Peter 5:13), and it was to Mark's house that Peter first went after his miraculous release from prison (Acts 12:11-12). Some have subtitled Mark's Gospel as Peter's Gospel, and certainly the second century church fathers Papias and Irenaeus described Mark as Peter's interpreter.

Some scholars believe Matthew's name may have been attached to the first Gospel because the assumed common source known as 'Q', consisting of the sayings of Jesus, was probably Matthew's work. It is known that Matthew was a tax collector and was, without doubt, used to keeping detailed records. The Gospel attributed to Matthew is certainly very Jewish and often focuses on the fulfilment of Old Testament prophecies. We have already noted that recent research suggests a much earlier writing of Matthew's Gospel than has been assumed for much of the twentieth century.

Luke was the only Gentile (non-Jewish) Gospel writer and was a physician (Colossians 4:14) and therefore an educated man. He travelled widely, accompanying Paul on some of his missionary journeys, which would have provided every opportunity and incentive for him to absorb the apostle's teachings about God's grace to the Gentiles. Luke's Gospel consequently majors on the theme of the universal scope of God's love, as illustrated by Luke's concern to mention the various 'outcasts' to whom Jesus ministered —women and children, tax collectors, lepers, Samaritans and Gentiles.

John's Gospel is quite different from the other three. Readers are immediately struck by his theological emphasis, literary style and vocabulary. Jesus is presented first and foremost as God's Logos ('Word') made flesh. All Jesus' great "I am" statements are found in John. His claims about Jesus' deity are more outspoken than in the other three Gospels. Recent writers have commented on the 'Jewishness' of the Gospel whose writer was clearly familiar with contemporary Judaean and Galilean culture and geography, and is seen as being a historically reliable witness.

Such minor differences as appear to exist between the four Gospels in fact tend to suggest that their writers did not depend on each other. Had the four Gospels been entirely consistent in style and detail, no doubt they would have been attacked as collusion. It is difficult to avoid the conclusion, if the evidence is viewed frankly and fairly, that the Gospels are exactly as they present themselves, four accounts by four different witnesses of the same basic facts.

Notes

[1] John Stott *Understanding the Bible* Revised Edition (Scripture Union, 1984), p. 147.

[2] *Ibid.* p. 152.

[3] Michael Green *World on the Run* (InterVarsity Press, 1983), p. 43.

[4] John Stott *The Authentic Jesus* (Marshall Morgan and Scott, 1985), Chapter 1.

[5] *Op. cit. World on the Run*, p. 47.

[6] *Op. cit. The Authentic Jesus*, p. 21.

[7] *Ibid.,* p. 23.

[8] *Ibid.,* p. 25.

[9] *Ibid.,* p. 26.

[10] A successful prosecution and subsequent conviction was secured on the basis of this evidence.

[11] *Op. cit. World on the Run*, p. 48.

APPENDIX 6

MAKING THE MOST OF CHRISTMAS

Tinsel

The word Christmas is derived from the old English *Cristes maesse*, "Christ's Mass". We have seen elsewhere in these studies (see especially Chapter 13) that there is no completely certain history of when the festival became commonly observed, but that the first written record of a feast associated with Christ's birth was in Rome in the year AD 336. This was twenty-four years after the emperor Constantine's conversion to Christianity in AD 312. From the ancient Roman pagan festivals of Saturnalia (December 17) and New Year have evolved the merrymaking and the exchange of gifts. Christmas has today become the most popular of the Christian festivals among believers and non-believers alike.

Old Germanic midwinter customs were progressively grafted onto the Roman celebration, so that the lighting of a Yule Log and the adornment of evergreens are now common features. The Christmas tree comes from the medieval German mystery plays centred on the tree of life (see Genesis 2:9), and Francis of Assisi popularised the Christmas crib in his celebration at Greccio, Italy, in 1223.

Another popular medieval feast was that of St Nicholas of Myra (c. 340) on December 6th, when the saint was believed to have visited children with gifts and admonitions, in preparation for the gift of Jesus at Christmas. It was through the Dutch that the tradition of St Nicholas (Sinter-klaas, hence Santa Claus) was brought to the USA in their colony of New Amsterdam, now New York. The sending of greetings cards at Christmas began in Great Britain in the 1840s and was introduced to the United States in the 1870s.

The Christmas carol is a largely Victorian invention, although the origin of some carols goes back hundreds of years. A *carole* was originally a form of dance rather than a Christmas hymn and, as people often dance as part of their celebrations, there grew up a tradition of simple popular songs suitable for celebrating the birth of the Lord Jesus. One of the most famous carols is *Stille Nacht* (Silent Night) which was, goes the story, composed in a single evening. On Christmas Eve in 1818 the organ in the village church of St Nicholas- in-Obendorf was found to need repairs —mice had eaten into the bellows and the organ was unusable! This meant that planned musical arrangements could not take place the following day. The curate Joseph Mohr wrote a poem and asked the organist if it could be set to an arrangement by guitar, which it duly was. So was born one of the most famous carols of all time!

Mid-winter feasting has a long history. The Romans and other ancients celebrated the shortest day of the year with feasting. It kept them warm and in good cheer and helped them forget for a few days the long winter nights past, giving them instead the encouraging prospect of shorter nights and the advent of spring a few months ahead. The original Roman mid-winter festival lasted from 17 December until the Kalends of January —the Roman new year when business accounts were settled. Kalends is the word from which our modern word 'calendar' is derived. So in our modern Christmas celebrations and traditions there is much 'tinsel' —a great deal that is showy but, for all too many, has little substance.

The gospel

Contrast these Christmas traditions with the underlying reason for them: "Christ's mass". Should we celebrate joyously or look to a more subdued remembrance of Christ's Nativity? No hard and fast rule is possible – it is very much up to the individual – but practising Christians often wish for a little space in their own lives over the Christmas period in which to reflect and offer their own worship to God for the gift of His Son. In Western societies, most struggle quite hard to find that space amongst all the festivities!

We have referred many times in this series of studies to the *Gospel writers* and *Gospel witnesses* - but what is this gospel, exactly? The word gospel comes from the old English *god* = good, and *spell* = news or, 'good news' and is simply the good news of salvation in Christ, available to all who genuinely seek Him, and who turn to Him in faith and repentance. There are many good books and pamphlets which set out the gospel in a clear and concise manner. Rather than emulate these in the next few pages, the reader may wish to see what the Bible itself says about the gospel. This will take the form of a short Bible excursion to examine what God's word lays down on this vitally important matter. These are not, it should be added, 'proof texts' —they are the author's own selection and ideally should be read as part of a wider reading of an entire Gospel. Many think that the Gospel of Luke is a good one to start on.

The whole Bible, Old and New Testaments, is a gospel. It shows how we humans were created for a relationship with our Creator God, who loves us with a love we frankly do not deserve. It shows how humans rebelled against God, something that is true for each individual as well as society as a whole. The Bible calls this rebellion 'sin'. To show humans that there is only one way to peace and a right relationship with God, He gave us His law against which we again rebelled. So God proved to us that we cannot earn our way to a right relationship with Him. We are by nature rebels —sinners.

The Bible shows how God determined on a plan of salvation from the earliest of times, and that His plan would be most costly to Himself, as it involved surrendering His own greatly beloved Son to our needs and interests. And as Jesus is a person of the 'godhead' it ultimately means that God *Himself* paid the price. Only by costly sacrifice could we humans begin to see the enormity of the crime of our rebellion against our Holy and spotless Creator. The only sacrifice that could possibly be acceptable to God was His own dear sinless Son. That is why Jesus had to die in our place (for the 'wages' of sin is death —Rom 6:23). The cross of the Lord Jesus now stands between us and God's wrath. By accepting the free gift of salvation earned for us by the Lord Jesus, we become part of His family —*saved from* the consequences of our sin and *saved to* a new life of worship and service as His Own people.

A one verse Gospel

A one verse Gospel is Acts 16:31 — **"Believe in the Lord Jesus and you will be saved."** You cannot get more straightforward than that! There are a few points to note about it:

1. An act of faith: "Believe in...."

What is faith? It is not just saying that you believe. It is believing "in" —an act of will, surrender, commitment and real trust.

2. The object of faith: "the Lord Jesus...."

To whom do we trust and commit our lives? —Jesus. He was a human being and His name means Saviour. The Lord —His title is a divine title; He is God's Son.

3. The outcome of faith: "...and you will be saved."

What does it mean to be saved?

NOW it means:

* forgiveness of all our sins and a clear conscience
* friendship instead of enmity with God
* being a member of God's kingdom and family, instead of Satan's
* the gift of His Spirit and His power to be different

THEN it will mean:

* going to heaven instead of hell when we die
* having a new body in heaven
* being made perfect
* seeing Christ and worshipping God face to face

ETERNAL LIFE is the term that links the NOW and the THEN together.

Some key Bible Passages which explain the Gospel

1. Born again
New life in Christ is so radical that it is not *like* being born again, it *is* being spiritually reborn. See John 3:1-21. (See also Ephesians 4:22-24; 1 Peter 1:23; Colossians 3:3).

2. Salvation
We are 'saved' by God's gift – the Bible calls this grace – and grace is God's free unmerited favour. It cannot be earned in any way. This, frankly, is a stumbling block to many. See Romans 3:21-26. Note that grace cannot be effective *apart* from a seeker's personal faith in Jesus Christ. (See Acts 2:38-41; Acts 8:36; 1 Corinthians 11:29; Hebrews 4:2).

3. Atonement
To 'atone' for some wrong done to another means to make amends for that wrong. In the Christian sense the idea of atonement is that we humans have wronged God by sinning against Him, and it is the Lord Jesus who makes atonement for that sin by taking our guilt upon Himself. So, Jesus' death on the cross in our place is *the* atonement —the acceptable sacrifice to God. Once our sins are atoned for by Jesus, we become 'at-one' (by no means a definition of the word *atone*, but quite helpful, nevertheless!) with God —see Ephesians 2:1-10. (See also 1 John 2:2; Colossians 1:13; Hebrews 9:24-29).

4. How to be saved
No matter how sinful we have been, God, in the person of Jesus Christ, died for us and if we repent (i.e. genuinely turn away from our rebellion against God in our lives), God will forgive us. What do we need to do in order to accept God's free gift of salvation? As someone once said, we need to go through three simple steps, A, B and C:

A – Admit our need of salvation. **B** – Believe in the Lord Jesus. **C** – Commit our lives to Him.

At a practical level, this means consciously praying to God, asking His forgiveness for past sins and asking Him for His power to live a new life for Him.

Once we are saved, do we stop sinning? Sadly we do not completely stop sinning this side of heaven. The old sinful nature tries to reassert itself as God's enemy (and our enemy), the devil, tries to make us rebel against God. But being a Christian in the sense of John 3:16 does help us to *sin less*. As we go on in the Christian life, God graciously and patiently reveals to us areas of our lives where we need specifically to yield to Him. So God slowly and surely and perceptibly makes us more like Himself. The process is ultimately completed when we are called to our permanent home —heaven. When, after having become a Christian, we sin, we need to repent of (turn away from) that sin and ask His forgiveness. We might think of this in terms of a child and its parent: although a child might rebel against its parent, this does not alter the fact that the child is, and always will be, the child of its parent. Jesus promised that those who are part of His family will never be lost (see for examples, John 6:37; John 10:28; Matthew 28:20).

The Lord Jesus Himself referred to the fact that His followers would continue, from time to time, to sin (see John 13:10) and would therefore need to be 'washed' in respect of these later sins. Plainly, it is not His desire that Christians sin, but He has recognised that we are 'flesh' and therefore weak and will sometimes yield to temptation. This is not the same, it should be added, as living in a state of complete and permanent rebellion against God. It is difficult to see how a true believer could continue to live in this way, but Christians can become misled, or have wrong notions —or simply be weak. These deficiencies the Lord Jesus has made provision for. Once we have been saved (i.e. our whole being is 'clean' and does not need to be cleaned again —which is the meaning of John 13:10), which Jesus likens to having been bathed, we will continue to journey through life during which our 'feet' will become soiled (i.e. we occasionally sin). We do not need to be bathed again, but we do need to 'wash our feet' —or repent of particular, known sins. Once we repent of such known sins, God has made wonderful provision for us to be restored (see Lamentations 3:22-23; Gal 6:1; 1 John 1:9 and Proverbs 28:13).

Exactly how do we go through steps A, B and C? There is no 'approved' form of words for a prayer asking the Lord Jesus to save us and make us part of His family. God looks more on the heart than any precise words used. But the following prayer may be helpful to those who truly want to commit their lives to the Lord Jesus:

Dear Heavenly Father, I sadly recognise and acknowledge that I have rebelled against you. I am a sinner. I do believe that Jesus came to this world to be my Saviour and He has died in my place. Please forgive me for all my past sins. I turn from them to you, now. Please take me into your family, and may Jesus now be my Lord, as well as my Saviour. From now on I will acknowledge you publicly as my Lord and ask your strength to follow you each day. I thank you from the bottom of my heart for hearing my prayer and saving me. I ask this in the Lord Jesus' name, and for His sake. Amen.

Anyone who has prayed such a prayer for the first time (and it may be good, though by no means necessary, to do this with a trusted Christian friend) should do two things. Firstly, find a good church, one that will help to build you up as you grow in the Christian faith. Ask God to help you find such a church, quickly. Second, let at least one other person know that you are now a Christian, preferably someone who will not be hostile to the idea! It is important that you learn to let other people know about your new life, and it will help to make the step more real to you. And don't feel overwhelmed by the step you have just taken —the God who planned from pre-history to bring His Son into the world to be our Saviour is more than a match for any opposition you may face or any inadequacies you may feel!

This book has examined the biblical account of the Nativity

of the Lord Jesus and shown, it is hoped, that we have excellent grounds for believing that the accounts we have been given are complete and trustworthy. There is a real poignancy in the Christmas story. God willingly surrendered His beloved Son to be the seal of salvation, completed on the cross at Calvary —once for all. The birth in Bethlehem some two thousand years ago was the beginning of a life like no other. Perhaps this is what we need to reflect upon each Christmas. We can take real joy in and mightily celebrate the fact of the birth of the Lord Jesus! But His birth was only the beginning of the most wonderful story ever told! And the story will not be completed until Jesus returns again in glory!

We began this book with the opening verse of H. J. Gauntlett's famous carol *Once in Royal David's City*. (See Chapter 1). Hopefully, by this stage, we will have a clearer grasp of the 'Christmas story' and where it fits into God's great plan of salvation. It is possible to intellectualise and theorise about the Christian faith, but ultimately, if it is to be accepted at all, it must be accepted with the simple faith of a child, as Jesus Himself made clear. (See Luke 18:16-17.) Perhaps, then, it is especially appropriate that we should finish with the last verse of Gauntlett's famous carol:

> Not in that poor lowly stable,
> With the oxen standing by,
> We shall see Him; but in heaven,
> Set at God's right hand on high;
> When like stars His children crowned.
> All in white shall wait around.